The Philosophy of Keynes's Economics

John Maynard Keynes was arguably the most influential Western economist of the twentieth century. His emphasis on the nature and role of uncertainty in economics is a dominant theme in his writings.

This book brings together a wide array of experts on Keynes's contributions to the philosophy of probability and to economics, including Gay Tulip Meeks, Sheila Dow and John Davis. Themes covered include:

- Keynesian probability and uncertainty
- the foundations of Keynes's economics
- the relationship between Keynes's earlier and later thought

The Philosophy of Keynes's Economics is a readable and comprehensive book that will interest students and academics interested in the man and his thought. Given the continuing relevance of Keynesian thought, this book will be an important source for years to come.

Jochen Runde is Senior Lecturer in Economics at the Judge Institute of Management, Cambridge, Fellow and Graduate Tutor (Arts) at Girton College, Cambridge and Associate Director (Professional Practice) of the Cambridge-MIT Institute. He has published widely on a variety of topics including the philosophy and economics of J.M. Keynes, probability, uncertainty and decision theory, Austrian economics and social ontology.

Sohei Mizuhara is Professor of Economics at Ryukoku University, Japan. His main research interest is the economics of Keynes and Kalecki. His books and most of his papers have been published in Japanese. His works in English include a paper in *Post Keynesian Econometrics, Microeconomics and the Theory of the Firm Vol 1: Beyond Keynes* (Edward Elgar 2002) edited by Sheila C. Dow and John Hillard.

Economics as Social Theory
Series edited by Tony Lawson
University of Cambridge

Social Theory is experiencing something of a revival within economics. Critical analyses of the particular nature of the subject matter of social studies and of the types of method, categories and modes of explanation that can legitimately be endorsed for the scientific study of social objects are re-emerging. Economists are again addressing such issues as the relationship between agency and structure, between economy and the rest of society, and between the enquirer and the object of enquiry. There is a renewed interest in elaborating basic categories such as causation, competition, culture, discrimination, evolution, money, need, order, organization, power probability, process, rationality, technology, time, truth, uncertainty, value, etc.

The objective for this series is to facilitate this revival further. In contemporary economics the label 'theory' has been appropriated by a group that confines itself to largely asocial, ahistorical, mathematical 'modelling'. 'Economics as Social Theory' thus reclaims the 'theory' label, offering a platform for alternative, rigorous but broader and more critical conceptions of theorizing.

Other titles in this series include:

Economics and Language
Edited by Willie Henderson

Rationality, Institutions and Economic Methodology
Edited by Uskali Mäki, Bo Gustafsson and Christian Knudsen

New Directions in Economic Methodology
Edited by Roger Backhouse

Who Pays for the Kids?
Nancy Folbre

Rules and Choice in Economics
Viktor Vanberg

Beyond Rhetoric and Realism in Economics
Thomas A. Boylan and Paschal F. O'Gorman

The Philosophy of Keynes's Economics

Probability, uncertainty
and convention

Edited by Jochen Runde
and Sohei Mizuhara

Routledge
Taylor & Francis Group

LONDON AND NEW YORK

First published 2003
by Routledge
11 New Fetter Lane, London EC4P 4EE

Simultaneously published in the USA and Canada
by Routledge
29 West 35th Street, New York, NY 10001

Routledge is an imprint of the Taylor & Francis Group

Typeset in Palatino by Taylor & Francis Books Ltd
Printed and bound in Great Britain by TJ International Ltd,
Padstow, Cornwall

British Library Cataloguing in Publication Data
A catalogue record for this book is available from the British
Library

Library of Congress Cataloging in Publication Data
Runde, Jochen, 1959–
The philosophy of Keynes's economics: probability, uncertainty and
convention / Jochen Runde & Sohei Mizuhara.
p.cm — (Economics as social theory).
Includes bibliographical references and index.
1. Keynsian economics. 2. Probabilities, 3. Uncertainty.
I. Mizura, Sohei, 1969– II. Title. III. Series.
HB99.7R83 2003
330.15'6–dc21   2002037160

ISBN 0–415–28153–9 (hbk)
ISBN 0–415–31244–2 (pbk)

Contents

Contributors

Bradley W. Bateman teaches writing and economics at Grinnell College, Iowa. He is the author, most recently, of *Keynes's Uncertain Revolution* (University of Michigan Press 1996), and is currently working on a project on the changing role of religion in the formation of American economics.

Jörg Bibow is Lecturer in Economics at the University of Hamburg, where he teaches central banking and European integration, and a visiting scholar at the Levy Economics Institute, Annandale-on-Hudson. His current research focuses on the effects of monetary policy on economic performance, especially the monetary policies of the Bundesbank and the European Central Bank. This work builds on his earlier research on the monetary thought of John Maynard Keynes.

Anna Carabelli is Professor of Economics at the University of Eastern Piedmont, Italy. Her research interests are in the fields of methodology, epistemology and the history of modern economic thought, with particular reference to Keynes and Hayek. She is the author of *On Keynes's Method* (Macmillan 1988), and has published articles on Keynes's thought on probability and uncertainty and comparative studies of Keynes and Hayek's views on expectations. She is currently involved in the coordination of a research project on the financial structure and financing of innovation.

Paul Davidson is Editor of the *Journal of Post Keynesian Economics* and Professor Emeritus at the University of Tennessee. He has held positions at the University of Pennsylvania, Rutgers University, the University of Bristol, the Institute for Advanced Studies (Vienna) and the Continental Oil Company. His latest book, published in 2002, is entitled *Financial Markets, Money and the Real World* (Edward Elgar). He is the author, co-author or editor of twenty other books and over 200 professional articles.

John B. Davis is Professor of History and Philosophy of Economics, University of Amsterdam, and Professor of Economics, Marquette

University. He is the author of *Keynes's Philosophical Development* (Cambridge 1994), *The Theory of the Individual in Economics* (Routledge 2003), co-editor of *The Handbook of Economic Methodology* (Edward Elgar 1998), as well as the author of numerous journal articles. He is a former president of the History of Economics Society and editor of the *Review of Social Economy*.

Sheila C. Dow is Professor of Economics and Head of Department at the University of Stirling. She has worked previously for the Bank of England and the Government of Manitoba, and has also taught in Canada. She has published widely in the areas of the history and methodology of economic thought, money and banking, and regional finance. Particular current research interests include the philosophy and economics of Hume and Keynes and the methodological issues behind monetary policy. Her latest book is entitled *Economic Methodology: An Inquiry* (Oxford University Press 2002).

Stephen P. Dunn is a Policy Adviser in the Strategy Unit at the Department of Health, London, and a Senior Research Fellow in the Economics Faculty at Staffordshire University. He has published several articles on methodology, Keynesian economics and the theory of the firm. In 2000 he was awarded the K. William Kapp Prize from the European Association for Evolutionary Political Economy.

Guido Fioretti is a Research Associate at the Complex Systems Centre at the University of Siena, and at the Institute of Network Economics at the University of Modena. He took a Ph.D. in economics after graduating in electrical engineering, in order to bring cognitive models of decision-making into economics. He has worked on modelling animal spirits in investment decisions, credit rationing due to cognitive inability to classify loan applications that involve new technologies, and collective decision-making in industrial districts.

Athol Fitzgibbons has taught at a number of Australian universities and is currently working in the School of Economics at Griffith University. He was trained in neoclassical economics and, although he was eventually repelled by the narrowness of that system, he maintains a strong interest in macroeconomic policy and theory. Fitzgibbons is currently researching the interrelation between the economy and values, particularly the scope of self-interest and its changing limits. His books include *Keynes's Vision* (Oxford 1987), *Adam Smith's System* (Oxford 1995) and *The Nature of Macroeconomics* (Edward Elgar 2000).

Bill Gerrard is currently a Reader in Economics at Leeds University Business School. His D.Phil. thesis was on 'Keynes, the Keynesians and the classics: a suggested interpretation', and he has published extensively on methodology, Keynesian economics and behaviour under uncertainty. A consistent theme in his work is the necessity of encompassing alternative disciplinary and theoretical perspectives in order to provide a better understanding of complex realities. In recent years, he has concentrated on putting his methodological principles into practice in the study of the professional team sports industry.

Donald Gillies is Professor of Philosophy of Science and Mathematics at King's College, London. He has conducted research on a variety of topics, but probability has remained his principal interest. In conjunction with the Post Keynesian group and his wife, Grazia-Ietto Gillies, an economist, he has made a study of probability in Keynes and the influence of Ramsey, developing in this connection an intersubjective interpretation of probability. An account of this research is to be found in his recent book, *Philosophical Theories of Probability* (Routledge 2000).

Tony Lawson is Reader in Economics in the Faculty of Economics and Politics at Cambridge University. He has published numerous articles on philosophical issues in economics and is the author of *Economics and Reality* (Routledge 1997). He sits on the editorial boards of various journals and is the general editor of the Routledge series 'Economics as Social Theory', of which the present volume forms part.

Paul Lewis was educated at Peterhouse, Cambridge, and at Christ Church, Oxford. He was a Research Fellow of Emmanuel College, Cambridge, before becoming Director of Studies in Economics and in Social and Political Sciences at Newnham College, Cambridge. His research interests include the philosophy of the social sciences, the methodology of economics, economic sociology and Austrian economics.

Charles R. McCann Jr is a Research Associate in the Department of Economics at the University of Pittsburgh. He is the author of *Probability Foundations of Economic Theory* (Routledge 1994) and editor of *John Maynard Keynes: Critical Responses* (Routledge 1998), among other works. His main areas of interest are the history of economic thought, social and political theory, and the philosophy of probability.

Gay Tulip Meeks is a Fellow of Robinson College, Cambridge, and runs an M.Phil. paper on philosophical issues in economics, which she started in the early 1980s. Her primary research interest is in the philosophy of economics (social choice, rationality). She also works on information and regulatory problems in the company sector. Her publications include 'Utility in economics', in Turner and Martin (eds) *Surveys of Subjective Phenomena Vol. 2* (Russell Sage Foundation 1985), (as editor) *Thoughtful Economic Man: Essays on Rationality, Moral Rules and Benevolence* (Cambridge University Press 1991), and (with Geoff Meeks) *Towards a Cost-Benefit Analysis of Accounting Regulation* (ICAEW 2001).

Sohei Mizuhara is Professor of Economics at Ryukoku University, Japan. His main research interest is the economics of Keynes and Kalecki. His books and most of his papers have been published in Japanese. His works in English include a paper in Dow and Hillard (eds) *Post Keynesian Econometrics, Microeconomics and the Theory of the Firm Vol. 1: Beyond Keynes* (Edward Elgar 2002), and a book review in the *Eastern Economic Journal*.

Rod O'Donnell has been Professor of Economics at Macquarie University, Sydney, since 1995. His publications include *Keynes: Philosophy, Economics and Politics* (Macmillan 1989), *Macroeconomic Principles* (Mind to Mind 2002), and (as editor) *Keynes as a Philosopher-Economist* (Macmillan 1991), as well as articles in both economics and philosophy journals. Educationally, he is appalled by the resource starvation policies of the Australian government towards tertiary education and the accompanying destructive shift from academic to corporate values in Australian universities.

Jochen Runde is Senior Lecturer in Economics at the Judge Institute of Management, Cambridge, and Fellow and Graduate Tutor (Arts) at Girton College, Cambridge. He has published articles on various topics including the philosophy and economics of J. M. Keynes, probability, uncertainty and decision theory, Austrian economics, and social ontology. He is currently participating in a research project investigating the impact of technological disruption in the photography industry.

Ted Winslow is Associate Professor in the Division of Social Science, York University, Toronto. His current research focuses on the implications of continental philosophy, particularly German idealism and Husserlian phenomenology, and the Kleinian variant of psychoanalysis for social theory in general and political economy in particular. He has a continuing interest in the economics of Keynes and Marx as approaches to political economy capable of development along lines suggested by these traditions in philosophy and psychology.

Acknowledgements

Our thanks to the authors, to Ann Newton who did her usual meticulous job in putting the manuscript in order, to Nina Gehl for her remarkable portrait of Keynes, and to Andrew Norman for photographing it. We are also grateful to the *Keizai Seminar* for granting us permission to republish the papers originally published in Japanese, and to Cambridge University Press for allowing us to include an abridged version of Gay Tulip Meek's essay originally published in G. T. Meeks (ed.), *Thoughtful Economic Man: Essays on Rationality, Moral Rules and Benevolence* (Cambridge University Press 1991).

S. M.
J. R.

1 Introduction

Jochen Runde and Sohei Mizuhara[1]

John Maynard Keynes's emphasis on the nature and role of uncertainty in economic life is a dominant theme in his economic writings. Indeed, in an article published in the 1937 *Quarterly Journal of Economics* (CWXIVa),[2] he argues that the impact of uncertainty on investment demand lies at the heart of what he had tried to convey in his most famous work, *The General Theory* (CWVII). It is therefore unsurprising that there has been a long line of his followers, memorably described by Alan Coddington (1976) as 'Chapter 12 Keynesians', who have studied and attempted to build on and develop this theme. Some prominent early contributors to this literature include George Shackle (1961a, 1967), Brian Loasby (1976), various Post Keynesians (notably Paul Davidson (1978) and Hyman Minsky (1975)), and even members of the Austrian School (O'Driscoll and Rizzo 1985).

Given his stature in the profession, it is likely that Keynes's observations on uncertainty would have attracted attention anyway. But they are often imbued with special significance, and an important reason for this is that he had devoted much of his early academic life to a King's College fellowship dissertation on the foundations of probability, finally published in 1921 as *A Treatise on Probability* (CWVIII). Surprisingly, though, it was not until the mid-1980s that serious work began on tracing the connection between Keynes's earlier thinking on probability and his later economic writings. An important early contribution to this area of research was a paper by Gay Tulip Meeks, which had been circulating in Cambridge since the end of the 1970s (and later appeared as Meeks (1991), an abridged version of which appears in this volume).[3] This was followed by a collection of essays edited by Tony Lawson and Hashem Pesaran (1985), full-length book treatments by Anna Carabelli (1988), Rod O'Donnell (1989), John Davis (1994b), Brad Bateman (1996) and John Coates (1996), and various other edited collections, including O'Donnell (1991b), Dow and Hillard (1995, 2002), Cottrell and Lawlor (1995) and Gerrard and Hilliard (1993). There developed a lively literature, that even now shows no signs of abating.[4]

The Keynes-philosophy literature is striking for its diversity and complexity. There are a number of reasons for this. In the first place, many of the contributors come from different backgrounds and, quite naturally, emphasise and in some cases build on different aspects of Keynes's thought.[5] In the second place, the contributions are often aimed at different audiences. Whereas some of them are intended and written as exercises in the history of ideas, in philosophy and the foundations of probability as well as economics, others are written as contributions to contemporary economic analysis. Tony Lawson's (1985) *Economic Journal* article on 'Uncertainty and economic analysis', for example, which draws extensively on Keynes's *A Treatise on Probability*, is widely cited in all manner of contexts, including the methodology of economics, the history of economic ideas, Post Keynesianism and Institutionalist economics. A third complicating factor concerns the extent to which Keynes's views on probability changed between the *Treatise* and his later economic writings: the *Treatise* offered a logical interpretation of probability, which came under severe attack in a paper by Frank Ramsey in 1926, a paper which also sketched the first axiomatic formulation of subjective probability that now dominates modern decision theory (Ramsey 1978). A variety of positions has emerged on the extent to which Keynes actually yielded to Ramsey and, accordingly, on the extent to which Keynes's later views may be read into his earlier theoretical writings on probability.

The size and difficulty of the Keynes-philosophy literature, taken in conjunction with the fact that the logical interpretation of probability is hardly staple fare nowadays, make it difficult for newcomers to break into. The object of the present volume is to provide a means of facilitating such entry, by giving contributors to the debate who have developed distinct interpretations of Keynes the opportunity to give reasonably short and self-contained statements of their positions. A number of the chapters in this volume were initially commissioned by one of us (S. M.) for publication in Japanese in the *Keizai Seminar*, with the aim of introducing research in this area to a Japanese audience.[6] We then supplemented the original list of contributions by inviting other contributors to the field to participate in the project.

The volume has been arranged by grouping together the chapters under six broad thematic headings: 'Probability, uncertainty and choice'; 'Continuity issues'; 'Social ontology'; 'Convention'; 'Methodology'; and 'Looking ahead'. The categorization is not perfect, of course, as many of the chapters address a variety of themes and spill over into more than one category. We have therefore attempted to provide some indication of the overlap where it occurs in the summary that follows.

Probability, uncertainty and choice

The four chapters in this section are devoted to various aspects of Keynes's writings on probability, uncertainty and economic action. As we have already indicated, these are the areas in which much of the initial interest in his more philosophical writings took off. The section begins with the abridged version of Gay Tulip Meek's (1991) paper mentioned above, which did so much to precipitate subsequent work on Keynes's analysis of probability and its connections to his economics. Given its historical significance in setting the tone and questions for much of the literature that followed, we are especially pleased to be able to reproduce it here. In this chapter, Meeks dissects and lays out the separate elements of Keynes's position on the nature of the investment decision under conditions of uncertainty, and demonstrates how, on Keynes's account, decision-making procedures may be considered rational even when it is not possible to determine numerically definite probabilities of future states of the world. Meeks here emphasizes the role of conventions and habits which, 'buoyed up by animal spirits as we take the plunge, respresents a sensible strategy for doing as well as we can in the tight corner uncertainty condemns us to'. She goes on to show that there are significant parallels between Keynes's position and that of the philosopher David Hume on the unavoidability of our dependence on induction in day-to-day life, and closes with a finely drawn assessment of Keynes's position, concentrating on the rationality of inductive procedures under different circumstances.

Meeks's chapter is followed by Charles R. McCann Jr's careful summary of some of the basic concepts employed in Keynes's *A Treatise on Probability*. Readers unfamiliar with the foundations and structure of Keynes's theory of logical probability may find this a useful place to begin. McCann kicks off with a section on the frequency theory of probability and how Keynes's scepticism about this theory led him to reinterpret probability as part of the field of logic. He then goes on to unpack Keynes's distinction between belief and rational belief for which there is evidential support, the notion of probability relations as relations of partial implication analogous to implication proper (and the associated distinction between primary and secondary propositions), the respects in which Keynes's theory might be classified as objective and subjective, the issue of non-numerical probability, and, finally, Keynes's distinctive notion of evidential weight.

The subsequent chapters by Jochen Runde and Athol Fitzgibbons explore some links between *A Treatise on Probability* and Keynes's later economic writings. Jochen Runde's chapter is a straightforward attempt to trace and shed some light on the points at which Keynes refers explicitly to *A Treatise on Probability* in *The General Theory* and subsequent writings. The places in which these references occur are in Keynes's analyses of stock-market behaviour and liquidity preference, and the core theoretical idea from *A Treatise in Probability* that he redeploys in these analyses is the distinction between judgments of probability and judgments of evidential weight. Runde unpacks the role of evidential weight in Keynes's accounts of investor confidence, the instability of beliefs in asset markets, and liquidity preference. An important issue here, of course, is the extent to which it is legitimate to locate Keynes's later views in his earlier philosophical position in *A Treatise in Probability* and Runde closes with some thoughts on the so-called continuity thesis (see further below).

Athol Fitzgibbons argues that Keynes's epistemology, formally laid out in *A Treatise on Probability*, is put to work with adaptations in *The General Theory*. Keynes's achievement in the earlier book, according to Fitzgibbons, was to formalize the rules of practical reason, developing an account which denies that all probabilities are quantifiable and which suggests, moreover, that even pairwise comparisons of probability in terms of greater than, less than or equal to, may not always be possible. Furthermore, Fitzgibbons emphasizes how Keynes takes issue with the doctrine of mathematical expectation and naïve applications of the Principle of Indifference.[7] Fitzgibbons goes on to argue that these and some related ideas from *A Treatise on Probability* reappeared in Keynes's economic writings, but with one major difference:

> Whereas *A Treatise on Probability* expounded the possibility of *rational* decisions, *The General Theory* argued that the instability of capitalism arose from *irrational* decisions in the capital markets. Once again irrational meant a 'failure to think systematically' and not a 'failure to maximize'; in fact investors were irrational when they maximized in the absence of full information. Investors often relied on 'conventions' to paper over the gaps in their knowledge, and in particular they typically adopted the convention that the present situation would continue into the future.

As Fitzgibbons sees it, Keynes's later emphasis was on the arbitrariness of investment decisions in financial markets, the instability of market conventions, the role of animal spirits, and so on. At the same time he regards Keynes as having been the first to introduce a 'knowledge dichotomy' into macroeconomics, distinguishing between those who are driven primarily by irrationality, animal spirits and the like (ordinary participants in financial markets), and those who have the superior knowledge and insight to arrive at rational decisions on behalf of the system as a whole (government economists). Fitzgibbons closes with some observations on the connection between Keynes's epistemology and his political philosophy, a new form of Liberalism that was meant to replace Socialism and *laissez-faire*. This position, which

Fitzgibbons calls 'the Third Way', is Platonic in origin and might be regarded as having authoritarian overtones. Fitzgibbons tests whether Keynes avoids this criticism by way of an imaginary dialogue between Plato and Keynes.

Continuity issues

A significant problem that arises in analysing the body of work of an author that spans several decades is the extent to which his or her views remained constant or at least consistent over time and, accordingly, the extent to which later ideas can be read into earlier ones. This is the so-called continuity problem, one that has been a source of significant debate among Keynes scholars in general and the authors represented in this volume in particular (see Bateman (1991) and the review by Gerrard (1992)). This section of the book begins with chapters by Brad Bateman and Rod O'Donnell, who take strongly opposing views on whether or not there occurred radical shifts between Keynes's earlier and later philosophical views.[8] These are followed by contributions from John Davis and Donald Gillies respectively, two important proponents of the discontinuity view. The final chapter in this section comes from Guido Fioretti, a more recent entrant into the debate, who finds significant continuities *and* discontinuities in the development of Keynes's philosophical thought.

Brad Bateman sets out to attack the following three arguments: (1) that it was Keynes's early work on probability that led him to understand the importance of expectations and uncertainty in economic decision-making and that he gradually introduced expectations into his economic writings during the 1920s and 1930s; (2) that Keynes's emphasis on expectations in *The General Theory* came about as a direct result of his earlier work on probability; and (3) that Keynes was the theoretical revolutionary who first introduced expectations to macroeconomics. The true picture, according to Bateman, is a rather different one, involving two radical shifts in Keynes's views on the importance of uncertainty and expectations in macroeconomics. The first occurred during the 1920s, when Keynes decisively rejected the standard Cambridge theory of the trade cycle that he had formerly advocated, and in which expectations and uncertainty play a central role. Indeed, Bateman shows that, even as late as the beginning of the 1930s, Keynes was quite vehement in denying that pessimistic expectations or a lack of confidence were of any relevance in explaining the trade cycle. The second shift occurred in the run-up to the publication of *The General Theory*, when Keynes once again placed expectations and uncertainty at centre stage. But this second shift, according to Bateman, had little if anything to do with Keynes's earlier writings on probability and was instead the consequence of his work in policy-making and his experience as an investor during the 1930s.

Many of Bateman's criticisms of the continuity view, both here and perhaps even more so in his 1996 book, are directed at Rod O'Donnell's early and influential study *Keynes: Philosophy, Economics and Politics* (1989). In his own contribution to the present volume, O'Donnell has accordingly elected to respond to Bateman's 1996 criticisms and, in the process, restate his own interpretation of the continuity view. The argument proceeds on two broad fronts. First, O'Donnell questions Bateman's view that an adequate understanding of Keynes's ideas necessarily requires the kind of 'thick' history produced by professional historians, which place economic ideas in social and cultural contexts, and embrace both external and internal influences on an author's thought (as contrasted with the kind of 'thin' histories that O'Donnell's book is an example of, and which concentrate primarily on the analytical aspects and internal development of an author's thought). Secondly, O'Donnell provides various arguments against specific aspects of Bateman's interpretation of his book, particularly as these relate to the continuity controversy. Among the topics covered are *'Das Maynard Keynes Problem'*, the memoir entitled 'My early beliefs' (CWXb), and Keynes's treatment of probability, expectations and conventions. The upshot is that O'Donnell does not deny that there were changes in Keynes's thought, but maintains that these occurred within a general conceptual framework that remained largely unchanged throughout his lifetime.

John Davis traces Keynes's early thinking to the Platonic realism and intuitionism of G. E. Moore (1903a) and recounts how Keynes treated probability on the same lines as Moore had treated 'good', namely as a Platonic entity not definable in terms of simpler ideas and knowable through direct, rational intuition. Davis examines some of the philosophical arguments that led to the demise of Moore's intuitionism, as well as Ramsey's critique of *A Treatise on Probability*, which was also aimed at Keynes's Moore-inspired conception of logical probability relations.

Davis places particular emphasis on Keynes's essay 'My early beliefs' (CWXb), in which Keynes reflects on the extent to which he and his circle had accepted Moore's doctrine of intuition. Here, Keynes suggests that he and his friends may have overestimated their intuitive abilities in claiming the right to judge what is good in every individual case on its merits, and that this exaggerated confidence in their own judgment led them to neglect Moore's views on the importance of social rules of good conduct. But the shortcoming of intuitionism particularly emphasized by Davis is that it leaves no room for the possibility of error. Specifically, where two people disagree about what is good, and each claims to have direct insight into it, there is the problem of how to sort out their disagreement. An adequate theory of judgment, Davis argues, requires being able to distinguish when one is in error from when one is correct.

How, then, did Keynes reinterpret individual judgment in his later thinking? Davis's answer to this question is that when Keynes refers to 'introspection and values' he means to say that, whether as economists or as ordinary individuals, we each make assessments of other individuals' motives and behaviour by considering how we ourselves would act in similar situations. Judgment then becomes a highly interdependent affair, such as that described in Keynes's famous account of stock-market behaviour. Davis argues that nothing remains of Keynes's earlier concept of individual judgment as the product of an autonomous and intuitive apprehension of Platonic entities. Rather, as he presents Keynes's new view, judgment is social in the sense that it is the product of interdependent individual judgments. Davis presents Keynes's later emphasis on social conventions as evidence of this new view of judgment, and concludes that the concept of convention became the central organizing concept in Keynes's later philosophical thinking.

Conventions also play an important role in Donald Gillies's wide-ranging chapter, albeit arrived at in a different way. Gillies begins with a brief history of IS–LM Keynesianism,[9] the Post Keynesian response and Keynes's analysis of the investment decision (a crucial aspect of Keynes's theory, as he saw investment as the motor driving the level of economic activity). The investment decision depends on what Keynes, in *The General Theory*, calls the state of long-term expectation, which implicitly introduces a concept of probability. The question that Gillies addresses in his chapter is what constitutes the most appropriate interpretation of probability in *The General Theory*.

Gillies proposes to answer this question by considering three different versions of epistemic probability: the logical theory as proposed in *A Treastise on Probability*, the subjective interpretation associated with Ramsey (1978) and De Finetti (1931), and what Gillies calls the intersubjective or consensus interpretation of probability. The logical and the subjective theories are well known, the intersubjective theory perhaps less so. At the heart of this theory is the idea that social communities have consensus beliefs and that these consensus beliefs may be treated as probabilities through an extension of the Dutch Book argument associated with Ramsey and De Finetti.[10] The basic idea is that it will be in the interests of the members of the community if they settle on common degrees of belief, since a failure to do so will leave them open on a collective basis to cunning people betting against them. Gillies suggests that the intersubjective interpretation is in some ways intermediate between the theory of rational degrees of belief proposed in *A Treatise on Probability* and the theory of subjective degrees of belief proposed by Ramsey.

The remainder of Gillies's chapter is devoted to the interpretation of probability in Keynes's theory of long-term expectations. Gillies agrees with Bateman (1987, 1996) and Davis (1994b) that Keynes abandoned his logical interpretation in the wake of Ramsey's criticism, but maintains that, rather than embracing Ramsey's subjectivist theory, he moved towards an intersubjective theory. Like Davis, Gillies presents Keynes's later emphasis on conventions and conventional behaviour as evidence of a shift in his views towards a portrayal of investors as reaching consensus beliefs through a process of social interaction. But investors will nevertheless still be labouring under uncertainty rather than risk (which, following Frank Knight (1921), Gillies associates with situations in which people have objective frequencies to go on). And it is in their emphasis on uncertainty that Gillies sees the Post Keynesians as having a more accurate interpretation of Keynes than advocates of IS–LM Keynesianism.

Guido Fioretti's chapter follows on from his recent *Economics and Philosophy* paper, in which he demonstrates the remarkably strong influence of the German philosopher Johannes von Kries on the development of Keynes's thinking about probability (Fioretti 2001). For some reason, perhaps because most of von Kries's writings appear only in German, this link has received little attention in the literature on the development of Keynes's thought. In his contribution to the present volume, Fioretti compares the philosophical frameworks of the two authors, Keynes's neo-Platonism on the one hand and von Kries's cognitivism on the other, focusing on the issue of non-numerical and non-comparable probabilities and Keynes's treatment of induction (the difference being that probability relations are real objects apprehended by pure intuition in Keynes, and the outcome of mental processes in von Kries). Fioretti suggests that the transposition of von Kries's ideas about non-numerical probabilities into a supposedly objective Platonic world required Keynes to adopt an atomistic ontology. However, Keynes's stance had changed by 1926, as evidenced by his denial of the atomic hypothesis, at least with respect to the social sciences, and Fioretti argues that Keynes consistently rejected the idea that human reasoning is akin to formal logic (although in rejecting his earlier neo-Platonism he later pleaded for human logic). Furthermore, Fioretti argues that Keynes's ideas about non-numerical and non-comparable probabilities, as well as evidential weight, carried through to his later writings.

Social ontology

One of the most significant aspects of the development of the methodology of economics over recent years has been the so-called ontological turn: whereas methodological discussions during the 1970s and 1980s dwelt primarily on epistemological issues involved in the construction and assessment of theories, currently there is much interest in investigating economists' underlying and often implicit assumptions about the nature of the entities and relations that make up the economic realm (see, for example, Lawson 1997a; Mäki 2001). The chapters in this next section fall into this category, and examine some of what Keynes had to say about the nature of social reality and how this bears on the tools with which economists tackle their subject matter.

First up is a chapter by Ted Winslow, who published an early account of the philosophy of Keynes's economics that may now be regarded as one of the earliest examples of the ontological turn in the methodology of economics (Winslow 1989). Winslow's contribution to the present volume, 'The foundations of Keynes's economics', rehearses some of the themes in his earlier paper and offers an account of the ontological and especially the psychological foundations of Keynes's thought. Winslow starts with *A Treatise on Probability* and shows that Keynes had there attempted to ground universal and statistical induction in the hypotheses of atomism and 'limited variety', and had given reasons why induction would be rendered useless in systems that display organic unity. As we have already noted, by 1926 Keynes had become quite explicit in his rejection of the atomic hypothesis with respect to the social realm, and, according to Winslow, had adopted a version of the hypothesis of organic unity compatible with rational inductive methods. (Winslow draws here on Alfred Whitehead's arguments about circumstances under which the internal relations that constitute an organic entity may be such as to make it possible to employ the frequency theory of probability.) Winslow goes on to show how fundamental the hypothesis of organic unity was to Keynes's economic modelling, albeit in a form that makes this hypothesis consistent with rational induction.

Tony Lawson has for many years sought to promote explicit ontological analysis in economics (Lawson 1997a, forthcoming). Part of this project has involved examining the work of authors such as Hayek, Marshall, Marx, Menger, Veblen and Keynes who, writing prior to what Lawson sees as the current era of 'ontological neglect' in mainstream economics, pay explicit attention to ontological issues in their work. In his contribution to the present volume, Lawson concentrates on what he calls 'Keynes's realist orientation' and specifically on Keynes's views on the ontological presuppositions of induction. Lawson argues that Keynes's sensitivity to ontological questions was not only in evidence long before he started on *A Treatise on Probability*, in various responses to Moore's (1903a) *Principia Ethica*, but indeed explains why he embarked on *A Treatise on Probability* at all. The main impetus here, Lawson argues, was Keynes's reaction to G. E. Moore's reliance in the *Principia* on the frequency interpretation of probability. Lawson portrays Keynes's criticisms of Moore as being based on an ontological consideration, namely that the frequency theory presupposes a closed system whereas moral issues usually have to be addressed in an open system. Lawson goes on to show how Keynes's discussions of inductive methods in *A Treatise on Probability* involve an explicit consideration of the nature of the physical and social world (for example, his discussion of the atomic character of natural law), and specifically that he consistently attempts to ground method in the nature, structure or properties of the system to which the method is to be applied.

According to Lawson, Keynes's later methodological conclusions are also underpinned by ontological analysis, although by the middle of the 1920s he had moved from being 'somewhat non-committal regarding the extent to which the material of the natural world can be regarded as atomic' to being reasonably definite that social phenomena cannot be. *The General Theory* implicitly adopts a view of the social world as an open system, Lawson maintains, and constitutes a clear example of how Keynes fashioned his substantive theories and methods to 'fit' with this position on the nature of social reality. Lawson offers a variety of arguments in support of this contention, but places special emphasis on the views that Keynes expresses in his review of Tinbergen's early econometric work on the business cycle, which drew heavily on his own (Keynes's) social ontology. The upshot for Lawson is that we should follow Keynes's example by attempting to craft our methods and practices in the light of what we find out about the social material to which they are applied.

Steve Dunn's chapter, 'Keynes and transformation', differs from those of Winslow and Lawson in that it takes as its point of departure not Keynes's ruminations about the ultimate nature of reality, but some implications of his emphasis on uncertainty in economic decision-making. Stripped to its essentials, Dunn's argument is that economic decision-making under uncertainty is guided by images of possible future states that exist only in the imagination of the decision-maker at the point of decision. Given that the imagination is not fully determined by the decision-maker's present circumstances, it then follows that the actions of decision-makers guided in this way may affect the future in non-predetermined ways. Dunn thus takes a line strongly reminiscent of G. L. S. Shackle (1972), that choice and the actions it guides are the source of history and novelty in human affairs. Like Winslow and Lawson, then, Dunn regards Keynes as having adopted a view of the social world as open (or 'transmutable' in the terminology that, following Paul Davidson, Dunn employs).

But Dunn is critical of Keynes for not having pushed this theme as hard as he might have done. As Dunn points out, *A Treatise on Probability* does not address the psychology of action or the emergent novelty, creativity or reproducibility associated with the imagination and action. On these issues it is necessary to turn to the places in Keynes's economic writings that consider the institutional contexts in which he saw the impact of uncertainty as being so decisive. Although Keynes does adopt a view of social reality as transmutable here, Dunn criticizes him for failing to pay sufficient attention to the way in which the actions of people generate uncertainty for others, and in particular how market competition, the activities of entrepreneurs and the process of accumulation generate uncertainty. In Dunn's view, Keynes's particular take on uncertainty in financial markets leads to the neglect of the creative and uncertainty-generating potential of the competitive process. He concludes that Keynes's own discussions of the competitive process need to be augmented by a philosophy of emergence and transmutability.

Convention

In various places in his economic writings Keynes suggests that, when confronted with significant uncertainty about the consequences of their actions, people tend to fall back on conventions. We have already seen that many of the authors in this book pick up on this theme in different ways (see also Davis 1994b; Lawson 1993; Littleboy 1990). Indeed, there is even a school of economic thought in France ('the French School') that styles itself as developing an 'Économie des conventions' (Orléan 1989; Dupuy 1989a, 1994, forthcoming) and which regards Keynes's observations on the topic as a major source of inspiration.

The first chapter in this section, co-authored by Jörg Bibow, Paul Lewis and Jochen Runde, explores the different practices that Keynes describes as conventions and then compares Keynes's account with the influential conception of conventions as focal point solutions to coordination games with multiple Nash equilibria proposed by the philosopher David Lewis (1969). The comparison is conducted by way of a commentary on an important paper by Jean-Pierre Dupuy, a leading member of the French School mentioned above, in which the differences between Lewis's and Keynes's analyses of conventions are discussed at some length (Dupuy 1989a). It is argued that although Dupuy's account of the differences between the two approaches is in many ways a highly illuminating one, his analysis raises some difficult questions of its own, questions that a fully satisfactory account of convention should be able to address.

Sohei Mizuhara regards the concept of convention as a cornerstone of Keynes's economics, and devotes the first part of his chapter to analysing Keynes's observations about the nature of convention in *The General Theory* and to fixing an interpretation of what he may have meant by the term. The second part of the chapter is devoted to developing some aspects of this interpretation, drawing on an earlier exchange between John Davis (1994a) and Jochen Runde (1994c) on exactly what Keynesian conventions are. In this exchange, both Davis and Runde regard the practice of trying to fall back on the judgment of others in attempting to form expectations under conditions of uncertainty (what Davis calls 'interdependent judgment') as essential to Keynesian convention. But Runde (1994c) insists on a further restriction, namely that it must be in the interest of everyone in the relevant social group to follow the convention in question if everyone else in that group is following it. Mizuhara asks what this additional restriction might amount to in situations of fundamental uncertainty and, drawing on *A Treatise on Probability*, proposes that drawing on conventions is the best that people can do in situations of extreme uncertainty, and therefore the rational or reasonable thing for them to do.

Methodology

The two chapters that follow, by Sheila C. Dow and Anna Carabelli respectively, also touch on the subject of convention. But as their primary focus is on questions of methodology, we have grouped them separately here. Dow addresses the intriguing question of the parallels between what economists know and what they assume that economic actors know. In her view, *A Treatise in Probability* is applicable to both how ordinary economic actors go about their business and how economists go about their business as economists, as it is concerned with what it is rational to believe in situations in which knowledge is incomplete. According to Dow, this concern of Keynes's with the rational grounds economic actors have for their beliefs, and particularly his emphasis on their limits, carries over to his economic writings. The difference, she argues, is that Keynes's explicit treatment of probability in *A Treatise on Probability* is replaced by an explicit treatment of convention in *The General Theory*. Dow suggests that there are close parallels between Keynes's methodological approach as an economist and his understanding of the way that economic actors acquire knowledge of the circumstances in which they are operating. The key issue here is his recognition that the economist, no less than the ordinary economic actor, faces a complex, open and often highly unpredictable world, and is therefore often forced to operate under conditions of significant uncertainty. And it is this recognition, she argues, that accounts for his pluralism in method, 'his awareness of the significance of persuasion, his reservations about mathematical formalism, his reference to psychology and social convention'.

Anna Carabelli is well known for her emphasis on the continuity of Keynes's thought between his earlier and later writings, and her interpretation of *A Treatise on Probability* as strongly foreshadowing his later views on economics as a branch of 'probable logic' (Carabelli 1988). In her contribution to the present volume she portrays Keynes as a staunchly rationalist critic of the scientific method in economics, an opponent of determinism who consistently took a strong anti-empiricist line on the construction and evaluation of economic theory. In her view, Keynes saw economics both as a moral science, insofar as it deals with ethical values and introspection,[11] and also as a branch of logic that helps economists to draw conclusions that avoid fallacious reasoning.

However, this logic is something distinct from mathematics, which she portrays Keynes as having opposed in economics. Rather, it has to do with constructing abstract theoretical models from 'the elements found in our own thought', models that are intended to facilitate the segregation of semi-permanent or relatively constant factors from those that are transitory.

Carabelli devotes the latter parts of her chapter to some reflections on Keynes's response to Ramsey's critique, maintaining that while Keynes accepted Ramsey's scepticism about the existence of logical probability relations, he nevertheless continued to insist on the distinction between what people actually believe and what it is reasonable to believe. On the basis of this distinction, she argues that Keynes continued in his later economic writings to emphasize the role of personal individual judgment made on the basis of the available evidence, even when describing economic decision-making in situations of uncertainty. Unlike the contributors who are grouped in the section on convention, she downplays the importance of conventional behaviour in Keynes's thinking and is sceptical about people simply – she might say blindly – imitating each other in situations of uncertainty. It is only in situations of complete ignorance and as a last resort that she believes Keynes saw people falling back on conventions, and even then she reminds us that conventions are often a source of instability rather than something stable around which individual views can coalesce.

Looking ahead

The final two chapters are devoted to issues surrounding the development of Keynes's ideas and how they might be tailored to fit into contemporary economic analysis. Paul Davidson, a leading member of the Post Keynesian school, has contributed a chapter on the terminology of uncertainty employed in economic theory and the role of activist government policies. The key contrast in this chapter is between what Davidson calls classical and Keynesian concepts of uncertainty. On the classical view, situations of uncertainty are represented as ones in which economic decision-makers know the objective probability (frequency) distributions of random events. On the Keynesian view, by contrast, situations of uncertainty are ones in which economic decision-makers have neither objective nor subjective probabilities to go on.

Davidson is a strong proponent of Keynes's economic analysis, but fears that the profession will not take much notice of Keynes's own ideas on probability and uncertainty because they are offered in terms of what are now unfamiliar concepts and terminology (Davidson 1988, 1991, 1996). He therefore offers a formulation of Keynesian uncertainty on the basis of a contemporary, and ultimately ontological, distinction between ergodic and nonergodic systems. The key difference is that whereas it is possible to derive stable statistical averages of random events in ergodic systems – averages which may then be used as a basis for predicting future events – this is not the case in nonergodic, or what Davidson calls 'transmutable', systems. Davidson's point is that the social world is indeed transmutable and that economic actors are consequently often faced with having to make decisions in the face of Keynesian uncertainty. Davidson argues that persistent long-term unemployment cannot occur in a classical 'immutable' world, only in a 'transmutable' world. Indeed, drawing on Hicks (1979), Davidson argues that Keynesian uncertainty lies at the heart of the need for activist fiscal policy. For it is such uncertainty that leads decision-makers to suspend judgment and keep their options open by holding liquid assets even over the longer term, leading to deficient aggregate demand and, thereby, to long-term unemployment.

Bill Gerrard is critical of both old and new Keynesian fundamentalists for what he sees as their fixation on historical, philosophical and methodological issues at the expense of attempting to draw on Keynes's ideas in a more constructive way to build a general theory of economic action under uncertainty. The aim of his chapter, 'Keynesian uncertainty: what do we know?', is accordingly to outline how these ideas might be so exploited. Gerrard concentrates on Keynes's remarks on using probability as a guide to conduct in *A Treatise on Probability*, where Keynes criticizes the then version of the 'Doctrine of mathematical expectation' (prior to subsequent axiom-based versions of expected utility theory) for assuming the numerical measurability of probability and 'good' and for neglecting risk and evidential weight. Some of these criticisms have a decidedly modern flavour, and Gerrard shows how the distinction between judgments of probability and evidential weight reappears in mainstream decision theory in discussions of the Ellsberg Paradox in expected utility theory (Ellsberg 1961).

Gerrard goes on to present Keynes's analysis of investor behaviour in Chapter 12 of *The General Theory* as an attempt to 'generalize the theory of economic behaviour to deal with cases of fundamental uncertainty in which choices are unique and the evidential base is very limited'. Like a number of the other authors in this volume, he argues that the key concept that carries over from *A Treatise on Probability* is the distinction between probability and evidential weight, which re-emerges in Keynes's famous observation that the state of long-term expectation depends not only on the most probable forecasts that investors can make, but also on the confidence with which they make those forecasts (CWVII: 148). The opportunity to develop Keynes's views, Gerrard argues, lies especially in what he had to say about (the precariousness of) conventions and conventional valuations on the stock market. A key issue here is what Keynes had to say about the determinants of what Gerrard calls the propensity to act on such valuations, which include the state of confidence and animal spirits,[12] but also the nature of the firm as an organization and the competitive environment in which it operates. Gerrard concludes that there are two avenues in particular that offer scope for the constructive development of Keynes's ideas. The first is the idea that fundamental uncertainty might usefully be expressed in terms of both Keynesian probability and evidential weight, which Gerrard presents as encompassing the more narrow mainstream conceptions of risk and ambiguity. The second is Keynes's emphasis on the precariousness of stock-market conventions, which Gerrard suggests might serve as a starting point for a more satisfactory account of stock-market bubbles than has been provided so far.

Conclusion

As we indicated at the beginning of this introduction, our main aim in producing this volume was to provide a means of facilitating entry to the subject, by giving authors who have developed distinct interpretations of Keynes the opportunity to present reasonably brief and accessible statements of their positions. At the very least, we hope that this collection will provide an interesting and useful demonstration of the richness and diversity of the literature on the philosophy of J. M. Keynes. At best, we hope that it will go on to stimulate further work in this lively and fascinating field.

Notes

1 We are grateful to Paul Lewis for his comments on a draft of this chapter.
2 CWXIV refers to volume 14 of the *Collected Writings of John Maynard Keynes* published by Macmillan. This notation is employed throughout the book.
3 Bateman (this volume) suggests that G. L. S. Shackle (1961b) was the first to argue for the possibility of a relationship between Keynes's work in *A Treatise on Probability* and *The General Theory*. To the best of our knowledge, Marshak (1941) was the first to recommend *A Treatise on Probability* to economists interested in investment decision-making under uncertainty.
4 We shall not attempt to provide a comprehensive list here, but some particularly interesting recent and forthcoming additions to the literature include Baccini (forthcoming), Dequech (1999a, 1999b, 2000), Fioretti (2001), Franklin (2001) and Weatherson (2002); see also Favereau (1988).
5 The contributions in this volume are interesting not only for what they take from and highlight in Keynes, but also for the diverse range of perspectives and issues they bring to their interpretations of Keynes. For example – and this is only indicative – Ted Winslow makes connections with psychoanalysis and Freud, Tony Lawson with issues concerning realism and social ontology, Fioretti with the writings of the German philosopher von Kries, and Gillies and Davis with questions of intersubjectivity and human agency.
6 The original papers were by Bateman, Carabelli, Davis, Gerrard, Gillies, Lawson, Mizuhara, Runde and Winslow.
7 The Principle of Indifference states that 'if there is no *known* reason for predicating of our subject one rather than another of several alternatives, then

relatively to such knowledge the assertions of each of these alternatives have an *equal* probability' (CWVIII: 45). The attraction of the Principle of Indifference lies in that it facilitates the calculation of numerical probabilities (where applicable in respect of an exhaustive and mutually exclusive set of outcomes or statements). However, unguarded applications of the Principle of Indifference can easily lead to contradictions, many of which Keynes was well aware of (CWVIII: Ch. 4). For more on the Principle of Indifference, see also the chapter by Donald Gillies in this volume.

8 The continuity problem is also addressed in other chapters in this volume. Carabelli, a staunch proponent of the continuity view, considers the impact of Ramsey's critique on Keynes's position as set out in *A Treatise on Probability*. She maintains that although Ramsey managed to convince Keynes to abandon the logical probability relations he had posited, Keynes continued to maintain the distinction between the actual beliefs that individuals might hold and what it is reasonable for them to believe. This distinction, she maintains, was all that was needed for him to remain consistent with his earlier writings on probability in his later economic writings. Ted Winslow and Jochen Runde also touch on the issue, and argue that although Ramsey's critique led Keynes to give up on the idea that there exist logical probability relations, this admission left untouched many other aspects of his theory (for example, his ideas about rational degrees of belief relative to the available evidence, non-numerical probabilities and evidential weight). Gerrard takes an even stronger line, arguing that Keynes did not reject his early beliefs so much as incorporate them into a more general framework. Indeed, Gerrard presents Chapter 12 of *The General Theory* as an attempt by Keynes to 'operationalize' his logical theory of probability.

9 IS–LM Keynesianism refers to the standard textbook account of Keynesian economics, precipitated by Hicks (1936).

10 According to the subjectivist approach, a person's degree of belief in some event E is measured by his or her betting quotient q, where q is the fraction of some stake S he or she would be prepared to pay in order to receive S if E occurs. A person's betting quotients are *coherent* if they meet the no-Dutch Book requirement, in which case they (and the subjective beliefs they measure) will satisfy the axioms of probability. A Dutch Book is a sequence of bets on a series of events that would result in a certain loss for the person who accepts them, whatever actually happens.

11 For Carabelli, Keynes saw economics as concerned primarily with non-observable phenomena, expectations, beliefs, and so on, and as a subject in which explanations are based on reasons rather than material causes.

12 Keynes describes animal spirits as 'a spontaneous urge to action rather than inaction' (CWVII: 161).

Part I
Probability, uncertainty and choice

2 Keynes on the rationality of decision procedures under uncertainty

The investment decision

Gay Tulip Meeks[1]

Introduction

The future is yet to come (as a Member once solemnly informed Parliament). But indubitable though this claim is, it cannot be said to furnish the kind of specific information on which we might base our plans. What else do we really know about the future course of events? Precious little, sceptics assure us, and much less than we tend to assume. Suppose they are right: what then?

Keynes's answer forms the subject of this chapter. The analysis shows him as endorsing the sceptical claim that we cannot acquire sure knowledge of the pattern of future events and as particularly concerned with how economic agents manage to cope with problems of perhaps woefully limited information. This is common ground with Shackle (1967) and Minsky (1975), but here more is made of the parallel with sceptical philosophy and a formal statement of Keynes's approach is presented. A dimension of the argument missing from those interpretations can then be explored; for it emerges that, crucial though Keynes thought the impact of uncertainty on action and especially on the investment decision to be, he did not view the resulting behaviour as unreasonable or (in an important sense) irrational – rather the reverse.[2] While stressing the role of some unreasoned elements in decision-making, he can also be seen as offering an account of economic agents' *rational* response to conditions not just of risk but of gross uncertainty.

The strategy is, first, to present a diagrammatic analysis of Keynes's argument; secondly, to draw together some of his own statements of it; thirdly, to relate it to antecedents in Humean sceptical philosophy; and finally, to examine some puzzles and weigh up what it depends on for success.

Structure of Keynes's argument

This section summarizes my account of Keynes's position, representing it by a 'structure diagram'[3] (Figure 2.1 below), where the notation *pq* indicates that *p* is *held by the arguer* to be a ground for believing *q*, and letters stand for propositions to which the accompanying 'dictionary' provides the key. The propositions relate both to Keynes's general argument about future-regarding decisions and his specific argument about investment, presented side by side because he tends (confusingly?) to switch from one to the other.

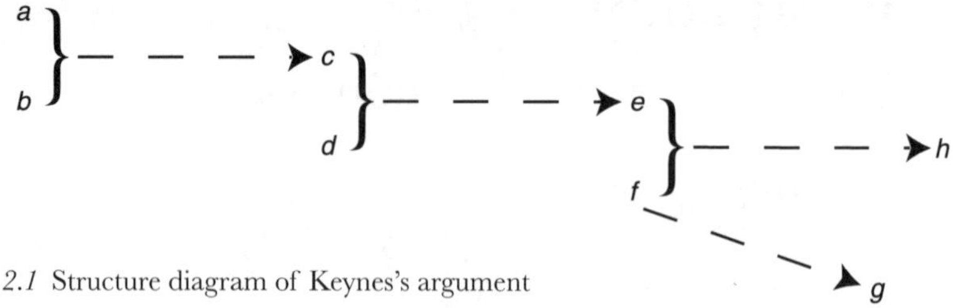

Figure 2.1 Structure diagram of Keynes's argument

Dictionary to Figure 2.1

a   It is impossible for us to deduce from our data what the future course of events will be; for instance, we cannot acquire (certain) knowledge, *ex ante*, of the future stream of returns from an investment.

b   It is impossible for us to establish a quantitative probability for every possible future state of the world; in particular, we cannot measure satisfactorily the probabilities of the various possible future returns from a capital asset.

c   Since actions have consequences in the future, we can deduce from our data neither which actions are best (given our goals), nor, in general, even which promise to be best; for example, if we are seeking to maximize profit, we face the difficulty that we cannot prove mathematically just from known facts or likelihoods which investment projects to favour.

d   We have to act and to choose between possible courses of action; similarly, investing is imperative and decisions where to invest have to be made.

e   In general, we must select a course of action by some means other than pure deduction from our data; and again this applies to the investment decision.

f   In practice our method of choosing actions is routine, in the sense that in the last analysis we rely on a set of habits and conventions (following the crowd) and especially on the custom of assuming that the future will be like the present and recent past; for example, the entrepreneur of an unquoted company assumes for practical purposes that the yield he expects from an investment project on the basis of the present state of affairs will in fact accrue, while in general those investing on the stock market act as if its existing valuations or trends give a largely correct guide to future prospects.

g   Since the basis of decision-making is merely conventional, subjective factors – including temperament, fashion, and even panic and hysteria – exert an influence, and in markets speculation is likely; thus, the extent to which the entrepreneur of an unquoted company invests depends partly on impulse or mood, and the stock market is subject to waves of optimism and pessimism.

h   But even so, our method of judging how to act isn't unreasonable in the circumstances; and where investment activity depends on private initiative, the way it is pursued under uncertainty is as good as can reasonably be expected.

As the diagram indicates, the argument has four premises, *a*, *b*, *d* and *f*, and two conclusions, *g* and *h*, with *c* and *e* as intermediate steps.

Textual evidence

What warrant is there for interpreting Keynes's position in this way? In this section, propositions *a* to *h* will be linked to Keynes's writings, taking the argument in three stages.

Stage 1: a *and* b, *leading to* c

'We do not know what the future holds', proclaims Keynes – premise *a*.[4] If there are to be changes, 'generally speaking, our imagination and our knowledge are too weak to tell us what particular changes to expect' (CWXIVd: 124). So in making estimates of prospective yield, 'the outstanding fact' is

> the extreme precariousness of the basis of knowledge on which [they] have to be made. Our knowledge of the factors which will govern the yield of an investment ... is usually very slight and often negligible ... we have to admit that our basis of knowledge for estimating the yield ten years hence of a railway ... a textile factory ... a building in the City of London amounts to little and sometimes to nothing; or even five years hence.
>
> (CWVII: 149–50)

He cites the fact that '[t]he orthodox theory assumes that we have a knowledge of the future of a kind quite different from that which we actually possess' as one of his two 'main grounds of ... departure' from it. Its 'false rationalisation follows the lines of the Benthamite calculus' and 'leads to a wrong interpretation of ... [our] principles of behaviour' (CWXIVa: 122).

Premise *b* is explicit as Keynes pours scorn on the tradition of assuming 'facts and expectations ... to be given in a definite and calculable form', 'the calculus of probability' being supposed 'capable of reducing uncertainty to the same calculable status as that of certainty itself'. But '[a]ctually', says Keynes, 'we have, as a rule, only the vaguest idea of any but the most direct consequences of our acts' (*ibid.*: 113). The general difficulty of assigning exact probabilities to possible outcomes is especially acute for investment decisions because

> The whole object of the accumulation of wealth is to produce results, at a comparatively distant, and sometimes ... *indefinitely* distant, date. Thus the fact that our knowledge of the future is fluctuating, vague and uncertain, renders wealth a peculiarly unsuitable subject for the methods of the classical economic theory ... By 'uncertain' knowledge ... I do not mean merely to distinguish what is known for certain from what is only probable. The game of roulette is not subject, in this sense, to uncertainty; nor is the prospect of a Victory bond being drawn. Or, again, the expectation of life is only slightly uncertain. Even the weather is only moderately uncertain. The sense in which I am using the term is that in which the prospect of a European war is uncertain, or ... the rate of interest twenty years hence, or the obsolescence of a new invention ... About these matters there is no scientific basis on which to form any calculable probability whatever. We simply do not know.
>
> (*ibid.*: 113–14)

Proposition *c* then finds expression in a passage which summarizes the whole first stage of the argument, where Keynes insists that 'human decisions affecting the future, whether personal or political or economic, cannot depend on strict mathematical expectation, since the basis for making such calculations does not exist' (CWVII: 162–3).

Stage 2: c, d *and so* e

The introduction of *d* – the idea of the 'need for action' and the 'necessity for decision' – enables the next stage of the argument to proceed: if we *have* to decide between courses of action, the 'ideal' calculus having been ruled out, we are forced (*e*) to fall back on some cruder way of judging.

So although we 'do not know' the future course of events, '[n]evertheless, the necessity for action and for decision compels us as practical men to do our best to overlook this awkward fact' (CWXIVa: 114). Similarly, the principles of behaviour that orthodox calculating theory misinterprets are 'principles of behaviour which the need for action compels us to adopt' (*ibid.*: 122). Or again: 'as living and moving beings we are forced to act. Peace and comfort of mind require that we should hide from ourselves how little we foresee. Yet we must be guided by some hypothesis' (CWXIVd: 124). The argument extends to all production, for 'the entrepreneur (including both ... producer and ... investor) has to form the best expectations he can as to what consumers will be willing to pay when he is ready to supply them ... and he has no choice but to be guided by these expectations, if he is to produce at all by processes which occupy time' (CWVII: 46).

Stage 3: e *and* f, *whence* g *and* h

But how are we to 'form the best expectations [we] can'? We 'substitute for the knowledge which is unattainable certain conventions [f], the chief of which is to assume ... that the future will resemble the past' (CWXIVd: 124). '[O]ur usual practice' is 'to take the existing situation and to project it into the future, modified only to the extent that we have more or less definite reasons for expecting a change' (CWVII: 148). This means assuming that 'the present is a much more serviceable guide to the future than a candid examination of past experience would show it to have been hitherto' and 'largely ignor[ing] the prospect of future changes about the actual character of which we know nothing'. Another form of conventional behaviour is to see safety in numbers and try to take refuge in the crowd. With organized investment markets, 'we endeavour to fall back on the judgment of the rest of the world ... to conform with the behaviour of the majority or the average', creating 'a society of individuals each of whom is endeavouring to copy the others' (CWXIVa: 114).

Take then the move from *f* to *g*. If the method of making future-regarding decisions is merely conventional, those decisions will strictly speaking lack 'an adequate or secure foundation' (*ibid.*: 118), however reassuring the method may feel. When we project the existing situation into the future, 'the facts of the existing situation enter, in a sense disproportionately, into the formation of our long-term expectations' (CWVII: 148). Yet organized investment markets have been able to develop with tacit reliance on the maintenance of this convention, although it is 'in an absolute view of things so arbitrary' (*ibid.*: 153).

But the inevitable weakness of a merely conventional basis of judgment opens the way for other factors (mood, dynamism, fashion, speculation, and sometimes panic and hysteria) to influence expectations, and so decisions (*g*). This is the cue for some of the most famous passages in *The General Theory*. 'If human nature felt no temptation to take a chance', writes Keynes, 'no satisfaction (profit apart) in constructing a factory ... or a farm, there might not be much investment merely as a result of cold calculation' (*ibid.*: 150). It is

> characteristic of human nature that a large proportion of our positive activities depend on spontaneous optimism rather than on a mathematical expectation ... Most, probably, of our decisions to do something positive, the full consequences of which will be drawn

out over many days to come, can only be taken as a result of animal spirits – of a spontaneous urge to action rather than inaction, and not as the outcome of a weighted average of quantitative benefits multiplied by quantitative probabilities. Enterprise only pretends to itself to be mainly actuated by the statements in its own prospectus, however candid and sincere. Only a little more than an expedition to the South Pole, is it based on an exact calculation of benefits to come. Thus if the animal spirits are dimmed and the spontaneous optimism falters, leaving us to depend on nothing but a mathematical expectation, enterprise will fade and die ...

(*ibid.*: 161–2)

'This means', he continues, 'that economic prosperity is excessively dependent on a political and social atmosphere which is congenial to the average business man' and that 'in estimating the prospects of investment, we must have regard ... to the nerves and hysteria and even the digestions and reactions to the weather of those upon whose spontaneous activity it largely depends.'

Just as individual psychology affects the enterprise of entrepreneurs, so also 'mass psychology' affects stock-market behaviour (*ibid.*: 170). Because the man in the street will have even fewer clues about prospective yield than the investing entrepreneur, contends Keynes, 'the element of real knowledge in the valuation of investments ... has seriously declined' as financial markets have grown. And,

A conventional valuation ... established as the outcome of the mass psychology of a large number of ignorant individuals is liable to change violently as a result of a sudden fluctuation of opinion due to factors which do not really make much difference to the prospective yield; since there will be no strong roots of conviction to hold it steady. In abnormal times in particular, when the hypothesis of an indefinite continuance of the existing state of affairs is less plausible than usual even though there are no express grounds to anticipate a definite change, the market will be subject to waves of optimistic and pessimistic sentiment ...

(*ibid.*: 154)

Our conventional assessments are flimsily based, then, and at the mercy of 'the forces of disillusion' (*ibid.*: 149, 153; CWXIVa: 114–15). Nor are the activities of relatively well-informed professional stock-market investors likely to exert a stabilizing influence; for 'most ... are, in fact, largely concerned, not with making superior long-term forecasts of the probable yield of an investment over its whole life, but with foreseeing changes in the conventional basis of valuation a short time ahead of the general public' – they are engaged in 'speculation', not 'enterprise', and (as in the well-known beauty contest analogy) even 'faith in the conventional basis of valuation having any genuine long-term validity' is not needed for this speculative activity of 'anticipating what average opinion expects the average opinion to be' (CWVII: 154–8). So Keynes holds that 'the vague panic fears and equally vague and unreasoned hopes are not really lulled, and lie but a little way below the surface'; and he claims it a major defect in orthodox theory that it involves 'an underestimation of the concealed factors of utter doubt, precariousness, hope and fear' (CWXIVa: 155, 122).

There remains the move from f combined with e to h – to the conclusion that adopting conventional means of evaluation, buoyed up by animal spirits as we take the plunge, represents a sensible strategy for doing as well as we can in the tight corner uncertainty condemns us to, allowing us to 'save our faces as rational, economic men' (*ibid.*: 114).

For Keynes, then, the entrepreneur who refuses to dwell on fears of possible ultimate loss is not acting wantonly but is akin to 'a healthy man [putting] aside the expectation of death' (CWVII: 162): it would be morbid to let an insecure future paralyse rewarding present pursuits. And when we come to form our expectations,

> It would be foolish … to attach great weight to matters which are very uncertain. It is reasonable, therefore, to be guided to a considerable degree by the facts about which we feel somewhat confident, even though they may be less decisively relevant to the issue than other facts about which our knowledge is vague and scanty.
>
> (*ibid.*: 148)

Moreover, if the average stock-market investor follows this practice, taking existing valuations as reliable – even though 'the actual results of such an investment over a long term of years very seldom agree with the initial expectation' – there is a self-sustaining mechanism. The 'conventional method of calculation will be compatible with a considerable measure of continuity and stability in our affairs', explains Keynes, '*so long as we can rely on the maintenance of the convention*'. For then the investor (who can sell his shares at short notice) 'can legitimately encourage himself with the idea that the only risk he runs is that of a genuine change in the news *over the near future*, as to the likelihood of which he can attempt to form his own judgment, and which is unlikely to be very large'; and 'he need not lose his sleep merely because he has not any notion what his investment will be worth ten years hence'. Thus the problem of selecting investments on the stock market reduces to one of foreseeing changes only a little time ahead. With this convention-based, market-induced stability, then, though the system is inherently fragile, still 'investment becomes reasonably "safe" for the individual investor over short periods'; and his routine assessment of the prospects is sensible (*ibid.*: 152–3).

Once organized capital markets exist, with their liquidity-enhancing role, wisdom seems to dictate that the entrepreneur too should abide by the conventional, mass valuation of the market, even if he believes himself to have a somewhat superior knowledge of the real prospects of his assets; 'for', writes Keynes,

> there is no sense in building up a new enterprise at a cost greater than that at which a similar existing enterprise can be purchased; whilst there is an inducement to spend on a new project what may seem an extravagant sum, if it can be floated off on the Stock Exchange at an immediate profit.
>
> (*ibid.*: 151)

Likewise, the activity of the professional investor is

> not the outcome of a wrong-headed propensity. It is an inevitable result of an investment market organised along the lines described. For it is not sensible to pay 25 for an investment of which you believe the prospective yield to justify a value of 30, if you also believe that the market will value it at 20 three months hence.
>
> (*ibid.*: 155)

In this sense, 'the professional investor is forced' by principles of good sense into his practice of trying 'to guess better than the crowd how the crowd will behave': he who instead attempts 'investment based on genuine long-term expectation ... must surely lead much more laborious days and run greater risks'; so the former approach yields 'the higher return ... to a given stock of intelligence and resources'.

Furthermore, even the 'waves of irrational psychology' that sometimes sway the market, though 'unreasoning', are 'yet in a sense *legitimate* where no solid basis exists for a reasonable calculation' (*ibid.*: 154–7, my emphasis). Nor should we 'conclude ... that everything depends on [them] ... on the contrary the state of long-term expectation is often steady'. But the steadiness does not – cannot – come from dependence on strict mathematical expectation, and 'it is our innate urge to activity which makes the wheels go round, our *rational selves* choosing between the alternatives as best we are able, calculating where we can, but often falling back for our motive on whim or sentiment or chance' (*ibid.*: 162–3, my emphasis).

Humean antecedents

Keynes's treatment of our behaviour in the face of ignorance of the future proves strikingly similar to that of the sceptical philosopher, David Hume; and, as this clarifies and perhaps strengthens Keynes's case, this section outlines the correspondence between their patterns of argument. The resemblance is surely not accidental. Keynes had studied deeply 'the superb Hume', as he called him, was an acknowledged Humean scholar,[5] and, as Harrod notes in his biography, 'took Hume's scepticism seriously' (Harrod 1951: 107, 656). 'Hume showed', Keynes explains, 'not that inductive methods [allowing "inference from past particulars to future generalisations"] were false, but that their validity had never been established' (CWVIII: 302) and 'that, while it is true that past experience gives rise to a psychological anticipation of some events rather than others, no ground has been given for the validity of this superior anticipation' (*ibid*.: 88).

Stage 1

Hume is renowned for showing that, when we 'suppose the future conformable to the past ... however easy this step may seem, reason would never, to all eternity, be able to make it' (AT: 16; see *a*).[6] For, he writes, 'there can be no *demonstrative* arguments [deductions from necessary truths] to prove, that those instances of which we have had no experience, resemble those, of which we have had experience' (T: 89). Nor can we establish this with 'probable' arguments [deductions from matters of fact], because arguments from past experience are themselves 'built on the supposition that there is this conformity betwixt the future and the past, and therefore can never prove it' (AT: 15). He also draws a moral about action: if we had to rely just on 'reason' [deduction from the known], 'we should never know how to adjust means to ends ... there would be an end at once to all action' (E: 44; compare with *c*).[7]

Stage 2

Far from concluding that future-regarding judgments must be abandoned, however, Hume maintains that there is no choice but to persist in them: this is 'the whimsical condition of mankind, who [*d*] must act and reason and believe; though they are not able, by their most diligent enquiry, to satisfy themselves concerning the foundation of these operations' (E: 160). Inference from past experience is 'necessary to the subsistence of our species': nature triumphs over sceptical doubt (E: 55). But 'if the mind be not engaged by argument to make this step', then 'it must be induced by some other principle of equal weight and authority' (E: 41) (*e*).

Stage 3

How then do our minds make the 'so necessary' transition from the observed present to the expected future event? 'Nothing leads us to make this inference', says Hume, 'but custom or a certain instinct of our nature' (*f*): 'custom ... is the great guide of human life. It is that principle alone which renders our experience useful to us, and makes us expect, for the future, a similar train of events with those which have appeared in the past' (E: 44, 159; AT: 16).

This completes Hume's main argument; but other remarks he makes could have set Keynes thinking along the lines of the move from *f* to *g*. In particular, Hume explains how his attitude to sceptical argument is very much a matter of mood. Reflecting on the force of sceptical philosophy leads him into a state of 'philosophical melancholy and delirium' which however is soon cured, for a time by his 'natural propensity, and the course of [his] *animal spirits* and passions ... I dine, I play a game of back-gammon, I converse, and am merry with my friends; and when after three or four hours' amusement, I would return to these speculations, they appear so cold, and strained, and ridiculous, that I cannot find in my heart to enter into them any farther' (T: 268–71, my emphasis). But just as the 'vague panic fears' that Keynes detects beneath the smooth veneer of the investment market 'are not really lulled', so also 'sceptical doubt', Hume believes, 'can never be radically cured, but must return upon us every moment, however we may chase it away, and sometimes ... seem entirely free from it' (T: 218).

Does Hume nevertheless think we behave wisely in relying on experience, despite unsquashable doubt? This is open to debate, although maintaining Hume's opposition to proposition *h* would be more orthodox.[8] Here I merely note as – to my mind rather strong – casual evidence for the unorthodox position Hume's remark that 'for [his] conduct' (acting, living, and so on) the sceptic 'is not obliged to give any other reason than the absolute necessity he lies under of doing so' (D: 9); his suggestion that the natural, instinctive force of habit or custom may sometimes have advantages over the working of deductive reason (E: 55); his acceptance that an anticipated effect may '*justly* be inferred' from the observation of an apparent cause (E: 34, my emphasis); and his admission that, be sceptical objections what they may, 'none but *a fool or a madman* will ever pretend to dispute the authority of experience, or to reject that great guide of human life' (E: 36, my emphasis).

Evaluation

So far, I have given my account of Keynes's argument and have tried to show that it is fair; and I have indicated his debt to Hume. The question now is: how well does the argument work?

Take first the acceptability of its four premises: *a*, *b*, *d* and *f*. There seems good reason to accept them but the first three might have been given more explanation. The fourth, *f* (reliance on conventions), is quite persuasively presented by Keynes and Hume as an accurate behavioural description.[9]

Premise *d* (necessity of action etc.) generates more doubt. A prolonged period of inaction is not inconceivable – is deciding not to act still to count as a form of action? But here Hume's reference to what is 'necessary to the subsistence of our species' is suggestive: such a period must yield to one of positive action in the *end* – if human agents are to survive. Grant then that survival requires action: does it also require investment? It is a pity that Keynes does not give explicit justification of this. But presumably his point is that rather similarly investment is indeed imperative for the *community* if the system of production is to survive.[10]

Premise *a* seems plain sailing given the backing of Hume's two powerful points against the claim that the future will conform with the past:[11] first, that this is not a necessary truth; and, secondly, that it cannot be deduced from past experience without circularity. Two vivid passages from Russell emphasize these Humean moves. First, the future collapse of past physical regularities is always logically possible:

> We have a firm belief that [the sun] will rise in the future, because it has risen in the past ... [But] expectations of uniformity are liable to be misleading. The man who has fed the chicken every day throughout its life at last wrings its neck instead ... Thus our instincts certainly cause us to believe that the sun will rise tomorrow, but we may be in no better a position than the chicken which unexpectedly has its neck wrung.

And secondly, it is circular to argue that, where there has been uniformity in the past, we know the future will resemble the past 'because what was the future has constantly become the past ... so that we really have experience of the future, namely of times which were formerly future, which we may call past futures'. Such an argument 'begs the very question at issue. We have experience of past futures, but not of future futures, and the question is: Will future futures resemble past futures?' (Russell 1912: 33–6). As Hume maintained, then, 'all reasonings from experience' ultimately depend on a non-deductive step; and *a* is home and dry.

Premise *b* needs more discussion, for a natural response to *a* is to suggest that *in*duction rather than *de*duction from past experience may permit us to judge future events probable. Keynes agrees but maintains that our information is generally too thin to enable us to use the mathematical calculus of probabilities to determine what it is rational to do. His basis for this can be gleaned from *A Treatise on Probability* (CWVIII),[12] in which he had set out a logical theory of probability, arguing that probability 'is concerned with the degree of belief which it is *rational* to entertain', but that often this degree will not be precise. Only 'in a very special type of case' can 'a meaning ... be given to a *numerical* comparison' between probabilities, while 'there are ... many cases in which ... probabilities are, in fact, *not comparable*' at all: 'a rule can be given for numerical measurement when the conclusion is one of a number of equiprobable, exclusive alternatives [as in throwing a die – or drawing a 'Victory bond'], but not otherwise' (*ibid.*: 4, 36–7, 122).[13] On this analysis, although 'some inductive arguments are stronger than others and … some are very strong', still 'how much stronger or how strong we cannot express' (*ibid.*: 288, see also 30–1). Ordinal ranking of probabilities will sometimes be elusive too (as in comparing propositions each based on a different type of evidence; *ibid.*: 31–2).[14] Nor is it always possible even to make comparisons with a 50:50 benchmark:

> Is our expectation of rain, when we start out for a walk, always *more* likely … or *less* likely … or *as* likely as not? I am prepared to argue that on some occasions *none* of these alternatives hold … If the barometer is high, but the clouds are black, it is not always rational that one should prevail over the other in our minds, or even that we should balance them …
>
> (*ibid.*: 32)

There is much more to Keynes's analysis of probability (for the full story, see CWVIII, especially Part I, Chapter 3).[15] It is controversial – although the prime objection of Jeffreys, a strident early Bayesian opponent, appeared to amount to little more than a complaint of intractability and 'vagueness': brushing aside Keynes's argument, he wrote, 'it seems to me that all probabilities actually are comparable and that Keynes is merely creating difficulties' (Jeffreys 1931: 223). There may be modern critics, however, prepared to argue more extensively that Keynes's claims on probability are open to attack.[16]

Suppose, though, that we accept all four premises, at least provisionally. How does the rest of the argument fare? The moves to *c* and *e* seem straightforward; so remaining queries centre on Stage 3 – the derivation of the, at first glance incongruous, twin conclusions: scope for non-rational or irrational elements (*g*) in reasonable or rational behaviour (*h*).

Can rough-and-ready convention-following behaviour under uncertainty really qualify as rational? One immediate problem is the meaning of 'reasonable' and 'rational'.[17] Acceptance of *h* depends on rationality being extended beyond deductive reasoning, a step Keynes certainly approves. Complaining that philosophy, preoccupied with demonstrative certainty, has tended to neglect 'the study of arguments, to which it is rational to attach *some* weight', he insists that 'in the actual exercise of reason we do not wait on certainty, or deem it irrational to depend on a doubtful argument'. Indeed, '[i]n metaphysics, in science, and in conduct, most of the arguments, upon which we habitually base our rational beliefs, are admitted to be inconclusive in a greater or less degree' (CWVIII: 3).

But if deduction does not set the standard, what does? Keynes views actions as rational if they are justified with respect to the beliefs it is reasonable for the agent to form on the available information[18] – recognizing that sometimes this will subsequently prove to have been misleading. On occasions when information is more seriously lacking or points in contradictory ways (as in the perplexing conjunction of auspicious barometer reading and darkened sky), there is no point in the façade of a 'pseudo-rationalistic' approach: rather, 'it will be rational to allow caprice to determine us and to waste no time on the debate' (*ibid.*: 32).[19] And rational action can sometimes rely on 'unconscious memory', a 'habit' of the mind, rather than conscious deliberation (*ibid.*: 15) – an idea backed by Hollis, who writes:

> to insist on conscious deliberation is to miss the place of habit in rational action. The rational way to drive a car is precisely not to deliberate each change of gear but to master the skill so well that no deliberation is needed. There are rational habits and, were there not, we could not talk, plan, associate, build, reason or perform many other tasks which make social life possible … if the point is missed, large areas of social action are wrongly classed as non-rational.
>
> (1977: 17)

Keynes's broad understanding of the rationality concept could, I think, find a fair measure of support within philosophy.[20] But orthodox economic theory has typically used 'rational' in a narrower sense,[21] and this is another point where opponents might seek to challenge him.

With 'reasonable' understood in a wide sense, a possible justification of inductive conventions goes back to Hume's claim that when we draw a well-grounded inductive conclusion nature gives us no viable option. Building on this, Lenz maintains that if we 'cannot avoid making' such inferences 'any injunction not to do so is beside the point' (1958: 183). If taking past experience as our guide is a convention 'none of us could possibly do without' (CWXIVd: 125), then at least it cannot be unreasonable in the sense that we should *give it up*.

Keynes did allow 'the inductive method' to be embedded in 'the organon of thought' (CWVIII: 294), acknowledging it as 'part of our human outfit, perhaps given us … by natural selection' (CWXa: 339).[22] But, believing induction could be given a more ambitious defence, perhaps he might have welcomed the solution constructed by Strawson, who argues that the statement 'induction is rational (reasonable)' is not only true but is a *necessary* truth. Strawson's appealing claim is that 'the rationality of induction … is a matter of what we mean by the word "rational"' when we assess procedures for 'forming opinions about what lies outside our observation or that of available witnesses. For to have good reasons for any such opinion *is* to have good inductive support for it' (1952: 261–2, my emphasis). On this basis, where past experience offers a clear guide, it is *by definition* rational to follow it.

On either of these justifications of induction, it makes sense (*h*) to base action on 'probable' knowledge, although this never in principle escapes the risk of, as Russell puts it, 'failure at the last'. 'We cannot be sure that [observed uniformities] will persist', writes Keynes, but 'if we find them in the past, we have at any rate some basis for an inductive argument' (CWXIVe: 316). The argument will occasionally be strong,[23] yielding inductive conclusions of which 'we are very well assured' and 'upon which it is rational to act with the utmost confidence' (CWVIII: 275). However, 'most ... of our decisions to do something positive' will depend on weaker inductive evidence, increasing the need for 'animal spirits' (*g*) to fill the confidence gap.

This helps to explain some of Keynes's remarks that may otherwise appear anomalous. 'We do not know what the future holds'; yet we do seem to 'know' something, for Keynes also speaks of 'the future about which we know so *little*' and of our having '*as a rule*, only the vaguest idea of any *but the most direct consequences of our acts*' (CWXIVa: 121, 113, my emphasis). Again, we assume indefinite continuance of the existing state of affairs 'except insofar as we have specific reasons to expect a change' (CWVII: 152); but if we are truly ignorant of the future, on what grounds *can* we expect this? Not on logically compelling grounds, but on inductive ones. For instance, Keynes allowed that it was 'known' in 1937 that there would shortly be a 'change-over' in the trend of population, this 'unusual degree of knowledge concerning the future' resulting from the 'time-lag in the effects of vital statistics' (CWXIVd: 125).

Inductive procedures must also enter into Keynes's classification of the expectation of life or the weather as only 'slightly' or 'moderately' uncertain. Here Keynes's intertwining of his general argument about all future-regarding decisions with his case about investment may create some further confusion of terminology. While Humean sceptical doubt affects even the most secure inductive conclusions (such as that the sun will rise again), we can rationally place confidence in them – theoretical uncertainty alone need not (Hume's 'philosophical melancholy' apart) leave us feeling uncertain. But in the context of long-term decisions and so investment, we may face the *pressing* doubt and intrusive uncertainty that arises when there is next to nothing for inductive procedures to go on,[24] leaving us deciding on the basis of 'whim or sentiment or chance' (*g*).

Yet inductive reasoning may after all get some grip. Once more there are apparently conflicting statements: we 'do not know' when a new invention will become obsolete (CWXIVa: 113–14); but still, the investing entrepreneur is held to enjoy an 'element of real knowledge' of the prospects; and again, the professional stock-market investor may possess 'judgment and knowledge beyond that of the average private investor' (CWVII: 153–4). The puzzle persists, as Keynes writes of 'socially advantageous' investment based on '*genuine* long-term expectation' (*ibid.*: 157, my emphasis).

More direct claims on scope for attempts at forecasting come with Keynes's assertion of the advantage of drawing inductive conclusions over only a *short* time-horizon.[25] This means that 'certain important factors ... [can] somewhat mitigate in practice the effects of our ignorance of the future' – among them 'the operation of compound interest combined with the likelihood of obsolescence with the passage of time', because of which the prospective yield for many individual investments 'is legitimately dominated by the returns of the comparatively near future' (*ibid.*: 163).[26] And there is another reason why the near future may curiously turn out to be what drives purportedly long-term expectation: as the textual section reported, Keynes sees conventional forecasting and imitative behaviour as leading to the stock market also being dominated by short-term expectations, investors then not needing to 'lose [their] sleep' over worries a decade away. He is very effective, I think, in showing how the 'average private investor', following – reasonably enough in the absence of a better alternative – the convention of projecting recent valuations, meshes with others putting trust in the same procedure and so contributes to surface stability, setting a pattern of stock-market behaviour which neither 'informed' entrepreneurs nor professional investors can rationally afford to ignore.

But in spite of this, fragility still lies at the heart of Keynes's account of investment. There is the ever-present possibility of an explosion of doubt because, below the surface, deep uncertainty remains: in investing, we do not 'really believe' in the conventional assumption 'that the existing state of affairs will continue indefinitely. [Indeed] we know from extensive experience that this is most unlikely' (*ibid.*: 152). Thus again *h* and *g* co-exist: the delicate market balance of convention-based stability seems on the one hand – while it lasts – to validate inductive forecasts based on current prospects, and on the other, paradoxically, to facilitate rapid collapse, like a house of cards, if ever confidence falters.

Conclusion

I have tried to clarify, and suggest the strengths in, Keynes's complex argument on the rationality of the investment decision under uncertainty, while also pointing out where it might be thought vulnerable. Its radical economic conclusions, though not fully conclusive, are commonly reached with the aid of respectable philosophical tradition, and the picture given of decision-making is in many respects persuasive.

But the picture is a sombre one, for it portrays rather violent 'fluctuations in the market estimation of the marginal efficiency of different types of capital' (*ibid.*: 164) as endemic in the capitalist economy – a *natural* concomitant of decision behaviour that isn't unreasonable under uncertainty.[27]

Notes

1 The original version of this chapter was completed in 1976, widely circulated in Cambridge and beyond, and used in seminars and a graduate lecture series. (Anna Carabelli was already working on an allied topic; similar lines of thinking on rational behaviour subsequently appeared in O'Donnell (thesis and 1989) and in Lawson (1985); and Coddington (1982) took a hostile but lively line (without direct reference to my work) on the points I made about scepticism and uncertainty.) The essay, slightly revised, was then published by Cambridge University Press in *Thoughtful Economic Man* (Meeks 1991): further backing for and discussion of the analysis presented here can be found in that considerably longer piece. I repeat the thanks given there to Robin Carter, Phyllis Deane, Martin Hollis, Geoff Meeks, Joan Robinson, Amartya Sen and a number of Cambridge graduate students for their comments, and to the Calouste Gulbenkian Foundation and the former Social Science Research Council for their support on this topic through Research Fellowships from 1975. In the production of this new, shortened version, I owe thanks to my daughter, Kitty, for her essential computing skills, and a final large debt to Jochen Runde for his patient encouragement and for giving me this opportunity.

2 In contrast, Shackle writes, 'the message of the *General Theory*' is that 'investment is an *irrational* activity or a non-rational one', also referring to 'the nihilism' of Keynes's final position (1967: 130, 247); on his understanding of the term 'rational', see Meeks (1991: 149–50). The late 1980s saw a burst of interest in this dimension of the argument: Skidelsky documents and evaluates this development (understandably without reference to my original piece) (1992: 82–9).

3 A device developed by J.L. Mackie.

4 Possible ambiguities of 'know' are taken up in the evaluation section.

5 Together with Sraffa he identified, as not Adam Smith's but Hume's, and gained reprinting for a rare and anonymous pamphlet (*An Abstract of A Treatise of Human Nature*, reprinted in 1938), giving a version of the argument-pattern being discussed here. (A joint economists' coup in philosophy, coming from a generation of economists sharing philosophical interests, some of them, for example Harrod and Ramsey, philosophers in their own right: see Coates (1996) and O'Donnell (1989).)

6 The following abbreviations are used for Hume's writings: T for *A Treatise of Human Nature*; AT for the Keynes-discovered *An Abstract of A Treatise of Human Nature*; E for *An Enquiry concerning Human Understanding*; and D for *Dialogues concerning Natural Religion*.

7 The usage of terms such as 'reason' or 'probable' in Hume's day does not fully coincide with ours: see Stove (1965, 1973).

8 See, for instance, Stove (1973: 50) and Popkin (1951). Keynes himself sometimes seems to interpret Hume in a fairly orthodox way; on the other hand, he certainly was alert to Hume's 'common sense and hard-headed practicality' (CWXA: 339) in philosophy, seeing him as standing 'for the plain man against the sophisms and ingenuities of "metaphysicians [and] logicians"' (CWVIII: 56).

9 Modern work on induction and language gives convention a significant role, whereby 'well-entrenched' predicates (such as 'green') are readily projected into the future and poorly entrenched ones (such as 'grue') are not (see Goodman 1954). In philosophy more generally, a tradition going back at least to J. S. Mill grants significance to rules and norms in behaviour. In economics, see Heiner (1983) and Simon (1976).

But might we sometimes use more complex conventions than Keynes describes? The latter can at least gain from a comparatively high 'weight' of evidence, aiding confidence in them (CWVII: 148, 240; CWVIII: 77–85). Runde (1990) leads the way in giving prominence to the concept of the 'weight' of arguments.

10 The necessity argument would be considerably less strong for the *individual* entrepreneur: see Matthews (1991).

11 'Conform with' or 'resemble': Hume's usage is followed by Keynes (and Russell), and when Keynes says 'the future never resembles the past' (CWXIVd: 124), 'resembles' presumably means 'replicates'.

12 His first major work (of which he writes, 'Hume might have read what I have written with sympathy' (CWVIII: 468)).

13 Keynes sees measuring probabilities as analogous to measuring degrees of similarity; and he gives a diagrammatic illustration of incomparabilities, shown in Figure 2.2 below (from CWVIII: 42). In this diagram, numerical probabilities lie along the line *OAI*; points along, for example, *OVWXI* can be compared ordinally; *Y* and *V* are unusual in being ordinally comparable by means of a common reference point *W* (similarly *X* and *Z*); but no comparison is possible between *U*, *Z*, *V* (or *U*, *X*, *Y*).

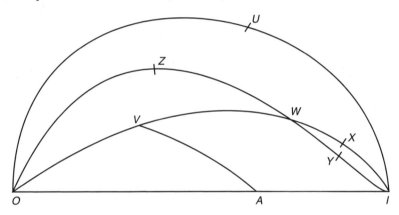

14 And ordinal rankings are insufficient, Keynes stresses, to ensure comparability between mathematical expectations or their sums as the Benthamite approach requires, even supposing the possible gains to be numerically measurable, and even supposing that both risk-aversion and the 'weights' of the arguments can be ignored. This is why Keynes sees *b* as so damaging for orthodox theory. It is because the Benthamite blueprint is held to rely on assuming that degrees of probability are 'wholly subject to the laws of arithmetic' that Keynes slates it as a theory 'no-one has ever acted on' involving a 'mythical system of probable knowledge' (CWVIII: 343–49; CWXIVd: 124).

15 See also Skidelsky (1992: 77–82) and Meeks (1991: 144–8).

16 Defeating (strongly-worded) *b* requires, however, very strong claims for numerical measurement. (More moderate opponents on probability might perhaps be able to use their ammunition in criticizing *f*; but see Runde (1995).)

17 Also 'not unreasonable'.

18 See Keynes (CWVIII: 246, 272–5, 339, 10–11). Keynes here avoids the possible von Mises pitfall of defining 'rational' action so as to eliminate the possibility of irrationality.

19 See Meeks (1991: 157–8).
20 See, for example, Raz (1975).
21 See Simon (1976), Sen (1987) and Sugden (1991).
22 Under strong pressure from Ramsey (and though still holding that induction was not *merely* 'a useful mental habit'). On his earlier but largely fruitless attempt to rebut extreme scepticism towards induction, see CWVIII (56 and Ch. 22) and Meeks (1991: 152).
23 But recall Keynes's 'how strong we cannot express'.
24 The 'double whammy' of unmeasurable, unrankable probabilities and negligible 'weight' of evidence.
25 Intuitively plausible, but not established in the argument (see CWVII: 51; CWVIII: 287–8).
26 Other examples of mitigation concern yields subject to some control or with an important social component.
27 In the context of the 1930s and unemployment, Keynes drew a political moral, saying: 'I expect to see the State … taking an ever greater responsibility for directly organising investment' – not because of greater foresight or gains from institutionalized decision processes (there may be losses) but because of its ability to press on with investment programmes whatever the state of confidence and so benefit the stability of effective demand.

    At the start of the twenty-first century, the analysis remains relevant to current policy concerns, such as stock-market volatility: see Shiller (2000) – Keynes's explanation of why rational investors participate in temporary 'waves of irrational psychology' can be related to what Federal Reserve Chairman Alan Greenspan called the 'irrational exuberance' of late 1990s markets.

3 On the nature of Keynesian probability

Charles R. McCann Jr

Introduction

John Maynard Keynes's 1921 *A Treatise on Probability* (CWVIII) is widely recognized as a significant contribution to the philosophy of probability that at once exposed the cracks in the foundation of the prevailing orthodoxy and succeeded in establishing the foundations of an alternative, *general* theory of probability. The positions advanced in this work, while important in their own right as having set the framework for the logical or necessarian approach to probability, take on an even greater significance when used as a lens through which to view Keynes's later economic writings. Only when seen in the light of the understandings and formulations of *A Treatise on Probability* can one truly appreciate the complexities of Keynes's accomplishments in economic theory.

A number of the other contributions to this volume address the connection between *A Treatise on Probability* and Keynes's economic works, and there is already a large literature on this subject which we need not confront here. The purpose of this chapter is more specific: to address the qualitative nature of Keynesian probability and to review its logical structure. As this is not a subject that is readily summarized in a brief overview, this chapter will merely cover some of its more important aspects, specifically those facets which differentiate it from its predecessor, the frequency theory, and which demonstrate its potential.[1]

Difficulties with the frequency approach to probability

At the time Keynes wrote on the subject, probability was dominated by the work of the frequentists, most notably John Venn in his 1888 *Logic of Chance*. On the frequency view, probability is the ratio of favourable to possible cases in a series or sequence of otherwise similar events, attributes, or observations. Probability then attaches to these events, attributes, or observations only as they are part of the well-defined series, and, thus, probability as frequency is entirely empirical. Keynes's criticism of the frequency view centred on his supposition that incomplete knowledge necessitates recourse to an *a priori* principle or some such similar criterion from which may be deduced an initial probability value. Once such a value is at hand, a comparison of propositions in terms of probability may be made. The frequency interpretation, however, neither requires nor can support an *a priori* proposition as a base; it relies *solely* on empirical data as the basis for the calculation of a probability value. In Keynes's estimation, experience alone is insufficient to serve as a basis for the formulation of probability judgments. A theory of probability, as a method by which one may intuit the probability of some conclusion based on incomplete knowledge, cannot rely on a reference class which is itself imperfect: 'where our experience is incomplete, we cannot hope to derive from it judgments of probability without the aid either of intuition or of some further *a priori* principle' (CWVIII: 94). Thus, one may concur that experience alone is unlikely to provide the necessary stationary and homogeneous series upon which such judgments as demanded by the frequency approach may be made.

Keynes's solution to the problems inherent in the frequency interpretation was to reinterpret probability as part of the field of logic. Keynesian probability then is essentially what may be termed a *relational* calculus, as it applies to the relations between arguments or propositions, not to the regularities of statistical series. According to Keynes, logical arguments are of two types, conclusive and inconclusive. Conclusive arguments are those of which where the certainty of a proposition is entailed by the premises; this is the realm of pure knowledge as distinct from belief. Inconclusive arguments are those of which a proposition stands to evidence (itself a proposition) in a relation of less than certainty, while still possessing a claim to some *degree* of certainty. It is to the realm of the inconclusive that Keynesian probability has its application, and it is here that one sees the clearest distinction between the epistemological stance of *A Treatise on Probability* and the received orthodoxy.

Belief

One of the more significant aspects of Keynes's approach is his exploration of the notion of belief, an understanding of which is central to the subjective (epistemic) nature of Keynesian probability. Important in this regard is the distinction between 'belief' and 'rational belief'. The 'belief' held in a proposition lies somewhere along a continuum extending from 'pure ignorance' to 'pure knowledge'. Belief, or 'mere belief', is entirely subjective, and so requires no support; it is of the nature of speculation or uninformed opinion. 'Rational belief' is something different, as it is coextensive neither with certainty nor with truth; such a belief may be certain or only probable. Rational belief is an objective concept, dependent upon the evidence we have amassed in its favour; it is something derived with respect to and with the support of a given body of evidence, and this derivation is logical in nature (as we shall see below). As employed by

Keynes, 'rational belief' may be distinguished from 'mere belief' based on the degree of knowledge (the evidence) we have regarding any proposition:

> If a man believes something for a reason which is preposterous or for no reason at all, and what he believes turns out to be true for some reason not known to him, he cannot be said to believe it *rationally*, although he believes it and it is in fact true. On the other hand, a man may rationally believe a proposition to be *probable*, when it is in fact false. The distinction between rational belief and mere belief, there-fore, is not the same as the distinction between true beliefs and false beliefs. The highest degree of rational belief, which is termed *certain* rational belief, corresponds to *knowledge*. We may be said to know a thing when we have a certain rational belief in it, and *vice versa* .
>
> (*ibid.*: 10)

A rational belief may then be held about a proposition the truth or falsity of which is unknown, but for which we have evidential support. There need be no connection to any actual occurrence, and our 'predic-tions' may in fact turn out to be wrong; but, nonetheless, based upon the evidence we have in our possession, we are *rational* to hold the beliefs we do. Any other conclusion would open us to charges of irrationality. Only when rational belief is certain is it to be regarded as knowledge. It is *knowledge* that in Keynes's view is fundamental, with belief being defined in relation to it. Still, Keynes noted that he was unclear as to whether certainty or probability should be the fundamental proposition: if certainty is fundamental, probability becomes that which possesses a 'lower degree of rational belief than certainty', while if probability is fundamental, certainty is definable as 'maximum probability' (*ibid.*: 16).

Primary vs secondary propositions

In Keynes's terms, probability relations are logical rather than the stuff of empirical regularities. All judgements of probability are relative to the knowledge possessed about a given proposition. This may be clarified using the formalism employed by Keynes. Let h represent an evidential proposition, that is, the premises of an argument. Let a represent another proposition, which we shall take to be the conclusions (partially) implied. Then we may hold that a stands in a strict relation to h, that is, a R h. Here it is clear that the evidentiary statements are inseparable from the conclusions derived. If we specify R as the relation of probability, P, then a P h represents the primitive, while undefined, *conditional* proba-bility relation.

The proposition a, which we have identified as the conclusion, Keynes termed the *primary proposition*. This proposition may be known directly, or indirectly through knowledge of the evidential propositions, *h*. The primary proposition is *derivative* from (actually partially or fully implied in) the evidentiary statement. Of utmost importance is the connecting link, the *secondary proposition, a/h*; this is an assertion that a probability relation *exists* (*ibid*.: 11). We are now in a position to distinguish probability and hence belief from knowledge. Knowledge requires that one possess direct and certain apprehension of the proposition *a* (so that *a* is in effect, and with apologies to those with positivistic sympathies, self-evident) or, failing that, requires that the proposition *h* be known with certainty and that a secondary proposition be known which states a certainty relation; the proposition *a* is known in this second instance with certainty, but this knowledge is indirect, that is, it is gained by argument. Keynes termed this knowledge *of* the proposition *a* (*ibid*.: 11–15, 17). In this instance, in which our judgment is beyond doubt, we may assert that $P = 1$.

But the secondary proposition may also assert a *probability relation*, according to Keynes, that warrants only some degree of rational belief in *a* relative to *h*. This he termed knowledge *about* the proposition *a* (*ibid*.: 13). Here, as we must rely on belief as opposed to having the security of knowledge, we can only infer that $P < 1$.

Keynes defined the conditional probability of *a* given *h*, *a/h*, as equal to $\propto$, where $\propto$ is the degree of rational belief in the primary proposition brought about through knowledge of its relation to the premises *h*. As *h* represents the complete (or at least complete *relevant*) knowledge set of the individual, he will not entertain a degree of rational belief of less than $\propto$; the degree of rational belief depends on *all* the evidence available at the time a judgment is made. To illustrate, let $h_1{}^c h$. It is obvious that the probability relation based on such incomplete knowledge or evidence a/h_1 is of a different order from the probability relation *a/h*, even though the probability *values* justified by these relations (to the extent that such are calculable) could conceivably be the same (*ibid*.: Ch.1; see also Russell 1948: 376–7). As rational belief requires that we account for *all* available relevant evidence, we should (ideally) be guided by *a/h* rather than a/h_1 when *h* is available to us.

Objective and subjective elements in Keynesian probability

For Keynes, probability is not a concept amenable to categorization as either objective or subjective, but comprises elements of both. Probability is a subjective concept in the sense that a proposition is capable of standing in relation to knowledge in varying degrees and is therefore dependent upon the knowledge to which it relates; the circumstances in which the actor finds himself and the very manner of his apprehension are in some degree unique to the individual. It is objective in that once the evidence is given, probability judgement is no longer 'subject to human caprice'. The objective component pertains to the probability relation itself. Once the facts are in, what is probable is determined objectively via the probability relation, the secondary proposition, and not related to opinion; it is of no consequence whatever what we may think or feel about the probability of any given proposition, for probability pertains to *rational* belief, which is itself an objective quality. Probability judgments are in a sense the product of a mechanical 'black box' process. 'The theory of probability is logical, therefore, because it is concerned with the degree of belief which it is *rational* to entertain in given conditions, and not merely with the actual beliefs of particular individuals, which may or may not be rational' (CWVIII: 4).

Yet for all this, Keynes himself viewed his work as fundamentally subjective: 'The method of this treatise has been to regard subjective probability as fundamental and to treat all other relevant conceptions as derivative from this' (*ibid.*: 312). Despite the perceived tension, there really is no discord between the two positions, that is, whether probability is of an objective or a subjective nature. The probability *relation* is objective and knowable in each and every instance by all possessed of a keen enough intellect (or rather sufficiently attuned cognitive abilities, which is not necessarily the same thing). The primary proposition, however, is known only through the evidentiary propositions, and the degree of belief warranted by knowledge of the primary proposition is determined *subjectively*. This is the reason for the subjective aspect of Keynesian probability being termed fundamental. As Roy Weatherford (1982) notes, 'Keynes explicitly denies that probability-relations are objective in the sense that any rational being would agree to them ... The validity of P depends, therefore, in a very Kantian sense, on the constitution of the human mind' (1982: 112–13).

The subjective element in Keynes's interpretation of probability enters via the apprehension of the premises that form the evidentiary component expressed in the probability relation. While the probability relation itself is not subjectively determined, subjectivity is reflected in differences in knowledge and even cognitive ability among and between individuals. We may regard the premises then as being both knowledge-dependent and situation-dependent, and hence, as they are relative to the 'observer', as subjective. As Keynes put it, writing explicitly of the inherently subjective nature of opinion and of knowledge:

> We cannot speak of knowledge absolutely – only of the knowledge of a particular person. Other parts of knowledge – knowledge of the axioms of logic, for example – may seem more objective. But we must admit, I think, that this too is relative to the constitution of the human mind, and that the constitution of the human mind may vary in some degree from man to man. What is self-evident to me and

> what I really know, may be only a probable belief to you, or may form no part of your rational beliefs at all. And this may be true not only of such things as *my* existence, but of some logical axioms also.
>
> (CWVIII: 18)

> What we know and what probability we can attribute to our rational beliefs is, therefore, subjective in the sense of being relative to the individual.
>
> (*ibid.*: 19)

Knowledge is not absolute, as it is impressed upon the mind through sensation or perception, which differ among individuals as do their cognitive and perceptual skills. All knowledge is subjective. Even knowledge of the axioms of logic varies according to the intellectual capacities of the individual and the intellectual constitution; they are perceived 'relative to the constitution of the human mind' (*ibid.*: 18). Yet the subjectivity and relativity of knowledge and opinion do not obviate the existence of a logical structure:

> But given the body of premises which our subjective powers and circumstances supply to us, and given the kinds of logical relations, upon which arguments can be based and which we have the capacity to perceive, the conclusions, which it is rational for us to draw, stand to these premisses in an objective and wholly logical relation.
>
> (*ibid.*: 19)

> Although a particular universe of reference may be defined by considerations which are partly psychological, when once the universe is given, our theory of the relation in which other propositions stand towards it is entirely logical.
>
> (*ibid.*: 142)

So, while the *premises* of an argument may be subjectively ascertained, the *conclusions* derived are objectively determined through the use of the logical calculus. Perhaps then we may regard Keynes's probability interpretation as *subjective epistemic necessarianism*.

From the above it may be objected that Keynes is involved in a contradiction as to the logical nature of probability, and indeed objections along these lines have been raised by, among others, Frank P. Ramsey (1978) and R. B. Braithwaite (1973). The objections highlight an inconsistency as to the status of the probability relation, namely whether the probability *relation* is objective and the probability *value* subjective, or whether the probability relation *itself* is subjective. Rod O'Donnell (1989: 64–6) claims that in fact no contradiction would ensue if it were accepted that: (1) the perceptive powers of individuals in regard to logical analysis are not uniform; and (2) there may be a general limitation on the powers of individual reason. This is significant in explaining Keynes's insistence that even knowledge of the axioms of logic is relative: while the logical relations of probability may be objective, they may well be *perceived* subjectively. As Keynes offered, 'logic can never be made purely mechanical. All it can do is so to arrange the reasoning that the logical relations, which have to be perceived directly, are made explicit and are of a simple kind' (CWVIII: 15). (Thus it may be the case that a P h is replaceable by a P$_i h$, where $i = 1, \ldots, n$ represents the n individuals under consideration. Then P$_i$ is still the logical relation of probability and is objective, but is, as are the premises, unique to the individual. This interpretation would seem to remove Shackle's (1972) objection to Keynes's theory, for it provides a basis for rational subjective judgements.)

There must then be three aspects to Keynesian probability: the logical relation, which is objective; the *knowledge* of this relation, that is, the manner in which it is perceived, which is relative and subjective; and the knowledge of the central propositions or premises of an argument, which is also subjective (CWVIII: 19). The objective aspect of Keynesian probability is thus defined solely with respect to the probability relation itself. The *relation* is objective; the *judgment* is subjective. Probability relations are neither certain nor probable; only their relation to knowledge is expressible in these terms (*ibid.*: 3–4).

Probability and measurement

Central to Keynes's general theory of probability is the notion that probability cannot be restricted in definition to a measurable function.[2] Probability in the most general sense allows for the possibility of unique instances, which cannot be eliminated from the set of probable events. In short, it accommodates surprise, as well as the incomprehensible.

Thus a justification for the construction of a probability relation must require more than measurability. It requires an acuity on the part of the individual sufficient to intuit the underlying relation:

> We might, that is to say, pick out from probabilities (in the widest sense) a set, if there is one, all of which are measurable in terms of a common unit, and call the members of this set, and them only, probabilities (in the narrow sense). To restrict the term 'probability' in this way would be, I think, very inconvenient.
>
> (*ibid.*: 36)

Yet despite his scepticism about the viability of numerical valuation of probabilities in general, Keynes did not wish to deny the possibility of comparisons of non-numerical probabilities. Comparisons are possible between non-numerical and numerical probabilities 'by means of greater and less, by which in some cases numerical limits may be ascribed to probabilities which are not capable of numerical measures' (*ibid.*: 132). It may be the case that order comparisons are possible: 'Objects can be arranged in an order, which we can reasonably call one of degree or magnitude, without its being possible to conceive of a system of measurement of the differences between the individuals' (*ibid.*: 32). Although numerical measurement may be neither practical nor possible, some form of order may be so.

Keynesian probability then may also be identified as an order calculus, but even here this conclusion is somewhat tenuous. Keynes himself maintained that probability relations may not even be 'comparable in respect of more or less' (*ibid.*: 37), as there may well be inherent tensions or inconsistencies among the various alternatives. The alternatives may, for instance, belong simultaneously to more than one (intersecting) series, or belong to mutually exclusive (non-intersecting) series, or belong to no series whatsoever. In addition, an order may not even be feasible: only where a probability relation is known, and a unique and homogeneous reference class is manifest, is an order possible. Comparisons are only feasible between probabilities 'when they and certainty all lie on the same ordered series' (*ibid.*: 38). All one can say in these cases is that probability lies somewhere between certainty and impossibility.

Weight

Finally, we come to consider the Keynesian concept of weight.[3] Keynes's solution to the problem of requiring an *a priori* condition as a consistency postulate, a condition absent from the frequency view he had criticized, was to distinguish between two situations: (1) where the evidence is the same, but the conclusions reached in respect of the evidence differ; and (2) where the evidence differs, but the conclusions reached are the same (*ibid.*: 58). The first situation represents a judgement of preferences, comparing x/h to y/h. In the case where $x/h = y/h$, that is, when the conclusions are equivalent and based on the same evidence, we are indifferent. Otherwise, we demonstrate a preference for one over the other.

The second situation represents a judgement of the *relevance* of the premises, that is, comparing x/h to x/h_1h. If the addition of h_1 to the existing evidence h makes no difference to the probability of the conclusion, h_1 is termed irrelevant; otherwise, h_1 is relevant and adds *weight* to the conclusion (whether or not the addition of h_1 to h increases or decreases the probability of the conclusion). The notion of weight was of particular interest to Keynes since it related conceptually to the degree of *confidence* one could express in a probability judgement as a guide to conduct: the greater the weight associated with a probability judgement, the more inclined we should be to be guided by it. While any additional relevant evidence *may* increase or decrease the degree of belief in a proposition, it will always have the effect of increasing the *weight* of the argument, meaning that there is in the accumulation of additional evidence always 'a more substantial basis upon which to rest our conclusion' (*ibid.*: 77). Increased weight, then, is perfectly consistent with increased, decreased, or unchanged degrees of belief; but increased weight always increases the *degree of confidence* in any conclusion derived. In other words, increased weight leads *pari passu* to increased validity in the efficacy, but not necessarily the truth, of a proposition. Weight is a function of the completeness, not the volume, of the evidence. The degree of uncertainty in a proposition can be reduced by the acquisition of additional relevant knowledge and hence lead to an increase in the confidence level, while it is unclear as to the effect of this increased confidence on the probability value.

Conclusion

Given the above presentation, one can see how Keynes's position on probability may be misinterpreted. By focusing on belief and weight, one may conclude that Keynes offers a subjectivist account, one centring on the epistemic nature of probability judgements; by focusing on the propositional calculus, and the discussion of knowledge and *rational* belief, by contrast, one gets the impression of an objective and ontological approach. In fact, each interpretation is correct as far as it goes, and yet it is only by considering both aspects that one sees the richness of the Keynesian project.

Notes

1 For more detail on the issues presented here, see McCann (1994).
2 Keynes allowed that probability may be numerically measurable in cases in which it is legitimate to apply the Principle of Indifference (such as in games of chance) or, and although he insisted that probabilities are not identical to frequencies, where it is legitimate to determine frequencies.
3 For greater detail, see Runde (1990).

4 On some explicit links between Keynes's *A Treatise on Probability* and *The General Theory*

Jochen Runde

Introduction

The last fifteen years or so have witnessed a steady flow of books and articles on the relationship between Keynes's economic writings and his earlier *A Treatise on Probability* (CWVIII, henceforth 'the *Treatise*').[1] As those who are familiar with it will know, the *Treatise* is as much a philosophical as it is a technical contribution to the theory of probability and statistics. And as such, it has provided a rich source for the literature focusing on the broader philosophical and methodological foundations of Keynes's later economic theorising, particularly his views on statistical inference in economics and the nature and impact of uncertainty in economic life. The purpose of the present note is to convey something of the flavour of this literature. Rather than attempting to provide a comprehensive survey, however, I shall restrict myself to an overview of the two places where Keynes makes explicit reference to the *Treatise* in *The General Theory*, in his discussions of long-term expectation and liquidity preference respectively. Readers interested in pursuing questions about the possible, but more implicit, impact on Keynes's economic theorising of the broader philosophical themes discussed in the *Treatise* are invited to consult Carabelli (1988), Davis (1994b), Lawson (1985) and O'Donnell (1989).

Probability and rational belief in the *Treatise*

The most distinctive feature of the *Treatise* lies in its conception of probability as a relation between propositions. In particular, Keynes analyses probability as a relation of *partial* implication between some hypothesis or conclusion h and some set of evidential propositions e (this 'probability relation' is written h/e and read 'h relative to e'). The probability relation is presented as a logical and therefore objective entity, the apprehension of which warrants some rational degree of belief between certainty (where h is a logical consequence of e and $h/e = 1$) and impossibility (where h is logically incompatible with e and $h/e = 0$). The formal theory that Keynes presents is essentially one of comparative probability, building on binary comparisons of the form $h_1/e_1 \geq^* h_2/e_2$ (where $\geq^*$ denotes the relation 'at least as probable as' and yields what we would now call a partially ordered set of probabilities).

Keynes's probability relations do not generally bear numerical values and are often not even pairwise comparable. But comparison may sometimes be possible, and Keynes gives conditions under which further comparisons of probability relations may be deduced from comparisons of probability relations already given. Only under special conditions, in this framework, is it possible to assign numerical probabilities. These conditions may be sketched as follows. Suppose we have a list of n exhaustive and mutually exclusive hypotheses $h_1, h_2, ..., h_n$. We then require: (i) that each h be 'indivisible', that is, that it cannot be split into subalternatives of the same form; and (ii) that $h_i/e =^* h_j/e$ for all i, j by appeal to the Principle of Indifference.[2] Let $H = h_1 h_2 ... h_m$ ($m < n$). The numerical probability of H is then $p(H/e) = m/n$ (this is effectively a version of what is sometimes called classical or *a priori* probability). Keynes also allows that numerical probabilities may sometimes be assigned to an outcome on the basis of a knowledge of the relative frequency of that outcome in a suitably defined series or group of otherwise similar outcomes. But he stresses that this assumes both the existence and the validity of our empirical knowledge of, such series or groups (CWVIII: 103), and maintains that these assumptions are too seldom met for the frequency theory to serve as a general theory of probability.

Uncertainty

Following Knight (1921), it has become conventional in economics to define uncertainty in opposition to risk: in situations of risk, decision-makers are guided by a knowledge of (numerically definite) *a priori* probabilities or statistical frequencies, whereas in situations of uncertainty they have no such knowledge to go on. This convention has led some authors to define Keynesian uncertainty as corresponding to situations in which decision-makers do not have knowledge of the relevant probability relations, either because they do not exist or because they are unable to perceive them (Lawson 1985; O'Donnell 1989). As we have seen, however, it is quite possible for decision-makers to have knowledge of probability relations and even to be able to compare them, on Keynes's account, without their bearing numerical values. To avoid confusion on this point, therefore, I shall follow the Knightian convention and define situations of Keynesian uncertainty also as ones in which decision-makers do not have access to numerically definite probabilities, be they of the *a priori* or the statistical variety. In terms of this definition it is possible for decision-makers to have knowledge of Keynesian probability relations, and perhaps even to be able to order them, and yet still to be choosing in situations of uncertainty in the Knightian sense.

In Chapter 6 of the *Treatise* Keynes introduces an additional non-probabilistic measure of evidential 'weight', which has also come to be interpreted as a measure of uncertainty (see Runde 1990). We have seen that he treats probability as measuring the strength of the logical relation between some hypothesis and the evidential propositions bearing on that hypothesis. But he suggests that when using probability as a guide to conduct, it is also rational to take into account the extent (in some sense), the degree of completeness, or the 'weight' of the evidence on which that probability is based. Other things being equal, he argues, we should prefer to act on probabilities in respect of which the evidence is 'more complete'. As with judgments of probability *per se*, Keynes believes that it is usually possible to make only qualitative comparisons of evidential weight. He is accordingly quite sceptical about the possibility of rational decision-makers being able to arrive at precisely determined valuations of choice options that take into account the 'good' of the associated consequences, their probabilities, weight and risk.[3]

It will be useful to take stock at this point. We have seen that *A Treatise on Probability* provides a theory of comparative probability in which numerical probabilities, be they of the *a priori* or the statistically based variety, are a special case. I have argued that Keynesian uncertainty is best interpreted on Knightian lines: that decision-makers should be seen as operating under conditions of risk where their decisions are informed by numerically definite probabilities of the kind just mentioned, under conditions of uncertainty when they have no such probabilities to go on (but which does of course not preclude their making qualitative judgments and comparisons of probability). Finally, in terms of Keynes's theory, probability judgments may be graded in terms of evidential weight, a measure which he interprets as a possible indicator of the extent to which the relevant probabilities might be trusted as a guide to conduct. I now turn to the two places in which these themes re-emerge in *The General Theory*, beginning with Keynes's famous 'Chapter 12' discussions of long-term expectation.

Long-term expectation

By long-term expectations Keynes means expectations 'concerned with what the entrepreneur can hope to earn in the shape of future returns if he purchases (or, perhaps, manufactures) "finished" output as an addition to his capital equipment' (CWVII: 47). Long-term expectations are distinct from short-term expectations, which are 'concerned with the price which a manufacturer can expect to get for his "finished" output at the time when he commits himself to starting the process which will produce it' (*ibid.*: 46). The 'state of long-term expectation' Keynes refers to in Chapter 12 of *The General Theory* is defined as 'the state of psychological expectation' concerning future events that may affect investment yields, and 'which can only be forecasted with more or less confidence': future changes in effective demand, type and quantity of the stock of capital goods, consumer demand, and so on (*ibid.*: 147–8).

What, then, is the relationship between Keynes's conceptions of probability, uncertainty and long-term expectation? We have seen that in terms of the theory of probability proposed in the *Treatise*, decision-makers only rarely have access to numerical probabilities. This same position provides the point of departure in his later writings on long-term expectations. In Chapter 12 of *The General Theory*, for example, Keynes argues that investors are generally not able to determine numerical probabilities of yields by invoking the Principle of Indifference (*ibid.*: 152), and, in his subsequent *Quarterly Journal of Economics* (*QJE*) defence of *The General Theory* (CWXIVa: 113), that the knowledge investors have at their disposal typically does not extend to statistical frequencies (such as might be derived from mortality tables or from the history of past weather patterns). It thus follows that the 'existing knowledge [of potential investors] does not provide a sufficient basis for a calculated mathematical expectation' (CWVII: 152) and Keynes therefore insists that it would be misleading to treat investment decision-makers 'as if' they were Benthamite calculators or what we might now call expected utility maximisers.[4]

But this is not to say, as is sometimes claimed, that Keynes fails to provide a theory of long-term expectations. In fact, he provides an extremely rich account of how investors form expectations by falling back on conventions: the practice of assuming that the existing situation will continue indefinitely except insofar as there are definite reasons to expect a change, the practice of taking current market valuations as 'correct' relative to existing knowledge, and the practice of copying the behaviour of other market participants who find themselves in a similar situation (for more on Keynes on conventions, see Davis (1994b)). The fact that investors often adopt conventions of this kind is quite consistent with their making judgments of probability about the possible outcomes of the courses of action open to them, although these judgments will typically be qualitative rather than quantitative in nature. Moreover, in an explicit footnote reference to the *Treatise* on the weight of evidence, Keynes (CWVII: 148) argues that the state of long-term expectation – and therefore the marginal efficiency of capital – depends not only on the most probable forecasts that investors make, but also on the confidence with which they make those forecasts. Although he does not go into very much detail on this point, his reasoning seems to be that investors, knowing that their judgments of probability are based on evidence that is highly incomplete, lack confidence in those judgments as a basis for choosing between alternative investments.

Keynes's account of the causes and the consequences of the precariousness of the state of long-term expectation then follows in a straightforward manner. Among the causes are the fact that investment expectations are informed, in a sense disproportionately, by the facts of the existing situation and are therefore unduly sensitive to changes in the 'news' and swings in confidence; that the self-referential nature of the conventional methods of calculation leads to 'bubble' phenomena and, if everyone is following everyone else's lead, to the possibility of dramatic fluctuations in asset prices; the short-termism that follows as a consequence of the liquidity provided by stock markets; and the subconscious and possibly irrational motivations of investors. The consequences, of course, are described in the familiar Keynesian proposition that a collapse in the state of long-term expectation may have a strongly negative impact on the marginal efficiency of capital, investment demand and hence the level of employment.

Liquidity preference

The second place in which there is an explicit reference to the *Treatise* in *The General Theory* appears in the theory of asset demand presented in Keynes's famous Chapter 17 on own-rates of interest. The own-rate of an asset over some period is defined as its yield q minus its carrying cost c plus its liquidity premium l:

$$r = q - c + l$$

where q, c and l are measured in terms of the asset itself (*ibid.*: 226).[5] The carrying cost component is straightforward, reflecting the physical depreciation and storage costs that affect certain classes of assets. The more important variables from our point of view are q and l. Keynes defines q as 'a yield or output' from 'assisting some process of production or supplying services to a consumer' (*ibid.*: 225). Since q is at best only probable it is adjusted for risk: 'The actuarial profit or mathematical expectation of gain calculated in accordance with the existing probabilities – if it can be so calculated, which is doubtful – must be sufficient to compensate for the risk of disappointment' (*ibid.*: 169, see also 240, 375). The risk premium is the difference between investors' estimates of the 'actuarial' value of an investment and what they would be prepared to pay for that investment when $c = l = 0$.

The crucial variable in Keynes's scheme is the liquidity premium, which reflects the 'potential convenience or security' provided by the liquidity or 'power of disposal' of an asset. The desire for such convenience and security is in turn related to investors' confidence in their estimates of probability:

> The liquidity-premium ... is partly similar to the risk-premium, but partly different – the difference corresponding to the difference between the best estimates we can make of probabilities and the confidence with which we make them.
>
> (*ibid.*: 240)

In a footnote to this passage, Keynes refers to the earlier footnote mentioned above, in which he links confidence to evidential weight (*ibid.*: 148). He is explicit about this link in a letter written after *The General Theory* was published:

> I am rather inclined to associate risk premium with probability strictly speaking, and liquidity premium with what in my *Treatise on Probability* I called 'weight'. An essential distinction is that a risk premium is expected to be rewarded on the average by an increased return at the end of the period. A liquidity premium, on the other hand, is not even expected to be so rewarded. It is a payment, not for the expectation of increased tangible income at the end of the period, but for an increased sense of comfort and confidence during the period.
>
> (CWXXIX: 293–4)

Keynes's theory of asset choice thus includes both probability-related and weight-related components. The probability component forms the basis of investors' calculations of risk and return (although Keynes insists that their probability judgments are seldom sharp enough to allow these calculations to be made in a very precise way). The second component reflects the evidential weight or degree of completeness of the evidence on which investors' probability judgments are based. The lower the evidential weight, the lower their confidence in the probability judgments that inform their asset choices. The motivational basis of Keynes's theory of liquidity preference may thus be summarised as follows. Whereas all situations of choice under uncertainty involve information that is incomplete in some way, they tend to differ in terms of (i) the extent to which this is so (evidential weight) and (ii) the scope that the choice options allow for responding to information acquired after the relevant action has been taken. In situations of risk, where decision-makers are actually in a position to determine *a priori* probabilities or statistical frequencies, they will have (close to) maximal confidence in their probabilities as a guide to conduct. Where their choices are of a one-shot kind they merely have to adjust for risk. And where their choices are ones that are repeated a large number of times even risk becomes irrelevant, since they can be almost certain that the aggregate payoff associated with any repeated option will lie in a narrow interval around the sum of the expected payoffs of the individual options.

In situations of uncertainty, however, particularly those involving long time-horizons, decision-makers may often have cause to revise their probability judgments after they have committed themselves to some course of action. They may find, for example, that future events that were initially regarded as probable become less probable over time. This possibility presents no problem where decision-makers are in a position to revise prior choices in a costless way. But many choices, once taken, are irreversible or at least costly to revise, particularly in the case of investment in fixed capital. In cases of this kind, decision-makers have reason to look not only for the most promising option in terms of risk and return, but also at the extent to which the different options open to them permit revision should forecasts fail. This is where the general incentive to liquidity enters in Keynes's account. When the information on which investment decisions are based is known to be highly incomplete, the readiness and terms on which commitments to previous choices may be dissolved assume importance. The degree to which this is possible, in the case of asset choice, depends on the ease with and terms on which assets can be disposed of, namely their liquidity. It follows, therefore, particularly in situations characterised by significant uncertainty, that more liquid assets will often carry a premium over less liquid assets.

Under conditions of extreme uncertainty, investors may even prefer to suspend judgment altogether and to delay committing themselves until more information becomes available. In Keynes's framework this last option takes the form of holding cash, an asset with no intrinsic yield and bearing zero risk. Again, and the transactions and speculative motives aside, the motivation for holding money and hence the liquidity premium is characterised in weight-related terms: the uncertainty that Keynes has in mind is not in respect of investors' beliefs about the possible outcomes of investment choices *per se*, but in respect of investors' distrust in their calculations and conventions concerning the future and/or the conventions adopted to get along without making such calculations:

> partly on reasonable and partly on instinctive grounds, our desire to hold money as a store of wealth is a barometer of the degree of our distrust of our calculations and conventions concerning the future … The possession of actual money lulls our disquietude; and the premium which we require to make us part with money is the measure of the degree of our disquietude.
>
> (CWXIVa: 115–16)

Concluding remarks

I have given a brief account of the places in *The General Theory* in which Keynes makes an explicit connection with his earlier *A Treatise on Probability*, but without saying anything about how his views on probability might have changed between the two works. As there is some controversy surrounding this question,[6] not to mention its obvious importance for the project of interpreting Keynes's economic thinking in terms of earlier work on probability, let me conclude with a brief indication of my own view on the matter.[7]

The controversy centres on Keynes's (CWXa: 338–9) response to Ramsey's (1978) famous critique of *A Treatise on Probability*, a response which has led a number of authors to argue that Keynes abandoned the objective theory of probability of the *Treatise* in favour of a subjective interpretation on Ramseyian lines (for example, Bateman 1987). Although Ramsey's paper is wide-ranging and complex, it is possible to isolate the two core aspects of his argument: (i) his view that beliefs about uncertain propositions are ultimately personal to those who hold them; and (ii) his seminal axiomatisation of subjective or personal probability, a system within which subjective probabilities can be shown to emerge as parameters of preferences over gambles that meet certain consistency requirements. Keynes does not have much to say about the second aspect, other than to acknowledge that Ramsey had succeeded in showing that 'the calculus of probabilities belongs to formal logic'. But I would argue that it is unlikely that Keynes accepted Ramsey's axiomatisation as either a descriptive or even a normative model of the rational decision-maker. For there is simply too much remaining in his later remarks on probability and uncertainty in economic life that is at odds with it, particularly his emphasis on the inability of investors to determine numerically definite probabilities or even compare probabilities in many situations; considerations of evidential weight and its impact on the confidence investment decision-makers have in their probability judgments; and the propensity of investors to suspend judgment and postpone investment decisions in situations of significant uncertainty.[8]

Keynes did accept (i), however, acknowledging that 'the basis of our degrees of belief ... is part of our human outfit, analogous to our perceptions and our memories rather than to formal logic'. And it is this remark that tends to be emphasised by authors who take the view that there is a strong discontinuity between Keynes's earlier views on probability and his later economic writings. In fact, however, and while it certainly raises some interesting questions about his later views on the basis of investors' probability judgments, Keynes's admission in no way compromises the themes from the *Treatise* that re-emerge in his economic writings. For the idea that (epistemic) probability judgments are essentially comparative, the validity of the formal structure of comparative probability provided in the *Treatise*,[9] that most practical decision-making is not informed by statistical frequencies, and the importance of evidential weight, are all largely independent of whether our degrees of belief are merely subjective, intersubjective (Davis 1994b), or do in fact correspond to objective relations of partial entailment. To this extent at least, therefore, it does not seem illegitimate to interpret Keynes's later remarks on probability and uncertainty in terms of the framework set out in the *Treatise*.

Notes

1   Some of the more prominent contributions to this literature include Bateman (1987), Carabelli (1988), Cottrell (1993), Davis (1994b), Lawson (1985), Meeks (1991) and O'Donnell (1989, 1991a, 1991b).

2   The Principle of Indifference states that 'if there is no *known* reason for predicating of our subject one rather than another of several alternatives, then relatively to such knowledge the assertions of each of these alternatives have an *equal* probability. Thus *equal* probabilities must be assigned to each of several arguments, if there is an absence of positive grounds for assigning *unequal* ones' (CWVIII: 45).

3   Keynes (CWVIII: 339–56). The measure of risk that Keynes proposes on p. 348 of *A Treatise on Probability* is closely related to what we now call the variance of a probability distribution.

4   For example, in his 1937 *QJE* defence of *The General Theory* he writes:

> The orthodox theory assumes that we have a knowledge of the future of a kind quite different from that which we actually possess. This false rationalisation follows the lines of the Benthamite calculus. The hypothesis of a calculable future leads to a wrong interpretation of the principles of behaviour which the need for action compels us to adopt, and to an underestimation of the concealed factors of utter doubt, precariousness, hope and fear.
>
> (CWXIVa: 122)

5   This section draws heavily on Runde (1994a). To compare assets in terms of own-rates, their expected rate of appreciation in terms of money a must be added to their 'intrinsic' returns. The 'commodity-rate of money interest' for any asset then becomes $R = q - c + l + a$. Unemployment occurs when the return on money l exceeds the commodity-rate of money interest on investment opportunities in physical capital not yet taken up. The return on money, in turn, is prevented from falling to a level consistent with full employment by its 'essential properties' of zero elasticities of supply and substitution with similar assets (CWVIII: 230–4).

6   Proponents of the so-called 'continuity thesis' who argue that there were no significant changes in Keynes's thinking on probability over time include Carabelli (1988), Lawson (1985) and O'Donnell (1989). Proponents of the opposing 'discontinuity' view include Bateman (1987), Davis (1994b) and Cottrell (1993).

7   A more comprehensive account appears in Runde (1994b).

8   Detailed accounts of why these 'Keynesian' phenomena are not easily accommodated within Ramsey's framework appear in Runde (1994b, 1995).

9   See Koopman (1940) for an influential interpretation and extension of Keynes's theory of comparative probability along subjectivist lines.

5 Keynes's epistemology

Athol Fitzgibbons

Introduction

Keynes's epistemology is formally laid out in *A Treatise on Probability* and applied with adaptations in *The General Theory*. These two books do not develop the connection that he saw between judgments of fact and judgments of value, or his growing disillusionment and belief in irrationality. They also omit his economic ideal, which was material prosperity sufficient to release the creative energies of humankind. I have concentrated here on the *Treatise* and *The General Theory*, but have mentioned the other ideas where they are relevant.

A Treatise on Probability

Keynes wrote the *Treatise* to advance what he called the 'logical theory of probability', but there ·are semantic disputes over the meaning of 'logical', and it is simpler to say that its real achievement was to formalize the rules of practical reason. The *Treatise* defined the circumstances in which it would be valid to derive probabilities and reach rational or logical decisions. Keynes gave common-sense meanings to the terms 'probability', 'rational' and 'logical', and he included doubtful arguments within the scope of logic. By 'rational', therefore, he did not mean rational as in an Aristotelian syllogism, or as in rational economic man. By 'rational' he meant, as in the language of everyday life, the systematic use of intelligence to advance a particular end.

Keynes was less interested in pure knowledge than in the knowledge relevant to decision and action. Aristotelian logic and strict microeconomics assume full information, but full information is rare in life. He believed that it was rational to draw conclusions, and act upon them, in the absence of proof or perfect information. 'In the actual exercise of reason we do not wait on certainty, or deem it irrational to depend on a doubtful argument' (CWVIII: 3).

The object of the theory of probability was to systematize processes of inference:

In particular it aims at elucidating rules by means of which the probabilities of different arguments can be compared. It is of great practical
importance to determine which of two conclusions is on the evidence
the more probable.

(ibid.: 121)

Probability was not necessarily reducible to a single figure. Keynes
believed that many probabilities could not be quantified, either by their
nature or because of insufficient information. For example, it was
impossible to quantify meaningfully the likelihood of an inductive
proposition:

A conclusion, which is based on three experiments in which the
unessential conditions are varied, is more trustworthy than if it were
based on two. But what reason or principle can be adduced for
attributing a numerical measure to the increase?

(ibid.: 30)

He believed that in the absence of quantification, individual feelings and
intuitions, which could not be justified on strict logical grounds, would
inevitably influence a probability estimate:

Without compromising the objective character of relations of probability, we must nevertheless admit that there is little likelihood of our
discovering a method of recognising particular probabilities, without
any assistance whatever from intuition or direct judgment.

(ibid.: 56)

Accordingly, non-quantitative estimates of probability were sometimes
subject to rapid fluctuation:

Consider, for instance, the reinsurance rates for the Waratah, a vessel
which disappeared in South African waters. The lapse of time made
rates rise; the departure of ships in search of her made them fall;
some nameless wreckage is found and they rise; it is remembered
that in similar circumstances thirty years ago a vessel floated, help-
less but not seriously damaged, for two months and they fall. Can it
be pretended that the figures which were quoted from day to day –
75 per cent, 83 per cent, 78 per cent – were rationally determinate, or
that the actual figure was within wide limits arbitrary and due to the
caprice of individuals?

(ibid.: 24–5)

Nevertheless, just as it was possible to compare degrees of similarity,
so it was also possible to compare degrees of probability. Judgments of

probability and judgments of similarity were rational responses to the evidence, and yet they also depended on the intuitive powers of the individual who made them:

> But the closest analogy is that of similarity. When we say of three objects *A*, *B*, and *C* that *B* is more like *A* than *C*, we mean, not that there is any respect in which *B* is in itself quantitatively greater than *C*, but that, if the three objects are placed in an order of similarity, *B* is nearer to *A* than *C* is.
>
> (*ibid.*: 39)

And just as disjoint objects could not be said to be more or less similar, some non-quantitative probabilities were not comparable:

> As in the example of similarity, where there are different orders of increasing and decreasing similarity, but where it is not possible to say of every pair of objects which of them is on the whole more like a third object, so there are different orders of probability, and probabilities, which are not of the same order, cannot be compared.
>
> (*ibid.*: 122)

A Treatise on Probability took issue with the doctrine of mathematical expectation, partly because that doctrine implicitly quantified all probabilities:

> The hope, which sustained many investigators in the course of the nineteenth century, of gradually bringing the moral sciences under the sway of mathematical reasoning, steadily recedes – if we mean, as they meant, by mathematics the introduction of precise numerical methods ... In the present case, even if we are able to range goods [utilities] in order of magnitude, and also their probabilities in order of magnitude, yet it does not follow that we can range the products composed of each good and its corresponding probability in this order.
>
> (*ibid.*: 349)

But although intuition was indispensable, there was a tendency to minimize its role, by misstating the degree of information. Information was frequently *overstated* by resort to the principle of non-sufficient reason (which Keynes called the Principle of Indifference). This Principle stated that uncertainty could be cancelled out, by assuming that each of two totally uncertain and mutually exclusive alternatives had a probability of 0.5. However, it was fallacious because it led to contradictions:

> If, for instance, having no evidence relevant to the colour of this book, we could conclude that ½ is the probability of 'This book is

red', we could conclude equally that the probability of each of the propositions, 'This book is black' and 'This book is blue', is also ½. So that we are faced with the impossible case of *three* exclusive alternatives all as likely as not.

(*ibid.*: 46)

The other way of minimizing the role of intuition was to show that incomplete information was equivalent to no information whatsoever. Keynes accused David Hume, who had promoted this practice, of unwarranted scepticism:

The judgments of probability, upon which we depend for almost all our beliefs in matters of experience, undoubtedly depend on a strong psychological propensity in us to consider objects in a particular light. But this is no ground for supposing that they are nothing more than 'lively imaginations'.

(*ibid.*: 56)

The error lay in assuming that we either know something fully or else not at all: 'Mr Moore's reasoning endeavours to show that there is not even a *probability* by showing that there is not a *certainty*' (*ibid.*: 342).

Some causal sequences were too unpredictable even for intuition to play a role. The *Treatise* analysed situations of 'objective chance', or chaos, in which there was not enough information for a rational response of any sort. So-called 'objective chance' was really subjective, because it concerned human ignorance and knowledge:

an event is due to objective chance if in order to predict it, or to prefer it to alternatives, at present equi-probable, with any high degree of probability, it would be necessary to know a great many more facts of existence about it than we actually do know, and if the addition of a wide knowledge of general principles would be of little use.

(*ibid.*: 319)

To summarize, *A Treatise on Probability* emphasized that practical action required the rational evaluation of non-quantitative probabilities, and that this evaluation would be influenced by intuition as well as the facts. It was erroneous to represent a situation as completely unknown when in fact there was information, and it was erroneous to quantify information by resort to the principle of non-sufficient reason. Keynes therefore took issue with utility maximization and other doctrines that wrongly minimized the role of intuition. And all these ideas were to manifest themselves again in Keynes's economic writings.

The General Theory

There was, however, one notable difference. Whereas *A Treatise on Probability* expounded the possibility of *rational* decisions, *The General Theory* argued that the instability of capitalism arose from *irrational* decisions in the capital markets. Once again, irrational meant a 'failure to think systematically' and not a 'failure to maximize'; in fact investors were irrational when they maximized in the absence of full information. Investors often relied on 'conventions' to paper over the gaps in their knowledge, and in particular they typically adopted the convention that the present situation would continue into the future. In this way they resorted to the fallacious principle of non-sufficient reason.

The General Theory noted that it was invalid to cancel out uncertainty:

> Nor can we rationalise our behaviour by arguing that to a man in a state of ignorance errors in either direction are equally probable, so that there remains a mean actuarial expectation based on equi-probabilities. For it can easily be shown that the assumption of arithmetically equal probabilities based on a state of ignorance leads to absurdities.
>
> (CWVII: 152)

Investment strategies that relied on the 'conventional basis of evalua-tion' had no substantive justification. When the prevailing conventions eventually collided with the facts, a new economic paradigm would emerge, and economic decisions would be predicated on a different future. The many different ways of cancelling out uncertainty validated many different strategies in the market:

> It has been, I am sure, on the basis of some such procedure as this that our leading investment markets have been developed. But it is not surprising that a convention, in an absolute view of things so arbitrary, should have its weak points. It is its precariousness which creates no small part of our contemporary problem of securing investment.
>
> (*ibid.*: 153)

Keynes accused the classical economists of abstracting away from the role played by 'animal spirits' and the intuition. Their utilitarian micro-foundations had excluded non-quantifiable probabilities, which were really of the essence, from consideration:

> But at any given time facts and expectations were assumed to be given in a definite and calculable form; and risks, of which, though admitted, not much notice was taken, were supposed to be capable of an exact actuarial computation. The calculus of probability, though

mention of it was kept in the background, was supposed to be
capable of reducing uncertainty to the same calculable status as that
of uncertainty itself; just as in the Benthamite calculus of pains and
pleasures or of advantage and disadvantage, by which the
Benthamite philosophy assumed men to be influenced in their
general ethical behaviour.

(CWXIVa: 112–13)

The process of investment also reflected an element of objective
chance. In order to predict the future of an investment, or to prefer it to
alternatives, it would be necessary to know many more facts than were
actually known, while a wide knowledge of general principles was of
little use:

professional investment may be likened to those newspaper compe-
titions in which the competitors have to pick out the six prettiest
faces from a hundred photographs, the prize being awarded to the
competitor whose choice most nearly corresponds to the average
preferences of the competitors as a whole; so that each competitor
has to pick, not those faces which he himself finds prettiest, but those
which he thinks likeliest to catch the fancy of the other competitors,
all of whom are looking at the problem from the same point of view
… And there are some, I believe, who practise the fourth, fifth and
higher degrees.

(CWVII: 156)

But even when the capital markets were often overwhelmed by chaos or
irrational behaviour, there was still a rational basis for *economic policy*.
The right method was to combine the policy-makers' intuitions with his
(Keynes's) theory:

Hence the extreme complexity of the actual course of events.
Nevertheless, these seem to be the factors which it is useful and
convenient to isolate. If we examine any actual problem along the
lines of the above schematism, we shall find it more manageable; and
our practical intuition (which can take account of a more detailed
complex of facts than can be treated on general principles) will be
offered a less intractable material upon which to work.

(*ibid.*: 249)

In *A Treatise on Probability* Keynes had suggested that some individuals
have superior powers of intuition:

Some men – indeed it is obviously the case – have a greater power of
logical intuition than others. Further, the difference between some

kinds of propositions over which human intuition seems to have power, and some over which it has none, may depend wholly upon the constitution of our minds and have no significance for a perfectly objective logic … The perceptions of some relations of probability may be outside the powers of some or all of us.

(CWVIII: 18–19)

One such superior individual had been Isaac Newton, who had inspired David Hume. Keynes argued in a biographical essay that Newton was 'not the first of the age of reason', but 'the last of the magicians' (CWXb: 364). However, the markets did not adequately reward insight and intuition:

Investment based on genuine long-term expectation is so difficult to-day as to be scarcely practicable. He who attempts it must surely lead much more laborious days and run greater risks than he who tries to guess better than the crowd how the crowd will behave; and, given equal intelligence, he may make more disastrous mistakes.

(CWVII: 157)

To summarize, the prevalence of rationality in the *Treatise* was replaced by the prevalence of irrationality in *The General Theory*. Keynes gave his own account for this shift in his essay 'My Early Beliefs':

As cause and consequence of our general state of mind we completely misunderstood human nature, including our own. The rationality which we attributed to it led to a superficiality, not only of judgment, but also of feeling.

(CWXb: 448)

The General Theory introduced the first *knowledge dichotomy* into macroeconomics, meaning that it postulated that one class of decision-makers (in the capital markets) was irrational, whereas another class (government economists) had the knowledge and capacity to arrive at rational conclusions. The subsequent inability of the Keynesians to justify this dichotomy would, but only after decades, lead to the demise of the Keynesian system.

Yet irrational behaviour was not of the essence, because *The General Theory* could have argued, as the *Treatise* had, that non-quantitative probabilities were capable of causing erratic fluctuations in even rational behaviour. The underlying philosophy in *The General Theory*, which was a reiteration of the philosophy in the *Treatise*, was disguised by references to the sociology of Wall Street. The assumption of irrationality did allow Keynes to explain how arbitrary changes in the conventional basis of evaluation led to *coordinated* swings in the markets. However, other mechanisms, such as misleading market signals, might have served the same purpose.

The central theme of the *Treatise*, which was that people without full information still try to act rationally, despite the personal aspect of their decisions, seems hardly objectionable. If it were possible to insulate scientific method from the method of practical reason, then Keynes's theme might be regarded as banal and trivially true. The usual experience is that life is a mixture of chance and calculation, with people making difficult choices and conducting their affairs as well as they can. But *A Treatise on Probability* was a polemical book because, by giving a role to judgment and intuition, Keynes restricted the scope of science.

It was all the more polemical because Keynes's real target was Hume, the most profound and influential Enlightenment philosopher, the disciple of Isaac Newton, and arguably the most substantial influence on modern philosophy. Hume had distinguished between positive and normative propositions because he wanted to claim that all knowledge, except of our own tastes and desires, was scientific. He claimed that there was a universal scientific method, which applied equally to the physical and social sciences. What was called probable reason was merely the expression of subjective value judgments:

> all probable reasoning is nothing but a species of sensation ... When I give the preference to one set of arguments above another, I do nothing but decide from my feeling concerning the superiority of their influence.
>
> (David Hume, *A Treatise of Human Nature*, quoted in CWVIII: 88)

A Treatise on Probability advanced a third category of knowledge, which was somewhere between positive and normative, namely rational belief. As I have noted, Keynes conceded that non-quantitative probabilities contain a subjective element, but he believed that Hume had overstated his case. Non-quantitative probabilities also contain information:

> Yet [Hume's] scepticism goes too far. The judgments of probability, upon which we depend for almost all our beliefs in matters of experience, undoubtedly depend upon a strong psychological propensity in us to consider objects in a particular light.
>
> (*ibid.*: 56)

Keynes regarded Hume's ideal as unworkable, because it was not always possible to abstract from the powers and limitations of the human mind. To this considerable extent Keynes was proposing to roll back the Enlightenment.

Reactions to Keynes's epistemology

The objections to the *Treatise* were consequently reaffirmations of the philosophy of the Enlightenment and the Humean vision. Frank Ramsey doubted the usefulness of non-quantifiable probabilities, which in any event had no scientific application. Even if we experienced such probabilities they had no validity: 'a [probability] relation about which so little can be truly said will be of little scientific use and it will be hard to convince a sceptic of its existence ... I might say "This is what I should think, but of course I am only a fool"' (Ramsey 1978: 64–5). In *The Nature of Macroeconomics* (Fitzgibbons 2000) I analysed Ramsey's concern that non-quantitative probabilities were unscientific because they are incompatible with prediction. I also analysed Ramsey's counter-argument that people are free to be irrational but obliged to be consistent: '[An intransitive decision-maker] could have a book made against him by a cunning better and would then stand to lose in any event' (Ramsey 1978: 84).

In a timeless world that might be true. However, for the following reasons it is wrong to say that people who act inconsistently *over time* would lose their money because they could have a book made against them: (1) financial penalties do not apply to many fields of decision-making; and (2) Ramsey implicitly assumes a bookmaker with perfect knowledge. A bookmaker who entered the share market, armed only with the knowledge that markets are driven by psychology, could lose a lot of money.

Nor do I see any point in R. B. Braithwaite's argument that unmeasurable probabilities lead 'to intolerable difficulties without any compensating advantages' (Editorial Foreword, CWVIII: xvii). And I have also explained elsewhere that there is no evidence (except for the 'surely Keynes wouldn't have thought *that*' reaction) to support the various inconsistent claims that Keynes came to realize that the *Treatise* was wrong and that he recanted. The reply to all these points is that if incomplete information *ipso facto* has any significant effects, then it is better to acknowledge them, even if they reveal that there are limitations to orthodox social science.

To say this is not to minimize the magnitude of Keynes's proposal, which was intended to change our views on the constitution of the modern mind. His *Treatise* declined into obscurity, though there was no major difference in philosophy between it and *The General Theory*, because it attacked positivist scientific method in the abstract, and without demonstrating a compelling need for what would have been a major change in culture and ideas.

By comparison, macroeconomics was an ideal field for the application of Keynes's epistemology, because the very nature of society was threatened by macroeconomic breakdown, while something was seriously and fundamentally wrong with the prevailing theory. Furthermore, the philosophy rebutted in *The General Theory* was not positivism but (though he is not mentioned by name) the Stoic method of Adam Smith. This conceived of a hidden order beneath the turbulent reality, which order was supposedly the proper object of science and thought. But although Stoicism had been an Enlightenment philosophy, it differed from positivism, and Smith's method had only been adopted in classical economics and nowhere else.

Keynes's macroeconomic theory only became a world doctrine after it was put into positivist terms. When the so-called Keynesian Synthesis became orthodox macroeconomic science, it dispensed with Keynes's philosophy of probability. Instead, it tried to explain changes in aggregate demand while retaining the micro-foundation of utility maximization and predictable market behaviour. The supposed 'economics of uncertainty' was based on assumptions that assumed uncertainty away.

The Keynesian Synthesis was eventually discredited when it was found to be inconsistent with the pursuit of self-interest in the capital markets, which are the very epitome of the self-interested pursuit of profit. There has since been a search for workable micro-foundations of macroeconomics, that is, for an account of the individual behaviour that generates business cycles and changes in aggregate demand. Although this search has proceeded unsuccessfully for decades, success would require changes in methodology that economists are not prepared to accept. An interesting new dichotomy is therefore emerging: macroeconomic policy is becoming Keynesian, while macroeconomic theory is not. This intellectual division allows macroeconomics to retain the status of a science, even though it is a science of nothing.

Politics and knowledge

The abstract question of 'Who knows what?' has a close connection to the tangible question of 'Who should have power?'; and Keynes's epistemology was an integral part of his political philosophy, which is now known as the Third Way (a term that I invented because Keynes's 'middle way' was misleading; see Fitzgibbons (1988: 63)). A new Liberalism that was informed by Keynes's epistemology was meant to replace Socialism and *laissez-faire*. Keynes objected to these doctrines, which he traced back to Hume, because they were materialistic and excluded probability and intuition; they reached pseudo-scientific conclusions about what should have been matters of moral and factual judgment.

The Third Way is clearly Platonic in origin. It emphasized the relevance of higher and universal Goods including justice, but these were indefinable and a matter for judgment and interpretation. Political decisions required knowledge of both universals and particular circumstances, and so no general rules could be given.

The obvious objection to this political doctrine is that it could have authoritarian implications. There was an innate tension between Keynes's genuine liberalism, with its stress on economic growth and individual choice, and his often-expressed belief that some individuals had a superior understanding of universals. For example: 'civilisation [is] a thin and precarious crust erected by the personality and the will of a very few, and only maintained by rules and conventions skillfully put across and guilefully preserved' (CWXb: 447). If the very few disregarded the value of money, or attributed little significance to the desires, then they would only be able to maintain power through authoritarian means. Keynes advanced different solutions to this tension over time. The Appendix juxtaposes passages from the social and political philosophy of *The General Theory* with some taken from Plato's *Republic*. Readers may therefore judge for themselves whether Keynes has successfully liberalized traditional epistemology.

Appendix: the Keynes–Plato dialogue

Democracy and individualism

Plato: Individualism is directed towards variety and the desires but, because it lacks a concept of personal evolution, it replaces moral knowledge with a one-dimensional utilitarianism.

> [Democracy and individualism] then, seems likely to be the fairest of states, being like an embroidered robe which is spangled with every sort of flower. And just as women and children think a variety of colours to be of all things most charming, so there are many men to whom this state, which is spangled with the manners and characters of mankind, will appear to be the fairest of states.
>
> (Plato 1892: 557)

> If anyone says to him that some pleasures are the satisfactions of good and noble desires, and others of evil desires, and that he ought to use and honour some and chastise and master the others – whenever this is repeated to him he shakes his head and says that they are all alike, and that one is as good as another.
>
> (*ibid.*: 562)

Keynes: The diversity arising from individualism allows us to select the best from the past, and transmit the best to the future. Its faults and abuses might be correctable, and the absence of individualism is one of the greatest defects of tyranny.

But, above all, individualism, if it can be purged of its defects and its abuses, is the best safeguard of personal liberty in the sense that, compared with other systems, it greatly widens the field for the exercise of personal choice. It is also the best safeguard of the variety of life, which emerges precisely from this extended field of personal choice, and the loss of which is the greatest of all the losses of the homogeneous or totalitarian state. For this variety preserves the traditions which embody the most secure and successful choices of former generations; it colours the present with the diversification of its fancy; and, being the handmaid of experiment as well as of tradition and fancy, it is the most powerful instrument to better the future.

(CWVII: 380)

Money and power

Plato: Societies organized around the accumulation of wealth become oligarchies, torn by an endless struggle between the rich and the poor.

[Oligarchical societies suffer] the inevitable division: such a State is not one, but two States, the one of poor, the other of rich men; and they are living on the same spot, and always conspiring one against another.

(Plato 1892: 551)

Keynes: The desire for wealth is related to the desire for power, but there is more liberty in societies organized around the accumulation of wealth.

Moreover, dangerous human proclivities can be canalised into comparatively harmless channels by the existence of opportunities for money-making and private wealth, which, if they cannot be satisfied in this way, may find their outlet in cruelty, the reckless pursuit of personal wealth and power, and other forms of self-aggrandisement. It is better that a man should tyrannise over his bank balance than over his fellow citizens; and while the former is sometimes denounced as being but a means to the latter, sometimes at least it is an alternative.

(CWVII: 374)

Plato: Money-driven societies are characterized by the very rich and the very poor.

So they make drone and pauper to abound in the state ... In democracies almost everything is managed by the drones.

(Plato 1892: 556–64)

Keynes: The desire to accumulate wealth is socially beneficial, and though inequality is excessive at present, society can make a decision to reduce it in future.

> I see, therefore, the rentier aspect of capitalism as a transitional phase which will disappear when it has done its work.
>
> (CWVII: 376)

> For my own part, I believe that there is social and psychological justification for significant inequalities of incomes and wealth, but not for such large disparities as exist to-day. There are valuable human activities which require the motive of money-making and the environment of private wealth-ownership for their full fruition.
>
> (*ibid.*: 374)

Money and virtue

Plato: In the ideal state the aim of life is virtue, which is expressed through the preservation of the state. In oligarchies wealth replaces virtue as the end of life.

> So [the rich and powerful] grow richer and richer, and the more they think of making a fortune the less they think of virtue; for when riches and virtue are together in the balance, the one always rises as the other falls.
>
> (Plato 1892: 551)

> [In the perfect state] no one is to have any of the ordinary possessions of mankind.
>
> (*ibid.*: 543)

Keynes: Virtue may be the aim of life in the ideal state, but since in actuality most people would rather have money it is sensible to let them acquire it within reasonable bounds.

> Though in the ideal commonwealth men may have been taught or inspired or bred to take no interest in the stakes, it may still be wise and prudent statesmanship to allow the game to be played, subject to rules and limitations, so long as the average man, or even a significant section of the community, is in fact strongly addicted to the money-making passion.
>
> (CWVII: 374)

Part II
Continuity issues

6   The end of Keynes and philosophy?

Bradley W. Bateman

Introduction

Writing the history of the ideas of John Maynard Keynes is a complex and difficult business. Keynes led a complex and busy life, and this fact alone would make the scholar's work complicated – all the more so since Keynes left so much of his paperwork behind: in addition to the thirty volumes of the *Collected Writings*, there are more than 100 boxes of original material deposited in the Modern Archives of King's College, Cambridge. Add to this the fact that most of the people in his personal and professional circles are themselves the regular subject of biographers and historians, and the size of the task involved in trying to place him in a clear and accurate historical focus is daunting.

Even these obstacles to writing about Keynes are not the *most* difficult ones, however. For, with enough time and patience, one can work through the cornucopia of material and, if nothing else, it can help to reveal patterns and influences that might not be obvious at first sight. By far the biggest problem for the Keynes scholar is that Keynes is an icon. For the social democratic Left, he is the great author of the theoretical justification for government intervention in the economy; for the conservative Right, he is the villain who undermined the traditional belief in *laissez-faire* during the Great Depression; and for the Marxian Left, he is the bourgeois apologist who helped capitalism to avoid the collapse that could have precipitated revolution. Thus, Keynes has a stature that makes his ideas sacrosanct for many people. Because of this, attempting to analyse his ideas critically always involves the risk that one will violate what is an article of faith for someone else.

Nowhere is the difficulty of interpreting Keynes's work more clear than in the fairly uncontroversial area of the actual influence of his ideas in shaping economic policy in response to the Great Depression. For we now know that in almost every country that tried to use government budget deficits to battle the effects of the Great Depression these policies were undertaken *without reference* to Keynes's writings. In the United States, in inter-war Germany, in Japan, in France and in Sweden, governments undertook budget deficits for a variety of reasons, but not because of Keynes or his great work, *The General Theory of Employment, Interest and Money*) (CWVII, referred to hereafter as *The General Theory*).[1] Yet Keynes is still regularly referred to in history books as the economist who influenced the capitalist world to use fiscal policy to stimulate its way out of the Great Depression. But if you consider the roles that the Left and the Right assign to Keynes as either hero or villain, it is necessary to each one of their myths that he did play such a role.[2]

So the first problem for Keynes scholars is getting past these myths and icons that have been constructed about him in order to get at the historical reality. One might suppose that this would not be so hard for the typical historian of economic thought who is also a Ph.D. economist and whose audience is other professional economists. After all, economists are notoriously empirical, as well as iconoclastic, so trying to persuade them of the 'facts' should not be so difficult as trying to persuade ideologues of the same. The unfortunate truth is that it is no easier to persuade economists to discard their myths and legends about Keynes. For some, this is because they are just as committed to the rights or wrongs of government intervention in the economy as any other citizen. The problem is also compounded, however, by the fact that so many economists *also* see Keynes as the authority behind a particular theoretical style. Thus, for economists, Keynes can be the godfather both of their politics and of their economic models.

Still, when we consider the historical 'facts', it seems impossible not to come to some conclusions that challenge the traditional mythologies about Keynes's life and work. In this chapter, I should like to undertake that challenge by looking at a part of Keynes's work that has traditionally been overlooked, but that has received particular scrutiny in the last twenty years: his philosophical work in probability and uncertainty and its possible influence on his economics.[3] This is a literature that is rife with controversies of its own, and I have been one of the controversialists; but I should, nonetheless, like to start here with an effort to explode some of the orthodoxies in this particular area and then show how it is possible to move on from this small area to explode some even bigger myths about Keynes and his work.

Exploding some small myths

The literature on 'Keynes and philosophy' has traditionally been marked by several fundamental controversies about the nature of Keynes's work in *A Treatise on Probability* (CWVIII). Controversy started almost immediately in the literature that began to appear in the 1980s; in particular, the doctoral dissertations written by Anna Carabelli and Roderick O'Donnell, both at Cambridge, took opposing stands on the nature of Keynes's work.[4] In a nutshell, O'Donnell argued that Keynes had constructed an objective theory of probability, while Carabelli argued that he had constructed a subjective theory of probability. No sooner had these two competing interpretations of Keynes's work started to gain circulation than a completely different argument was put forward: namely that Keynes had originally constructed an objective theory in *A Treatise on Probability*, but that later, in the 1930s, he had capitulated to criticism from Frank Ramsey (1978) and had accepted a subjective theory. These controversies shaped the first decade of the 'Keynes and philosophy' literature.

But my purpose here is not to review those early debates about the nature of Keynes's theory of probability.[5] Instead, I should like to make three strong statements that debunk several of the underlying assumptions that run through the 'Keynes and philosophy' literature and so are crucial to the arguments of virtually every writer in this area. Once these assumptions are overthrown, we shall be free to see that the 'Keynes and philosophy' literature can lead us in some new and unexpected directions. Thus, I shall go on in the next section to argue that the new understanding we gain of Keynes when we are freed from these stifling old assumptions allows us to come to some very different conclusions about Keynes and his ideas in the 1930s.

The three interrelated myths that I should like to challenge are: (1) that Keynes's early work in probability theory led him to understand the importance of expectations and uncertainty in economic decision-making and that he slowly introduced expectations to economics in his economic writings in the 1920s and 1930s; (2) that the use of expectations in Keynes's great book, *The General Theory*, came about as a direct result of his earlier work in probability theory; and (3) that Keynes is a great theoretical revolutionary who first introduced expectations to macroeconomics.

In their place, I should like to substitute the three following assertions: (1) that early in his economic writings, Keynes advocated a standard Cambridge theory of the trade cycle that, as had always been the case, depended on expectations and uncertainty as a means of explaining why capitalist economies are prone to booms and busts; (2) that Keynes abandoned the Cambridge trade cycle theory in the 1920s and maintained this position (with a vengeance) well into the 1930s; and (3) that Keynes placed expectations and uncertainty at the centre of his argument in *The General Theory* because his work in policy-making and his experience as an investor in the 1930s led him to do so *after years of denying that expectations or uncertainty had any relevance in macroeconomics*.

The thrust of my effort here, then, is not so much to enter into the debates about the nuances of Keynes's philosophical work as it is to question *how* that work came to manifest itself in his economics.[6] The explicit purpose of virtually everyone who writes in the 'Keynes and philosophy' literature is, after all, to employ their interpretation of Keynes's philosophical work in probability to gain a better grasp of his economics; but my purpose in this first part of the chapter is to question the very nature of that link. The standard way in which writers in the field have tried to explicate the link between 'Keynes the philosopher' and 'Keynes the economist' follows the general outline of the myths I am trying to debunk. Once his philosophical work is interpreted, a short argument follows in which the writer either offers a few quotations from the *Tract on Monetary Reform*, *The Treatise on Money* and *The General Theory* that seem to have some reference to expectations and uncertainty or, more usually, jumps straight to *The General Theory* to show how the ideas explicated from *A Treatise on Probability* illuminate Keynes's great book.

Perhaps the best (and shortest) way to support my three counter-claims to these myths is to look at Keynes's writings of the late 1920s and early 1930s, when he was working on *A Treatise on Money* and defending it after its publication.[7] Thus, I shall begin with the second of my alternative propositions about Keynes. Keynes's position in *A Treatise on Money* was that booms and busts are caused by disequilibria between the market and the natural rates of interest. If market rates are greater than the natural rate, then the economy will contract because of contracting investment; if the market rate is below the natural rate, then the economy will expand because of expanding investment. As Keynes himself later admitted, this is a very mechanical interpretation of the economy, but it followed directly from his style of theorizing.[8] The entire argument in *A Treatise on Money* depends on Keynes's Fundamental Equations, which he derives from the equation of exchange, $MV = Py$. In the grips of an unshakable self-confidence that led him to say to Montagu Norman, the then head of the Bank of England, 'I can only say that I am ready to have my head chopped off if it [his analysis] is false', Keynes churned out a dense theoretical argument that he used in the many venues in which he was working as an expert on the possible policy responses to the Great Depression (CWIX: 350–1). Keynes was sure that he had proved that the solution to the slump was to be had in the Bank of England's adjustment of the bank rate in line with the natural rate.[9]

For our immediate purposes, the main point is not the theoretical content of Keynes's argument *per se*, but rather what he said about those who offered opposing interpretations. As was always the case with Keynes, he laid considerable contumely upon his opponents in the battle of ideas. The objects of his greatest opprobrium were those who supported the theory that the explanation of the slump lay in uncertainty and expectations; in this case, it was the leading proponent of the Cambridge theory of the trade cycle, A. C. Pigou. In drafting *A Treatise on Money*, Keynes had referred to 'Professor Pigou's somewhat mythical "psychological errors of optimism and pessimism" on the part of the business world', but he was even more biting and mordant in the final draft.[10] There, Keynes offers a very humorous send-up of Pigou's version of the Cambridge trade cycle theory:

It is as though the family were to go on giving a child successive doses of castor oil every ten minutes until the first dose had done its work. Or – to take a better parallel – it is as though different members of the family were to give successive doses to the child, each in ignorance of the doses given by the others. The child will be very ill. Bismuth will then be administered on the same principle. Scientists will announce that children are subject to a diarrhea–constipation cycle, due, they will add, to the weather, or failing that, to alternations of optimism and pessimism amongst the members of the family.

(CWVI: 200)

Keynes's message here is very clear: confidence and expectations are an erroneous explanation of what drives the trade cycle. Keynes's attack did not stop with what he said in *A Treatise on Money*, however.

Shortly after the publication of *A Treatise on Money*, he encountered Pigou directly when Pigou was called to testify before the Macmillan Committee, of which Keynes was a member and where he was trying to use his arguments in *A Treatise on Money* to shape the Committee's conclusions. Throughout the many interviews conducted by the Committee with expert witnesses, Keynes gave nothing but withering replies to anyone who suggested confidence and expectations as the causes of the slump. With Pigou he was more polite, but no less dismissive. In an exchange about the Bank of England's policy of maintaining a high bank rate to support the pound sterling in the Gold Standard, Keynes wanted Pigou to acknowledge the argument in *A Treatise on Money* that it is these high rates, and they alone, that were causing insufficient investment:

Keynes: Does this not depend on the rate of interest?
Pigou: Undoubtedly, in part.
Keynes: Is not that fundamental?
Pigou: There is the state of mind of the business man. The business man might be in such a state that he would not borrow money or use money at 0 percent.
Keynes: That is an extremely abnormal state of things?
Pigou: It is the two things – interest and his state of mind.[11]

Keynes's adamant position is repeated throughout the proceedings of both the Macmillan Committee and the Economic Advisory Council.[12] But nowhere is his position (that confidence and expectations are not important in understanding the trade cycle) set out more clearly than in his correspondence with Hubert Henderson, the co-author with Keynes in 1929 of the famous campaign document 'Can Lloyd George do it?' (CWIXa), which had originally made the argument for a large-scale government deficit to combat the slump. Henderson, trained at Cambridge, and still an advocate of the Cambridge theory that the slump was caused by a lack of confidence, or poor expectations, argues with Keynes in their correspondence over this subject until late 1933. Their correspondence provides one of the most succinct statements of Keynes's position when Henderson paraphrases Keynes: 'You always say – "It's nonsense to talk about confidence"' (CWXXI: 166).

If all this only proves the second of my three points, that Keynes abandoned his advocacy of the traditional Cambridge theory of the trade cycle, it leaves my two other points still to prove. The first, that Keynes was originally an adherent of the Cambridge theory, is fairly straightforward, from the evidence. After studying with Marshall for his Civil Service exam, Keynes wrote often, in his early book reviews and essays, as an adherent of Cambridge monetary and trade cycle theory. Thus, he could say as early as 1910, when speaking of a businessman's decisions to invest, 'he will be affected, as is obvious, not by the net income which he will actually receive from his investment in the long run, but by his expectations. He will often depend upon fashion, upon advertisement or upon irrational waves of optimism or depression' (CWXV: 46). And it was Keynes's own student, Frederick Lavington, who came to Cambridge after starting a career in banking, who would publish the most definitive single statement of the Cambridge theory of the cycle, *The Trade Cycle: An Account of the Causes Producing Rhythmical Changes in the Activity of Business* (1922). Thus, when Keynes embraced his monetary theory of the trade cycle in *A Treatise on Money*, he was turning on the position that he himself had once been taught and had, in turn, taught to others. He was, literally, an apostate, and his criticism of Pigou was issued with the traditional fervour of a convert for those who have not followed the new path.

So now we have established my first two alternative propositions about Keynes, namely that he was originally an advocate of the Cambridge trade cycle theory and that he abandoned that position with a vengeance in the late 1920s and early 1930s. This, in turn, allows us to see why two of the myths we listed are just that. The Cambridge trade cycle theorists, who followed the more public writings of Overstone and Bagehot, were advocates of the importance of uncertainty and expectations in explaining booms and busts long before Keynes arrived on the scene. Thus, the argument that one finds repeated over and over in the 'Keynes and philosophy' literature, that Keynes was the person who introduced expectations to macroeconomics, is simply ridiculous. Keynes tried to make this claim for himself in his oft-quoted article in the *Quarterly Journal of Economics* in 1937, but as D. E. Moggridge has pointed out, Keynes frequently made grandiose and inflammatory statements to cause a stir.[13] This was a part of his strategy to draw attention to what he was saying. Dennis Robertson criticized him squarely for his unfairness to Marshall and Pigou in their correspondence, but Keynes was not concerned with historical accuracy. He wanted to have a good fight and persuade people of an old truth that he had recently returned to after having abandoned it many years earlier.

This brings us squarely to the question of how and why Keynes brought expectations back into his own theorizing about the economy. Why is it that in his Michaelmas lectures of 1933 he suddenly begins to talk about expectations in a pervasive way?[14] Why is it that in the spring of 1934 Keynes suddenly includes expectations throughout the draft chapters of *The General Theory* that he circulated among friends? Where did this sudden concern come from? There is no *one* place where we can look to find the answer, but it seems clear that the concern came from two primary sources: his long-standing feud with Pigou, Henderson and anyone else he encountered in policy-making circles who disagreed with him, and his ongoing work as an investor. The policy debates, which are discussed above, went on from late 1930 until mid-1933 and forced Keynes to face the question of uncertainty in his professional life and correspondence on a regular basis. Those debates with his friends and colleagues do not appear from the evidence, however, to have been enough on their own to convince him to change his mind.

Instead, it seems that it was the events that he was forced to examine in his capacity as a policy analyst that led him to this conclusion. And these same events – for instance, the abandonment of the Gold Standard, the Treasury conversion of War bonds – also affected him as an investor. It would take an essay longer than this one to detail these many events and Keynes's responses to them, but the responses are all in the public record and they point in one direction. Slowly and inexorably, as Keynes watched the financial markets during the early 1930s, he came to see the truth that they were driven by expectations and confidence.

Of course, as was noted above, he was not watching these events only from his perch as a policy analyst. They also affected him as an investor – as the Bursar for King's College, Cambridge, and as the portfolio manager for the Provincial insurance company.[15] From these perches, he was forced to judge the movements of the market, and what he saw from this perspective was that confidence drove markets. This was particularly the case with the bond markets after Britain went off the Gold Standard. Whereas Keynes had noted before the abandonment of the Standard that the Bank of England could not change rates because of the demands of the Standard, now he saw that there were no artificial restraints on rates. As he attempted throughout 1931–33 to explain the moves in the bond markets, he was forced to realize the centrality of expectations and confidence. Still, while recognizing the importance of expectations in this arena, he continued to argue against the importance of uncertainty with Hubert Henderson until early 1933. Then, suddenly, he stopped arguing with Henderson, and at exactly this same time expectations and confidence begin to suffuse Keynes's theoretical work.

While he does draw some vocabulary and ideas from his earlier philo-sophical work on probability (for example, the notion of evidential weight), there is simply no reasonable way to argue that it was that philosophical work that had brought him to see the importance of expec-tations in his economic theorizing. To make such an argument would require a massive effort to explain away the years of his *denying* that expectations and uncertainty were important to understanding the trade cycle. In any case, the documentary evidence seems clear enough on this point: Keynes introduced expectations and uncertainty into *The General Theory* in response to his experiences in policy-making and investment, not as an intellectual by-product of his work as a philosopher.

Exploding some bigger myths

Now, as regards the 'Keynes and philosophy' literature, the points I have made above change much of the terrain. If it is no longer possible to make an argument that the ideas in *A Treatise on Probability* get placed directly (slowly or quickly) into Keynes's work as an economist, then much of the style of argument in the literature must be changed. Now, instead, it must be explained why his theory of expectations lay dormant while Keynes actively and vociferously argued that expectations were not an important part of economic decision-making. There is also an embarrassing need to explain how Keynes abandoned his earlier adher-ence to the Cambridge trade cycle theory if expectations were such an integral part of his economic thinking throughout the 1920s and 1930s. In short, there is a lot of explaining that needs to be done to support the traditional premises of the connection between Keynes's philosophy and his economics.

I do not wish to labour this point. The important point here is not the state of the debate in the 'Keynes and philosophy' literature, but rather what we can learn through a better understanding of Keynes. Thus, the most important point of seeing that Keynes was not the first economist to understand the centrality of expectations and confidence in capitalist economies, and of understanding that he came to this realization for good through his work as a policy analyst and investor, lies outside the traditional 'Keynes and philosophy' debates *per se*. The most important points lie somewhere else altogether. It is important, first, to realize that the whole episode points to the incontrovertible fact that, throughout the nineteenth century and into the twentieth century, expectations, espe-cially unstable expectations, have been observed to be a part of what drives capitalist economies. And this observation has been made not by neophyte theorists, or radicals, but rather by some of the most sober and clear-eyed analysts on the scene: Overstone, Bagehot, Marshall, Pigou, Lavington and, finally, Keynes. It is also worth noting as a lesson from this episode that very good economists, like Keynes, can get tricked by their 'magic formula mentality' into denying this fact. Like many contemporary theorists of the first rank, Keynes denied for many years that confidence and expectations play a significant role in driving capitalist economies.

Keynes eventually abandoned his denial of the importance of expectations and uncertainty, however; and this points to another important lesson to be learned – namely that good economic theory comes from experience of the real economy. Keynes finally got it right, but not because he fiddled long enough with the mathematics or because he discovered a new econometric technique to apply to data. To be sure, he developed new models; and to be sure, he was empirical in his investigations. But what he learned, he learned by arguing over policy-making and by managing a portfolio. These activities are important empirical experiences and they taught Keynes a lesson, one that he employed to make better theory. This lesson is also one that could be posted, to great advantage, over the entrance door to all programmes that grant a doctoral degree in economics.

In addition to considering this lesson about capitalist economies and how best to do economics, there are still some important myths to be exploded. The two with which I should like to conclude are closely related and come out of a more careful look at the arguments that Keynes undertook with Henderson, Pigou and the other Cambridge trade cycle theorists between 1930 and 1933. When we see the political dimension of those arguments, we see some interesting facts about Keynes's eventual embrace of confidence and expectations that challenge the traditional understandings of his legacy.

What was the political dimension of those arguments between Keynes and his adversaries? In essence, the political dimension of the debate centred on the question of whether the government could do much if anything to help ameliorate the effects of the Great Depression. When Henderson, Pigou and the Treasury mandarins argued that confidence was central to understanding what was happening to the British economy, they would inevitably go on to say that this fact precluded the possibility of undertaking any large-scale government deficits ('loan financed public works projects', in their lexicon). And that, of course, was anathema to Keynes. He had argued in 'Can Lloyd George do it?' (CWIXa) and in 'The means to prosperity' (CWIXd) that such deficits were the best means of stimulating the economy, so he was not ready to hear that such plans would not work because they would 'scare' businessmen with the prospect of higher taxes and further government intervention in the economy. This political dimension is especially clear in the private correspondence between Keynes and Henderson, who was, after all, the co-author of *Can Lloyd George do it?*[16]

Thus, whatever else Keynes may have had at stake in the disputes over confidence and uncertainty, he was reluctant to give way on this

issue because of what were seen as the unacceptable political consequences of accepting the centrality of confidence in explaining the booms
and busts of capitalist economies. Keynes did, of course, eventually give
way to his critics and admit that confidence is central to understanding
the cycles in capitalist economies; however, this leads to the awkward
question of how he reconciled his acceptance of confidence with the
arguments against government deficits and public works projects. The
answer to how he made this reconciliation leads to my next two
debunking propositions (to be added to the three in the previous
section): (4) that *The General Theory* is not intended primarily as a polemic
in favour of fiscal fine-tuning; and (5) that after 1933, Keynes never again
endorsed discretionary fiscal deficits in the same way as he had in 'Can
Lloyd George do it?' and 'The means to prosperity'.

For some, of course, these propositions are simply unimaginable. For
people on both the Left and the Right, it is important that Keynes stay as
he was: the man who introduced discretionary fiscal policy to the capitalist economies. But the plain truth is that, even if his work was used
after the Second World War as an *ex post* defence of discretionary fiscal
policy, it was neither the driving force behind such policies in the inter-
war period, nor did Keynes himself offer his work as a simple defence of
such policies.[17]

For at least fifteen years, scholars have been noting the fact that *The
General Theory* is bereft of almost any mention of the policies that might
follow from the theory and, in particular, the fact that the book hardly
constitutes a ringing defence of the policies so closely associated with
Keynes's name.[18] A careful perusal of the recently completed *Collected
Works* shows that, in the years following the publication of *The General
Theory*, Keynes was no proselyte for an active fiscal policy, as he had
been earlier. Consider, for instance, this quotation from 1937, the year
after *The General Theory* was published:

> Public loan expenditure is not, of course, the only way, and not neces-
> sarily the best way, to increase employment. Nor is it always
> sufficiently effective to overcome other adverse influences. The state of
> confidence and of expectation about what will happen next, the
> conditions of credit, the rate of interest, the growth of population, the
> state of foreign trade, and the readiness of the public to spend are
> scarcely less important.
>
> (CWXXI: 429–30)[19]

Thus, while Keynes did not abandon all reference to fiscal policy, the
urgency of his appeals and their certitude changed drastically with the
publication of *The General Theory*. In fact, when he did talk about fiscal
policy after the publication of this book, what Keynes said was something altogether different. During the years of the Second World War, in

his work as an economic specialist in the British Treasury, Keynes came to advocate the view that the 'regular' budget, for items of current expenditure, should always be kept in balance: 'It is important to emphasize that it is no part of the purpose of the Exchequer or the Public Capital Budget to facilitate deficit financing, as I understand this term' (CWXXVII: 406, see also 352–3). Thus, in addition to the 'regular' budget, Keynes suggested that long-term public capital investment be put into a separate budget. He then argued that, if the government maintained an agenda of possible future public investment, it might sometimes be desirable to speed up, or slow down, the execution of projects from this list. He insisted, however, that the projects be financed by bonds that would eventually be paid off from the revenues generated by the projects themselves. This is hardly a ringing defence of discretionary fiscal policy.

In fact, Keynes came to support a whole range of policies for stabilizing the economy that really have little or nothing to do with discretionary fiscal policy. He termed this complex of ideas 'the socialization of investment'.[20] It was to consist of the careful use of the Public Capital Budget, mentioned above, together with the stabilization of private investment.[21] The crux for stabilizing private investment was to be the stabilization of the expectations of private investors. But how could the expectations of private investors be stabilized? Clearly, he believed that if the government could stabilize the flow of public capital expenditure, this would help to stabilize entrepreneurs' expectations of the future. And he believed that a stable monetary policy would also help in this regard. Thus, what Keynes proposed is the creation of long-run stable government policies to help maintain business confidence in the future. In recognizing that 'animal spirits' drive private investment, Keynes went a long way towards acknowledging the concerns of Hubert Henderson and his other early critics who had said that large, discretionary projects were just as likely to backfire as they were to help, because of their adverse impact on business confidence.

The end of Keynes and philosophy?

Keynes's move to arguing for long-run stable policies is perhaps best captured by his many references late in his life to creating 'conventions' and 'rules' that would stabilize capitalist society. As he said in his memoir, 'My early beliefs' (CWXb), 'civilization [is] a thin and precarious crust erected by the personality and the will of a very few, and only maintained by rules and conventions skillfully put across and guilefully preserved'. Now Keynes understood that the thin and precarious crust was not going to be preserved by simple, mechanical fine-tuning of the economy.

In effect, what happened to Keynes's thinking on economic policy was a complete volte-face. Whereas he had once believed that the government could successfully tinker with the economy to provide full employment, now he recognized that successful policies would have to take into account the unpredictable reactions of businessmen to those policies. The result was that he could no longer recommend large-scale fine-tuning with the same self-assurance and bravado that had character-ized his earlier position.

And this brings us to what I take to be the real end, or purpose, of the 'Keynes and philosophy' literature. The real lessons of Keynes's work on uncertainty, as it applies to economics, all stem from his inability to escape the simple fact that capitalist economies are subject to booms and busts because of the shifts in capitalists' expectations.[22] Confidence really does matter. But there is more to the story than this one insight; other important questions arise because confidence is so central to capitalist economies. What exactly are the limits of government policy-making in a capitalist economy? How far can the government go before it loses the confidence of business leaders? What does it mean about the relative power of capitalists and workers if capitalists' fears must always drive economic policy-making? If successful economic policy is always to take account of business leaders' fears about future profits, can workers get fair treatment? Are the answers to these questions different in different countries? What role do different cultures play in shaping the nature of business managers' expectations? What role do different cultural concep-tions of propriety play in determining the limits of economic policy? Will global capital markets dampen or exacerbate the effects of confidence on investment and the trade cycle?

All these questions flow naturally from a full understanding of this chapter in Keynes's life. In asking them, I do not mean to presuppose the answers. For we must remember that another lesson that may be learned from Keynes's experience of arguing about expectations and uncertainty is that ideology can be poison. Keynes kept himself chained to a mechan-ical conception of the economy for many years because of his ideological distaste for the apparent outcome of 'confidence' arguments about the trade cycle. The answers to the questions may change with time. There may be different answers for different nations. We may discover that the answers are not anything like what we thought they would be when we started our enquiry.

But we can say with some certainty that the questions are inescapable. Certainly, in the summer of 1998, when the Federal Reserve Bank of the United States cut interest rates three times in quick succession to help shore up the world financial system, it was in response to their fears about a collapse in confidence following the Russian default on interna-tional loans. So, can we afford to train future central bankers who do not understand the role of confidence in the global economy? No, we cannot. Not if we want to avoid serious bouts of unemployment and poverty. So, the fundamental questions raised by this episode will not leave us.

Despite the fact that many contemporary economists are uncomfortable with the philosophical dimension of their subject, it will not go away.

Thus, the end of 'Keynes and philosophy' is to bring us back to these critical questions and to help us shape our understanding of what is at issue in the modern capitalism that defines the world in which we live.

Notes

1 Canada may be the only country that undertook such policies after a debate explicitly informed by Keynes's writings. For detailed studies of the countries mentioned above, see Hall (1989).

2 In the period after the Second World War, after *The General Theory* became widely accepted, Keynes's name did become attached to counter-cyclical fiscal policy and his work can be seen in this sense as influential in many subsequent economic policy debates. It is the case, however, that during the 1920s and 1930s his work was conspicuously absent from the many national debates where government budget deficits were used.

3 G. L. S. Shackle (1961b) first argued for the possibility of a relationship between Keynes's *A Treatise on Probability* and *The General Theory*. The literature in this area really only took off after the oil price shocks in the 1970s and the subsequent attempts to introduce expectations into macroeconomic models. Don Patinkin (1990) provides an interesting, if biased, survey of the literature.

4 The revisions of these dissertations appeared in the mid-1980s, and they mark the beginning of the effort to figure out just exactly what Keynes was up to when he undertook his original philosophical enquiry in his fellowship dissertation (1907) and its revision, *A Treatise on Probability*. See Carabelli (1988) and O'Donnell (1989).

5 The theory that Keynes changed his mind about the nature of probability was originally put forward in Bateman (1987). Bateman (1991) is a long review essay of the published revisions of Carabelli's and O'Donnell's dissertations. Both of these articles provide easily accessible statements of the issues in the debate over the nature of Keynes's theory of probability.

6 I believe that the debates over the nature of Keynes's theory of probability are important for many reasons, but wish in this chapter to go a step further and look at where those debates lead.

7 I do not try to offer a full account of my defence here owing to lack of space. But the reader may find the fully worked out argument from all the relevant evidence in Chapters 4 and 5 of Bateman (1996).

8 Patinkin (1976: 53, 126) was the first to argue that Keynes employed a 'magic formula mentality' in *A Treatise on Money*. Clarke (1988: 313) makes a similar argument, as does Bateman (1996).

9 Because England was on the Gold Standard at the time, the bank was not at liberty to change bank rates freely, hence Keynes developed a long list of policy alternatives to a cut in the bank rate for the Macmillan Committee and the Economic Advisory Council.

10 This quotation from the draft manuscript of *A Treatise on Money* appears in Keynes (CWXIII: 89).

11 This exchange is QQ. 6613–16 in the Committee on Finance and Industry *Minutes of Evidence* (HMSO 1931).

12 For the quotations and citations, see Bateman (1996: Ch. 5).

13 See Moggridge (1986).

14 See Rymes (1989) for composite notes from Keynes's lectures of the 1930s.

15 Donald Moggridge's essay on Keynes's investment activity at the beginning of volume XII of the *Collected Writings* is the best overview of this subject available. To see how Keynes came to see effects of expectations in the bond markets, consider Oliver Westall's (1992) careful exploration of how he moved the Provincial's portfolio into consuls in 1931–32 in anticipation of a fall in interest rates.
16 The relevant letters, with references to the issue of whether the conservative aspects of confidence arguments were anathema to Keynes, are reproduced in the *Collected Writings*.
17 The source for the best readings on the adaptation of 'Keynesian' policies in the inter-war period is given in note 1 above.
18 See, for instance, Kahn (1984: 158), Meltzer (1988) and Peden (1988: 38).
19 For a full catalogue and discussion of such quotations, see Chapters 5 and 6 of Bateman (1996). This is only one of numerous examples.
20 Keynes first uses this term in the concluding chapter of *The General Theory*.
21 Keynes also mentioned an intermediate action between these two options. He argued that many large corporations, such as the port authorities, were effectively under public control and that they should be managed so as to smooth the flow of capital expenditure.
22 I do not mean to imply that unstable expectations are the only sources of instability in capitalist economies.

7   The thick and the thin of controversy

Rod O'Donnell[1]

Introduction

Controversy is the permanent companion of interpretation, just as it is of economics. We may never reach agreement in either area but, as rational beings, we are at least capable of doing our best to understand competing points of view. To do so, however, requires sufficient goodwill and respect for the tasks of comprehension and discussion. Clashes between protagonists will be intellectually more productive if they aim at better understanding and more informed dialogue.

In this chapter, I discuss some of the general and particular issues that arise in controversies and debates concerning Keynes's philosophy and its relation to his economics. Given space limitations, I concentrate on two interpretations only: Bradley Bateman's, as set out in his *Keynes's Uncertain Revolution* (1996); and my own, as set out in my *Keynes: Philosophy, Economics and Politics* (O'Donnell 1989). As well as seeking to contribute to the better understanding of aspects of both interpretations, the discussion also addresses issues that arise in Keynes scholarship regardless of the identities of the protagonists.

It may seem self-indulgent to dwell on my own interpretation, but I do so because some commentators evidently still do not understand it adequately, because it is based on all the available evidence, and because I still adhere to its main theses and overall structure. The reasons for choosing Bateman's is because his interpretation is in strong contrast to mine, because his book criticizes me more than any other author,[2] and because I should like an opportunity to discuss his views and rebut his criticisms. As always, space restrictions constrain coverage to a subset of the issues.

Histories

Bateman characterizes all prior efforts at exploring the links between Keynes's philosophy and his economics as works in the history of economic thought and hence as *histories* (Bateman 1996: 3). No other possibility is envisaged. Even books discussing Keynes's ideas and analyses are viewed as histories of doctrines or analytical constructs. Having forced them into the mould of being histories, he then finds much fault with them: they are only 'thin' histories and not 'thick' histories; they do not explore the origins of Keynes's thinking; and they do not pay enough attention to putting Keynes's ideas into historical context.

The task he sets himself, at the beginning of his book at least, is to write a better history, one that will adequately tell 'the story of Maynard Keynes's concern with probability and uncertainty' (*ibid.*). Despite all previous scholarship, he regards this story as remaining untold because previous authors have not addressed 'the question of *where* Keynes's interest in the ideas came from' (*ibid.*). And, instead of the 'thin histories of analytical constructs' produced by other writers, he seeks to produce a 'thick' history.

Bateman spends little time explaining the distinction between thin and thick histories. From his brief discussion, it emerges that thin histories are written by historians of economic thought, they focus on 'the pedigrees of specific analytical ideas', and they are primarily concerned with the internal influences on an author's thinking. Thick histories, by contrast, are practised by historians proper, they place economic ideas in social and cultural contexts, and they embrace both external and internal influences on an author's thought. A thin or purely internalist history has some value, but a thick history, one that 'tells a full story of a history of an idea', will almost always be more valuable (*ibid.*: 3–4).

In relation to its historical arguments, the main thesis of his book is that it is impossible to understand uncertainty and expectations in *The General Theory* without understanding the 'external' influence on Keynes's thought of his debates in the early 1930s with other economists over the role of business confidence in the Great Depression (*ibid.*: 4, 10, 124–5, 145). The main reason for this emphasis on thick history is his belief that it is impossible to understand ideas adequately without understanding their historical origins (on which see below).

Some observations on Bateman's introductory remarks are pertinent. First, it seems extraordinary to suggest that other writers still have not told stories of Keynes's concern with probability and uncertainty. Most of the well-known books Bateman refers to have done just that – related stories about how Keynes came to these issues in his early years and how these resurfaced, in full or in part, in *The General Theory*. Perhaps his criticism is that these efforts are incomplete or misleading, that they are only 'thin' and not 'thick' stories, or that each only recounts 'a' story whereas he will tell 'the' story. But if this is what is meant, it would help if it were made clear.

Secondly, my book (and possibly those of others) was not written as a historical work, even one in the history of economic thought. Its primary aim was always *analytical* – to explore the philosophy, and the links between this philosophy and the economics and politics, of one of the greatest economists of the twentieth century whose thought still has contemporary relevance. Of course, it had historical dimensions which entered the story as required, but it never claimed to be, and was never intended as, a history, thick or thin. Criticizing it for not being what it never sought to be is beside the point.

Thirdly, Bateman tells us that he is 'not certain that the full story is the one [he has] told here, for there is a *fundamental indeterminacy* in the retelling of that story' (*ibid.*: 12, my emphasis). The main reason for the existence of this indeterminacy is 'the fact that Keynes found himself by the late 1930s with a set of sentiments and ideas accumulated over a life-time but with no good way to express these' (*ibid.*). That is, 'Shorn of the certainty of his early beliefs, he was left to express himself imperfectly', and 'found himself prone to lapsing' into his old modes of speech (*ibid.*: 13–14). As a result, 'scholars will always be faced with the dilemma of trying to discern his actual beliefs from the imperfect approximations he found for his own thoughts' (*ibid.*: 14).

This distinction between Keynes's actual beliefs and their imperfect expressions is both troublesome and revealing. First, it shifts the discussion towards Keynes's mind. His mind was clear early on, but later struggled to express itself adequately. But how do we know this? Bateman does not provide any *relevant* textual evidence[3] and, to my knowledge, there are no passages in Keynes's later writings supporting this view in relation to the concepts surrounding probability and uncertainty. So it appears that we only know about it on Bateman's say-so. This is either an assertion or it implies that Bateman knows more about Keynes's mind than others. Secondly, Bateman is quite certain of his interpretation of various key passages in Keynes's writings, even though others have provided reasons for thinking these passages are ambiguous or imprecise. It must therefore be that Bateman can perceive what Keynes is really trying to say, even though Keynes could not find the proper words to say it. Again, this implies insight into Keynes's mind. And thirdly, assuming Bateman's distinction does accurately portray the state of Keynes's mind, how are we to decide between competing interpretations when they offer different dividing lines between his actual beliefs and their imperfect approximations? The absence of any criteria seems to be the reason for the fundamental indeterminacy. But if everything is fundamentally indeterminate, why is Bateman's interpretation better than any other? No pointers are given, other than an assertion or Bateman's own insight.

Finally, describing all previous works as thin histories and his own as a thick history conveniently massages the odds in his favour. Since thick history almost always outperforms thin history, his book is almost guaranteed to be a superior account.

Is history necessary to adequate understanding?

Is it possible to obtain an adequate understanding of ideas without knowing their history? My answer is yes – the adequate understanding of ideas is not dependent on a knowledge of their history, although such knowledge can broaden and deepen understanding. Hence productive discussions about ideas are possible without knowledge of the details of their origin and evolution.

Bateman's answer appears to be no – knowing their history, or at least the external factors in their history, is essential to the adequate understanding of ideas. This message is conveyed by the following remarks:

> But without considering the external [historical] influences, *it is simply not possible to get Keynes's ideas in clear focus.*
>
> (*ibid.*: 4, my emphasis)

> Likewise, it is *impossible* to understand Keynes's use of uncertainty in *The General Theory* without understanding his long and protracted battle in the 1930s over the importance of business confidence to the Slump.
>
> (*ibid.*: 4, my emphasis)

Our respective answers have influenced the kinds of books we have written. I wrote a book that pursued the analysis and investigation of Keynes's ideas, referred to their history and the historical context as the discussion required, but did not undertake a lengthy or detailed investigation of the historical development of these ideas. I also believe that before one can write a history of ideas, one must have a prior notion of what these ideas are. By contrast, Bateman's book seeks to be a thick history that will make adequate understanding possible by clarifying the historical evolution of Keynes's ideas. On his account, non-historical analytical works such as mine have merely mired themselves in misunderstanding, confusion and error through their neglect of history.

In fact, however, Bateman's book does not actually deliver on its promise of showing the *necessity* of history to understanding. This is because his account of the history of business confidence in Keynes's writings of the 1920s and 1930s is basically compatible with a number of interpretations, including my own. So if the same history can be embraced by his (correct) interpretation and my (incorrect) interpretation, how can it be that this history is essential to the adequate understanding of Keynes's ideas?

Does Keynes's philosophy drive his economics?

Bateman suggests that I maintain that 'Keynes had an overarching philosophical schema that drove his economics' and that 'changes in his philosophical ideas were a *cause* for the changes in his economic ideas' (*ibid.*: 10, and note 9). This is a misrepresentation. What my book argues is that there are strong links or continuities between Keynes's philosophy and his economics, such that a knowledge of the former clarifies parts of the latter, and that the way in which Keynes theorized parts of his economics was *influenced* by his philosophy. It also contends that these links do not take the form of linear translations or transferences of one body of thought into another.

In fact, Bateman uses exactly the same *kind* of argument as I used. When Keynes decided, *for whatever reason*, to make uncertainty a central theme of *The General Theory*, he turned to his philosophical beliefs, *whatever these were*, as a way of theorizing this theme. What divides us are our views on what these philosophical beliefs were – in the simplest of terms, I say the conceptual framework of *A Treatise on Probability* within which there was an internal shift, while Bateman says Ramsey's theory of subjective probabilities and Keynes's intersubjective version of this. If turning back to philosophical ideas, or saying that philosophy influences economics, means that philosophy 'drives' economics, then this characterization is equally applicable to Bateman's own book.

Changes in Keynes's philosophical ideas

Bateman contends that I argue that 'Keynes's philosophical ideas remain unchanged' between *A Treatise on Probability* and *The General Theory* (*ibid.*: 8), and that my story 'depends on Keynes having one unchanged conception of probability after 1921' (*ibid.*: 102, note 3). This is another poor representation because it implies that I think Ramsey had no impact on Keynes and because it confuses two things that are distinguished in my account. My basic argument is that, in philosophy, Keynes's *conceptual framework* remained unchanged, but that certain of his *ideas* within that framework did change in significant respects as a result of Ramsey's critique. The outcome is an internal shift within the existing framework away from a heavy emphasis on strong rationality, known probabilities, probabilistic uncertainty and determinate conditions towards a greater recognition of the role of weak rationality, unknown probabilities, radical uncertainty and indeterminate conditions. There are thus some significant changes in Keynes's ideas about the appropriate mix of concepts to be used in the analysis of behaviour under uncertainty.

Bateman does not mention these vital aspects of my interpretation except for a footnote reference to unknown probabilities (*ibid.*: 57, note 34) that misrepresents my argument and subjects it to misguided criticism. My view is that unknown probabilities are relevant to *The General Theory* in the context of long-term expectations and radical uncertainty because a dearth of relevant information about the long-term future means that agents with given mental abilities are unable to perceive logical probability relations; it is not, as Bateman puts it, that 'Keynes merely came to realise that more and more probabilities were unknown and fewer and fewer people had the ability to recognise them'. The first of his two criticisms is that Keynes's use of unknown probabilities was 'an unsatisfactory move in the first place that betrayed the unsatisfactory nature of his larger theory'. This is irrelevant because it is not a criticism of my view, but a criticism of Keynes's theory. His second criticism is that Ramsey's critique of Keynes's theory was 'directly aimed at' unknown probabilities, and that it was to 'this part of Ramsey's critique' that Keynes referred in his response. Yet unknown probabilities are not mentioned in Ramsey's critique of Keynes. He cites a passage from *A Treatise on Probability* which, while related to unknown probabilities, is used to launch a quite different criticism, namely the presence of a contradiction in Keynes's theory; as Ramsey (1978: 65) put it, it shows Keynes's 'inability to adhere to [his theory] consistently even in discussing first principles'. However, as argued at length in my book, this criticism is a mistake; Ramsey overlooked the role of limited logical insight in Keynes's theory.[4] And, finally, I am unable to find any passage in Keynes's response to Ramsey (CWXa: 336–9) that refers to an argument by Ramsey about unknown probabilities.

Das Maynard Keynes Problem

Bateman re-asserts the existence of a problem or 'paradox' in Keynes's writings analogous to the apparent paradox in Adam Smith's.[5] How could the author of *A Treatise on Probability* with its stress on rational individuals and objective probabilities have written *The General Theory* with its stress on 'irrational people who base their decisions on social conventions' (*ibid.*: 7)?

Superficially, it would seem that Bateman's solution to the alleged problem is the obvious one of saying that Keynes changed his philosophical beliefs between the two books. That is certainly part of his story. But, despite his claim that it is only possible to solve the problem on the basis of his understanding of the evolution of Keynes's views on probability (*ibid.*: 69, 73), by the end of his book the problem remains unresolved. The reason the reader is left in limbo is because nothing like an adequate explanation is given as to why agents in *The General Theory* are irrational.

Bateman says that Ramsey's critique of *A Treatise on Probability* converted Keynes to subjective probabilities, that subjective probabilities underpin uncertainty and expectations in *The General Theory*, and that the agents in *The General Theory* are irrational. It is the last of these claims that creates internal difficulties for his account. First, the subjective theory of probability, whether in Ramsey's or in later versions, does not assume agents are irrational but grants them the minimum amount of rationality necessary to support the theory (in the form of a consistency requirement). Secondly, when Bateman later discusses the behaviour of agents in *The General Theory* (*ibid.*: 128–39), not once does he characterize them as irrational. They now have (inter)subjective probabilities and follow social conventions, but the question of their rationality or irrationality is never addressed. There is enough in his discussion, however, to indicate that *some* element of rationality is present in their behaviour, but to admit this would destroy *das Problem*. Given his earlier stress on the problem and his claim that only his account can supply a solution, it is remarkable that he does not return to it and satisfy the reader by providing an adequate explanation of why the agents of *The General Theory* are irrational.

The only hints we are given come at the start of his book. Its first chapter states that, early in life, Keynes took rationality to have 'a very narrow meaning', namely that 'people always act so as to achieve what is objectively and recognisably *good*', and that, later in life, when people did not act in this way, 'he called them "irrational"' (*ibid.*: 13–14). The following page then adds a slightly different, but closely related, view, namely that Keynes's conception of rational behaviour in *A Treatise on Probability* depended on objective probabilities so that, when he threw these over, no basis remained for rational action (*ibid.*: 17). However, these brief, unexpanded arguments sit in a thicket of difficulties. Leaving aside the debatable issue of whether they adequately portray Keynes's early or later conceptions of rationality, they presume that Keynes only ever had one conception of rationality and that, when that was abandoned, he was incapable of making use of any other concepts of rationality. Hence the only alternative was irrationality. Unlike probability where he is portrayed as switching with relative ease from one theory to another, Bateman sees him as unable to make any movements or shifts concerning rationality. There is also no realization that, if he accepted subjective probabilities, Keynes also accepted the form of rationality required by that theory.[6] And, finally, by assuming that there is only one form of rationality in *A Treatise on Probability*, these arguments ignore Keynes's remarks in that work that point to the alternative forms of behaviour which I have labelled 'weak rationality'.[7]

By contrast, *das Problem* does not exist in my account. There is no paradox about the author of *A Treatise on Probability* also being the author of *The General Theory*. My characterization of the relationship between the two works is the different and more subtle one of saying that, by the time Keynes came to write *The General Theory*, he had made an internal shift or change of emphasis within the conceptual framework of *A Treatise on Probability*. This allows my account to embrace certain changes in the handling of uncertainty, expectations, probability and conventions, while maintaining that both works deal with rational agents operating in different environments. I agree that *A Treatise on Probability* emphasizes rationality based on objective probabilities, but it also refers to situations where this breaks down and alternative forms of behaviour can be followed by rational agents. However, the representation of *The General Theory* as populated by irrational individuals is nonsensical in my account. In my view, its agents behave as rationally as they are individually able given their circumstances. The typical circumstances in *A Treatise on Probability* are highly favourable, being rich in information and logical ability, but Keynes also mentions circumstances in which these precondi-tions are absent and rational agents are forced to follow different procedures. In *The General Theory*, the circumstances embrace *both* those of adequate information and ability as well as the better known, information-ally deprived circumstances which generate radical uncertainty and the need for alternative strategies such as convention-following.

It follows that *das Maynard Keynes Problem* is non-existent in my account and does not require a solution. My work provides an evidence-based explanation of why the person who wrote *A Treatise on Probability* could also write *The General Theory*, and why the agents in both books behave rationally. The problem only exists in Bateman's account, and his book does not provide an adequate solution.

'My early beliefs'

This 1938 memoir by Keynes plays a vital role in Bateman's argument for *das Maynard Keynes Problem*. There is much that could be said here but let me focus on just one of Bateman's key propositions, namely, his contention that the memoir makes it abundantly clear that Keynes rejected his earlier attachment to Platonism which he later came to regard as a 'mistake' and an 'absurdity' (*ibid.*: 8, 39). While claiming that Keynes 'offered ample evidence of ... the changes in his ideas' between *A Treatise on Probability* and *The General Theory* (*ibid.*: 9), Bateman actually provides no quotations from Keynes to support this claim. Passages are quoted from the memoir (*ibid.*: 13–14, 43, 162) but none of them lend credibility to his view. Given the key role this proposition plays in his interpretation, it is no wonder that he reacts so strongly to my opposing viewpoint and my description of the memoir as possibly the most decep-tive document in Keynes's *oeuvre*. He dismisses this as an unpersuasive 'allegation' (*ibid.*: 14, note 14) and takes no notice of the fact that it is actually the conclusion to a lengthy, reasoned, evidence-based case which draws on *history* to point out that the memoir mixes remarks which are accurate with others that are false.[8]

However, let us turn to the memoir itself. One of the three questions Keynes says he will address is whether 'one still holds by that youthful religion' (CWXb: 435), where religion primarily means Moore's ethics with its Platonist, intuitionist elements. Keynes's answer is pretty clear and direct:

It seems to me looking back, that this religion of ours was a very good one to grow up under. It remains nearer the truth than any other that I know, with less irrelevant extraneous matter and nothing to be ashamed of; though it is a comfort today to be able to discard ... the calculus and the mensuration and the duty to know *exactly* what one means and feels. ... It is still my religion under the surface.

(CWXb: 442)

I see no reason to shift from the fundamental intuitions of *Principia Ethica*; though they are much too few and too narrow to fit actual experience which provides a richer and more various content.

(CWXb: 444)

Would someone who had completely abandoned Platonism have written these passages? I read them as providing solid evidence against Bateman's proposition. If there is other relevant evidence that puts them in a different light and provides support for his proposition, Bateman does not reveal it in his book. But if, in fact, there is no other evidence, his argument degenerates into argument by assertion.

By contrast, my interpretation says that the memoir reveals *qualified reaffirmation* of Keynes's belief in his early Moorism. When I reflect on all the evidence and seek a consistent interpretation, I agree that Keynes criticized his earlier beliefs but contend that these criticisms represent immanent criticisms and qualifications rather than wholesale abandonment. The above passages seem to me to support this view and contradict Bateman's.

Classifications of probability theory

Bateman takes me to task for not following Hacking's 'very helpful' bipartite classification of probability theories, for 'creating' a tripartite division in which the third category is redundant, for being unable to see that the logical theory of probability is the same as an objective epistemic theory, and for allowing myself 'a false sense of distinction' between Keynes's and Ramsey's theories (*ibid.*: 49, and note 19, 51, note 21).

These criticisms are misguided. At the time I wrote my book (which refers to Hacking's volume), I was well aware of Hacking's distinction and where Keynes's theory would fit into his classification. However, I chose not to use it because the tripartite division used by several other philosophers seemed to me to offer more advantages in relation to Keynes. One of the advantages was that it made it very difficult to conflate Keynes's theory with Ramsey's theory, a mistake which Bateman recognizes as one that other people have made (*ibid.*: 50–1).

Bateman treats Hacking's bipartite (aleatory/epistemic) classification as if it were obviously the correct system. In fact, however, the system one uses for classifying probabilities ultimately has a large arbitrary element. Hacking cuts the cake in one way, but a different bipartite division could be made using an objective/subjective criterion which would group Keynes's logical theory and the frequency theory together, leaving the subjective theory on the other side. Or, following Gillies and Ietto-Gillies (1991: 393–4), we could change the meaning of objective and divide the terrain using an objective/epistemological split which, despite the non-standard terminology, results in groupings similar to Hacking's. The ultimate arbitrariness is also evident in the fact that Hacking's epistemic probabilities then have to be subdivided into objective ones (Keynes's theory) and subjective ones. So Bateman himself finishes up using a tripartite division, the only difference between his and mine being the route used to get there. And if we both end up with three distinct theories, why is one of them redundant in my account but not in his?

Intersubjective probabilities

Bateman's view is that, by 1931, Keynes had switched from logical probabilities to subjective probabilities and that, by 1933, he had also embraced intersubjective probabilities. The theory of intersubjective probabilities is borrowed from Gillies and Ietto-Gillies (1991). Leaving aside my deep disagreement with this interpretation, let me comment on the way Bateman handles intersubjective probabilities in relation to *The General Theory*.

There is a noteworthy difference between the arguments of Gillies and Ietto-Gillies, and those of Bateman. While Gillies and Ietto-Gillies propose a link between intersubjective probability and *The General Theory*, their view of this link is cautiously and circumspectly expressed. In relation to long-term expectations, their contention is that 'Keynes is implicitly making use of a concept of probability more or less equivalent to the notion of intersubjective probability'; that Keynes's theory 'implicitly involves the notion of intersubjective probability'; and that, in analysing these expectations, 'Keynes was moving towards a concept close to our intersubjective probability'.[9] Thus the most that is claimed is that intersubjective probabilities are something *implicit* in *The General Theory*; there is no claim that Keynes consciously developed them. Bateman, however, sweeps this tentativeness aside and replaces it with confident assertion. Intersubjective probabilities are definitely present in *The General Theory* because Keynes actually created and introduced them:

> When probabilities are formed according to group norms, they are referred to as intersubjective probabilities. After Keynes abandoned

his work in *Probability*, he embraced this idea of *intersubjectivity* and made it central to *The General Theory*.

(*ibid.*: 50, note 20)

Suddenly, two years after he had publicly abandoned his objective theory of probability and accepted Ramsey's criticisms, he had a place to use his own newly minted intersubjective probabilities.

(*ibid.*: 78)

But there is more to Keynes's achievement than this ... [He] was, at the same time, the first to introduce an analytical treatment of inter-subjective probability.

(*ibid.*: 131)

What Gillies and Ietto-Gillies see as implicit, Bateman sees as explicit. We move from something implicit in Keynes's thought, something towards which it was moving, something of which he may or may not have been conscious, to something of which he is definitely aware, some-thing which he had just recently created, and something to which he had given analytical treatment. Is there any independent evidence for Bateman's interpretation? One would think that if Keynes had newly minted a theory of probability (even as an extension of Ramsey's) and was the first to give it analytical treatment, there would be some remark somewhere relating to this, for Keynes was not backward in writing about his intellectual advances and innovations. But, in fact, there is total silence. All things considered, it looks as if we are again faced with either argument by assertion or argument by insight into Keynes's mind.

Confidence and expectations

Notwithstanding the interest of the historical debates over business confidence, Bateman's analytical treatment of the concept of confidence is loose and incomplete. Instead of regarding confidence and expecta-tions as separate concepts, he treats them as synonymous. He describes Chapter 12 of *The General Theory* as presenting 'Keynes's theory of the state of long-term expectation, or confidence, and its effect on invest-ment' (*ibid.*: 127), and observes that 'there was no necessity for Keynes to turn to confidence, or expectations about the future, as the final element' in pulling *The General Theory* together (*ibid.*: 78). This conflation, however, is at odds with *The General Theory*. In Chapter 12, Keynes says that the state of long-term expectations depends on *two* separate factors – fore-casts (or expectations) and confidence:

> The state of long-term expectation, upon which our decisions are based, does not solely depend, therefore, on the most probable

forecast we can make. It also depends on the *confidence* with which we make this forecast – on how highly we rate the likelihood of our best forecast turning out quite wrong.

(CWVII: 148)

This section of *The General Theory* is also notable for being one of two places where Keynes refers directly to *A Treatise on Probability* via its chapter on the weight of argument. In *A Treatise on Probability*, the concept of weight can be viewed as underpinning the amount of confidence that rational agents have in probabilities.[10] In my account, the remarks in *The General Theory* provide evidence of a link between *A Treatise on Probability* and *The General Theory* such that the probability-weight pair of the former has some connection with the expectation-confidence pair of the latter. Keynes's second footnote reference to *A Treatise on Probability* provides further relevant evidence in the context of liquidity preference. The difference between liquidity premium and risk premium is described as corresponding to 'the difference between the best estimates we can make of probabilities and the confidence with which we make them' (CWVII: 240). The distinction, and its relation to *A Treatise on Probability*, is even more explicit in Keynes's subsequent letter to Townshend in 1938:

I am rather inclined to associate risk premium with probability strictly speaking, and liquidity premium with what in my *Treatise on Probability* I called 'weight'. ... A liquidity premium ... is payment ... for an increased sense of comfort and confidence during the period.

(CWXXIX: 293–4)

Bateman is aware that Keynes's ideas on liquidity preference have a 'strong dependence on confidence' (*ibid.*: 124), but he remains silent about pursuing Keynes's own leads on the further analysis of confidence.

Bateman does not ignore the footnote reference to *A Treatise on Probability* in *The General Theory*, but gives it a novel twist which draws on his distinctive approach to interpretation. He maintains that probability and weight in *A Treatise on Probability* are Platonic entities, that when Keynes rejected Platonism he rejected the original meanings of these words, and that when he subsequently continued to use these words it was with new subjective meanings (*ibid.*: 59, note 38). It is notable that no grounds are given for this view that are independent of Bateman's interpretation. First, it rests on the contested proposition that Keynes rejected Platonism. Secondly, it rests on the claim that the reference to *A Treatise on Probability* was not to the original meaning of a phrase but to a new meaning that Keynes does not reveal. Most authors, including Bateman and Keynes elsewhere, when they refer back to their earlier work without qualification, refer back to its original meaning. But not Keynes on this occasion. Thirdly, nowhere in his writings does Keynes tell us, or even hint, that he is now using a previously distinctive concept with a new meaning. How, then, do we know that Keynes has injected a different meaning into an old phrase and now has a subjective theory of weight? Only on Bateman's say-so. Again, we appear to have argument by superior insight into Keynes's mind.

Conventions

Many recent scholars have recognized conventions as important in the discussion of economic behaviour under uncertainty in *The General Theory*. In Bateman's account, however, they are elevated to supreme importance. They are treated as the foundation of expectations formation: 'Keynes makes it perfectly clear that agents form their expectations by means of a *social convention*' (*ibid.*: 130). They are viewed as the foundation of the theory of intersubjective probabilities that Bateman believes Keynes developed out of Ramsey's theory: 'Keynes intended to represent his agents' beliefs via an extension of Ramsey's subjective probabilities as being determined intersubjectively by social conventions' (*ibid.*: 131). And they are central to one of the key themes of Bateman's book, the 'unexpected story of the importance of rules and conventions to Keynes's thought' (*ibid.*: 9), and the 'fine irony' associated with this that someone who started out rejecting general rules of conduct finished up championing rules and social conventions as necessary for the maintenance of civilization (*ibid.*: 162).

Several features of Bateman's treatment of conventions invite comment. First, in relation to *The General Theory*, their scope is not defined. Do they apply to all expectations, both short-term and long-term, and to all agents in all markets? Sometimes it is suggested that they are the unique foundation of expectations formation (*ibid.*: 130), while at other times it is suggested that Keynes's agents calculate expected values using probabilities (*ibid.*: 131–2). Whether the latter is separate from, or reducible to, conventions is left unexplained.

Secondly, Bateman's use of the term is astonishingly elastic. He offers no definition of the concept, which leaves him free to treat it like putty.[11] In the final two chapters of his book, its meaning undergoes extension and metamorphosis. Initially, the term is used uncontroversially to cover the techniques that Keynes outlined in 1936 and 1937 (*ibid.*: 130–1).[12] A few pages later, however, we encounter an extension in which social conventions become general rules or habits *of the human mind*. After quoting a passage from Ramsey's discussion of 'human logic' in which Ramsey says that the 'human mind works essentially according to general rules or habits', Bateman asks: 'What indeed are social conventions if not "general rules or habits"?' (*ibid.*: 139). To which the obvious response is: 'But are they general rules and habits of the way the human mind works?'. The next chapter then produces a breathtaking metamorphosis. Social conventions become synonymous with economic policy:

> [Keynes] came to see that maintaining the proper conventions was crucial to investment, too. Just as a well-established convention of low interest rates might be self-fulfilling, so, too, might be a well-established convention of stable, high levels of investment.
>
> (*ibid.*: 152)

> Thus the judicious use of public capital expenditure could be made a new convention that would yield more stability in the level of aggregate investment.
>
> (*ibid.*: 159)

And 'the three most prominent ways in which Keynes meant to socialise investment by creating new conventions' were through 'socialising public investment', 'public works and a balanced budget', and 'stabilising private investment' (*ibid.*: 152–9).

In all cases, 'convention' can be replaced with 'policy'. Where standard usage would talk of policies, Bateman substitutes conventions. The explanation for this Humpty Dumpty-like disdain for ordinary meanings is bound up, I think, with his story about the great irony of Keynes's life – the evolution, concerning rules and conventions, from repudiation to acceptance. Since Bateman sees the later Keynes as insisting that conventions and rules are essential to the maintenance of liberal civilization, then other things that Keynes also advocated to help create a better world, such as certain economic policies, are swept into the same conceptual basket. Conventions and rules then take pride of place as the central organizing concept of the thought of the later Keynes. The old cliché is apparently once again vindicated – those who start out being radicals finish up being conservatives in their final years.[13]

Conclusion

The valuable contribution of Bateman's book is to have advanced a history of the concept of confidence in Keynes's economic thought of the 1920s and 1930s. As he rightly suggests, previous works on Keynes had not addressed this question in sufficient historical detail. No doubt, further debate and discussion will test the robustness of his story.

Unfortunately, Bateman has wrapped up his valuable contribution in other analytical arguments, many of which are dubious, controversial and unsupported by the relevant evidence. The inclusion of these other arguments reveals that his agenda is not merely to write a 'thick' history of the development of some of Keynes's ideas, but also to advance a particular interpretation of the relationship between *A Treatise on Probability* and *The General Theory*. In my view, his book would have been far less controversial if he had not sought to tie its historical and analytical themes so tightly together, but had realized that its historical account of confidence is compatible with the main outlines of alternative interpretations of the analytical links between Keynes's two path-breaking works.

Notes

1 I am grateful to Wylie Bradford for comments on an earlier draft of this chapter.
2 Carabelli comes second as a target. Most of Bateman's criticisms are not discernible from the sparse index to his book. This only contains two references to me and one to Carabelli, whereas a more accurate index would record nineteen to me and ten to Carabelli.
3 The quotations he gives from 'My early beliefs' (CWXb: 433–50) are irrelevant in my view because they do not provide support for his proposition.
4 See O'Donnell (1989: 64–6), where an appendix is specifically devoted to explaining Ramsey's mistake, which Braithwaite repeats in his Foreword to the *Collected Writings* edition of *A Treatise on Probability* (CWVIII: xxi). Bateman (1991: 109, note 2) comments on this passage in my book, but his comments completely misunderstand my argument for they just restate Ramsey's points in different words.
5 He first raised the alleged problem in Bateman (1991).
6 For Keynes's recognition of the consistency requirement in his response to Ramsey, see Keynes (CWXa: 339).
7 See, for example, O'Donnell (1989: 59, 78, 121, 147, 254) and O'Donnell (1991a: 14–19, 40–5).
8 Misunderstanding of my position is also evident in relation to the proposition that Keynes undertook the study of probability in order to overthrow Moore's argument for rules. Bateman claims that I say this proposition is 'quite false' (Bateman 1991: 109, note 1). In fact, this is the *exact opposite* of what I say at several points in my book, including my account of 'My early beliefs'. See O'Donnell (1989: 12, 106–7, 109–12, 117–19, 135, 149–51).
9 The quotations are from Gillies and Ietto-Gillies (1991: 404, 407, 408; see also 395).
10 See O'Donnell (1989: 73).
11 In my account of Keynes, conventions, and the strategies of weak rationality more generally, are defined as 'practical measures for resolving theoretically undeterminate decision problems' (O'Donnell 1991a: 17).
12 See CWVII: 152 and CWXIVa: 114.
13 In this area, too, another strong contrast emerges between his account and mine; see, for example, Chapters 6, 13 and 14 of O'Donnell (1989).

8 The relationship between Keynes's early and later philosophical thinking

John B. Davis

Introduction

The relationship between Keynes's early and later thinking in general is a large subject that covers the domains of economics, philosophy, probability, politics and ethics. In this chapter I restrict myself to philosophy, comparing Keynes's early and later philosophical thinking. Admittedly, it is not entirely possible to discuss Keynes's thinking in only one domain at a time. But because philosophy involves foundational conceptual structures, it can be discussed in relative separation from these other domains. This chapter thus advances one view of Keynes's philosophical development, and then briefly considers some of the implications of this view for his later economics.

My main conclusion is that certain philosophical views that Keynes began to develop in his early unpublished Apostles papers (see Skidelsky 1983) – views which appeared in more mature form in his *A Treatise on Probability* (CWVIII) – were largely abandoned by the time he began work on *The General Theory* (CWVII). Specifically, I shall maintain that he gave up both the idea that there exists an ontological realm of Platonic entities populated by qualities (such as goodness) and relations (such as relations of probability), and the associated idea that this realm is accessible to us through pure intuition of a rational and unmediated kind. I also argue that Keynes's later philosophical thinking made the concept of convention its central organizing concept. This later philosophical thinking involved an understanding of behaviour as interdependent and dispositional, and focused philosophical investigation on the historical social world. I do not claim, finally, that Keynes gave up all his early philosophical commitments, and consequently allow that he retained his early *A Treatise on Probability* characterization of the form of probability judgments as essentially qualitative and comparative in nature (see Runde 1994b). This characterization carries over into his later view of uncertainty, but it operates in the changed philosophical framework created by his understanding of behaviour as interdependent and dispositional.

I proceed as follows. The first section describes factors that give us good reason to believe that Keynes changed his mind about his early philosophical commitments. The second section describes Keynes's early philosophical views, emphasizing the influence of G. E. Moore. In the third section I summarize important problems in the early philosophy of Keynes and Moore, and show how Frank Ramsey's criticism of Keynes bears on these problems. In the fourth section I discuss the change in Keynes's philosophical thinking through his own eyes, as recorded in his essay 'My early beliefs'. In the fifth section I explain what changed in Keynes's philosophical thinking, and then turn to how these changes were manifested in *The General Theory*, especially in connection with his important concepts of radical uncertainty and convention. I conclude by pointing to a possible connection between Keynes and the later Wittgenstein for future research.

Factors influencing the development of Keynes's philosophical thinking

An important feature of Keynes's intellectual development is that he did most of his work in philosophy and economics at different stages of his career. Though Keynes began economics early, his early thinking was nonetheless more focused on philosophy, especially the moral philosophy of G. E. Moore. After the publication of *A Treatise on Probability*, however, his attention shifted from philosophy to economics. Of course, this is not to say that Keynes ceased to hold philosophical views, but rather that what views he had were not explicitly articulated. Thus to the extent that we can speak about Keynes's later philosophical thinking, it must be in terms of what may be argued to underlie his later economics.

Let me note the problems this creates for explaining Keynes's philosophy over his entire career. First, obviously, inferring Keynes's later philosophical views from his economics is more difficult than simply reading his explicitly philosophical early writings. Secondly, these later philosophical views also need to be translated out of a particular intellectual framework, since economics as a body of ideas has its own specific form of conceptual and theoretical organization. The overall problem in trying to explain Keynes's philosophy over his entire career consequently lies in linking his early philosophical views in their more traditional mode of presentation to his later philosophical views that are removed from direct view and are also formulated within the distinct intellectual structure of economics.

An additional important fact about Keynes's intellectual development is that he dramatically changed his mind about economics. While scholars dispute the nature of this change, it is clear from the Preface to *The General Theory* that Keynes believed his economic ideas had changed substantially from what they had been before. Thus when considering Keynes's philosophical thinking over his entire career, in addition to the problems noted above, we must also consider the problem created by the shift in his thinking in economics. Not only, therefore, must Keynes's later philosophical thinking be inferred from the different intellectual framework of his economics, but it must be inferred from an intellectual structure of economic thinking that underwent important changes.

To summarize, two forces operated on Keynes's philosophical development across his career: his shift to economics and his shift within economics. Both suggest that Keynes's early philosophical views would not carry over into his later thinking without change. That Keynes himself thought his philosophical thinking changed is indicated by (1) his response to Ramsey's (1978) critique of Keynes on intuition of probability relations – Keynes said 'I think he is right' (CWXa: 338–9) – and (2) his 1938 statement about his early philosophical views in 'My early beliefs' where he said one did not know things by relying on 'direct unanalysable intuition about which it was useless and impossible to argue' (CWXb: 437). It is true that the meaning of these passages has often been debated (Bateman 1987; Carabelli 1988; Cottrell 1993; Davis 1994b; Gillies and Ieto-Gillies 1991; O'Donnell 1989; Runde 1994b). However, the issue appears to be not whether Keynes changed his views, but in what ways he changed his views. To see how this might be understood, we turn first to Keynes's early philosophical views.

Keynes's early philosophical thinking

The primary influence on Keynes's early philosophical thinking was the philosopher G. E. Moore (Skidelsky 1983). Moore and Bertrand Russell were in the forefront of a reaction against British neo-Hegelian idealism as developed by F. H. Bradley, Bernard Bosanquet, T. H. Green and J. E. M. McTaggart at the end of the nineteenth century (Urmson 1956). For these philosophers the mind-dependent character of the world implied that all things and objects were internally related, so that the truth of any given proposition or statement depended upon the truth of all other propositions. Knowledge for the idealists was an interconnected organic whole, and individual truths always possessed a provisional character. Moore and Russell, in contrast, believed individual propositions or statements stood on their own, and could be known to be true in virtue of their correspondence to reality. Moore's early paper, 'Refutation of idealism' (1903b), laid the basis for a new realist philosophy.

Moore's philosophy had its direct impact on Keynes through Moore's *Principia Ethica* (1903a; Davis 1994b: 10ff.). There, Moore added to his realist view a theory of definitions. Definitions do not reflect the ways words are used in ordinary communication, but 'describe the real nature of the object or notion denoted by a word' (Moore 1903a: 7).

Furthermore, definitions 'are only possible when the object or notion in question is something complex' (*ibid.*). Then, in giving a definition of something, one breaks down that complex into a set of simple properties and qualities that can be reduced to nothing more simple. These ultimate simple properties and qualities compose the definition of the term in question. These ultimate simples are also indefinable. Some terms of our language, however, are already in simple form: examples are 'yellow' and 'good.' Thus 'good' cannot be defined as, say, the utilitarians define it ('productive of pleasure'), and indeed any attempt to define good in terms of something else committed what Moore termed the naturalistic fallacy. When we use the term 'good' we simply refer to a simple quality of the world called goodness. Moreover, as an indefinable, simple quality, goodness can occupy neither time nor space, and is consequently a non-natural type of thing that belongs to what some philosophers term the Platonic realm.

How, then, did one recognize goodness or know something was good when intending to refer to something as 'good'? Essentially Moore believed one exercised one's intuition, an intellectual capacity for seeing into the ultimate nature of things. 'In fact, it follows from the meaning of good and bad, that such propositions ["this or that is good"] ... all must rest in the end upon some proposition which must be simply accepted or rejected, which cannot be logically deduced from any other proposition' (*ibid.*: 143). That is, one simply accepts that at some point saying something is 'good' is sufficient, because there is nothing further we can say about the simple quality of goodness. Moore's theory of definition in terms of simple qualities and properties thus had as its necessary accompaniment a theory of intuition as a form of rational insight into the ultimate constituents of the world.

Keynes adopted Moore's thinking in his own early writings. Historically, probability theorists had debated over the meaning of the concept of probability. In his 1908 fellowship dissertation and then in *A Treatise on Probability*, Keynes regarded the concept of probability as indefinable. Using Moore's reasoning, Keynes argued that '[w]e cannot analyse the probability-relation in terms of simpler ideas' (CWVIII: 8). Thus, just as 'good' denoted a unique, indefinable quality, so 'probable' denoted a unique, indefinable relation. Similarly, Keynes adopted an account of intuition that built on the key features of Moore's view. Within the realm of knowledge, he argued, we must distinguish between direct and indirect knowledge. Direct knowledge depends upon direct acquaintance with three types of things: our sensations, the ideas or meanings we understand, and relations between sense-data or meanings we perceive (*ibid.*: 12). Probability relations as a type of relation are thus something we perceive and are directly acquainted with; probability statements expressing probability relations are something we have direct knowledge of (*ibid.*: 13).

Interestingly, Moore had not thought the probability relation indefinable, and had defined probability in terms of what he regarded as the simpler notion of frequency. This had implications for his view of right conduct, since he explained right conduct as what would be likely to produce the greatest amount of goodness, and used the frequency view of probability to explain likelihood. Keynes, however, in his early Apostles paper, 'Ethics in relation to conduct' (1904), argued that when we say something is probably right in terms of its ability to produce more good, we are making a rational judgment, not predicting that in the long run one thing will occur more often than another. He retained this view in *A Treatise on Probability*. Thus, in his early philosophy up to and including the *Treatise*, Keynes sought to extend Moore's basic philosophy by emphasizing probability reasoning as part of the domain of rational belief. As he put it, that part of our knowledge which concerned what is only probable was the subject of rational belief, the highest degree of which he termed '*certain* rational belief [that] corresponds to *knowledge*' (CWVIII: 3).

Problems with the early philosophy of Moore and Keynes

Moore's theory of definition presupposes a theory of the meaning of language that is now known as the referential theory of meaning (see Schwartz 1977). The principal idea of this theory is that the meaning of a term is that to which it refers. The theory has an apparent plausibility when used in connection with proper names. Thus the meaning of the expression 'G. E. Moore' could be that real individual who was a philosopher in Cambridge in the first half of the twentieth century. But most philosophers now no longer think the referential theory adequate as a general theory of language-meaning. In the first place, too many terms and expressions in our language do not appear to name anything. Secondly, since the later work of Ludwig Wittgenstein, most Anglo-American philosophers have sought to understand meaning in terms of use. As Wittgenstein (1953: Pt. I, s. 421) put it: 'Look at the sentence as an instrument, and at its sense of employment'. He also argued in criticizing his own early philosophy, which had shared doctrines with Moore and Russell, that when we concentrate on how people use language, we are not tempted to search for meanings as some peculiar set of entities existing in a metaphysical realm beyond ordinary experience.

Moore and Keynes had indeed understood language-meaning in referential terms when they agreed that the meaning of the term 'good' was a simple quality called goodness. Wittgenstein's criticism was that there was no need to posit some transcendent Platonic entity, goodness, occupying neither time nor space, to understand the meaning of the term 'good'. One simply looked at how the term good operated in our ordinary discourse, and established its meaning in that way. The same criticism applied to Keynes's idea that 'probability' named some transcendent Platonic entity, namely the relation of something being probable. One could understand the term 'probability' by seeing how it was used. But Wittgenstein's argument was stronger than simply saying that language-meaning could be understood in terms of use, and that this made reference to a realm of Platonic entities such as qualities and relations unnecessary. The real force of Wittgenstein's critique was in the charge that the whole idea that one might speak coherently about a realm of Platonic entities was unsupportable. In his view, there simply was no basis for saying that such things as qualities and relations populated some non-natural realm removed from human experience. Indeed, the only reason philosophers had thought such a thing was that they had been saddled with a mistaken view of the nature of language that had led their thinking down a dead end.

Wittgenstein is most famous for the shift in thinking about the nature of language and meaning, but other philosophers also saw that the type of view Moore and Keynes had adopted was implausible. C. D. Broad (1934) attacked Moore's view of 'good' by saying that there was no evidence that the term actually stood for anything at all. Later, emotivist philosophers argued that since there was no evidence that 'good' actually stood for anything, we might just as well believe that people employed the term 'good' to express nothing more than a sense of approval. This highly subjective view made nonsense of ethics, and was as far from the thinking of Moore and Keynes as was possible. But the irony was that there was nothing in Moore's theory of definition that prevented such doctrines from emerging.

Frank Ramsey, who was also an emotivist in ethics, made a similar criticism of Keynes's understanding of the meaning of 'probability'. The heart of Moore's theory of definition when applied to the meaning of 'probability' was that one had to use intuition as a form of rational insight to grasp logical relations between propositions. Ramsey asserted, 'I do not perceive them, and ... I ... suspect that others do not perceive them either' (1978: 63). Ramsey thus cast doubt on there being a Platonic realm of logical relations by exposing intuition as arbitrary and unfounded. People simply did not have perceptions (as he termed intuition) of logical relations. Keynes's understanding of the meaning of probability was consequently shown to be baseless. It was to this criticism that he later responded in his obituary of Ramsey, saying, 'I think he is right' (CWXa: 338–9). Note, however, that Keynes's admission did not concern his understanding of the *form* of probability judgments as essentially non-quantitative and comparative in nature. All that Keynes abandoned in response to Ramsey was his early Moorean view of the meaning of 'probable' as a Platonic logical relation knowable through intuition.

Keynes's self-criticism in 'My early beliefs'

Keynes's admission to Ramsey raises the question of how Keynes's philosophical thinking might have changed. Important evidence in this regard may be found in Keynes's memoir, 'My early beliefs' (CWXb). Though some commentators on Keynes's philosophy believe that this essay should not be taken seriously (see, for example, O'Donnell (1989)), this does not seem to be the right conclusion to draw, since it was one of only two pieces unpublished in Keynes's lifetime that he requested be published after his death (the other was a recollection of a German friend from the time of the Versailles negotiations). There are other reasons to take 'My early beliefs' seriously. One was that when Keynes read the memoir, he was primarily addressing younger friends and children of friends to whom he wanted to pass an understanding of how he and his friends had come to see the world. The other reason is that 'My early beliefs' was read after the publication of *The General Theory*. Thus not only was Keynes's mature economic thinking set by then, but he had good reason to want to set the record straight about early philosophical views for which he was known.

In the memoir, Keynes discussed his early years at Cambridge in terms of the views and values he and his friends had held. He was generally quite critical of himself and his friends, saying that they had been young and naïve about the world. But the main object of his criticism was their adherence to Moore's doctrine of intuition. Not blaming Moore, Keynes said that he and his friends had overemphasized their intuitive abilities: 'We claimed the right to judge every individual case on its merits, and the wisdom, experience and self-control to do so successfully' (CWXb: 446). This exaggerated confidence in their own judgment led them to put aside Moore's views about the importance of social rules of good conduct, and it was not until much later in Keynes's life that he and his friends came to appreciate that 'civilisation was a thin precarious crust erected by the personality and the will of a very few, and only maintained by rules and conventions skillfully put across and guilefully preserved' (*ibid.*: 447).

What Keynes tells us in 'My early beliefs' is that individual judgment generally needs to operate within a framework of social rules. This conclusion is a dramatic departure from Keynes's early Apostles paper, 'Ethics in relation to conduct' (1904). There Keynes had criticized Moore for not explaining rules of right conduct in terms of intuition (Moore had relied on the frequency theory of probability for this part of his ethics). Now we find Keynes saying that intuition in the form of individual judgment is often unreliable, and individuals should be more observant of society's rules and conventions which are the product of a delicate historical process. Indeed, Keynes says he and his friends were mistaken in setting 'on one side ... Moore's fifth chapter on "Ethics in Relation to Conduct" ... but also the part which discussed the duty of the individual to obey general rules' (CWXb: 446). But while Keynes absolved Moore of the extremes to which Keynes and his friends had taken the doctrines of *Principia Ethica*, he did not say that Moore was right in emphasizing intuition as the basis for individual judgment. Keynes treated the idea of intuition as a form of rational insight sarcastically in 'My early beliefs', and clearly believed that individuals possessed other resources when exercising judgment. The problem with intuition, I argue for Keynes, is that it lacks an account of how we err. On the view of intuition that Moore developed one saw into the essential nature of reality when one grasped such things as goodness. But if two individuals disagree about what is good, and each claims to have direct insight into the underlying nature of reality, how do we sort out their disagreement? When the only understanding one has of judgment is of unmediated insight, this question is irresolvable. Thus, an adequate theory of judgment requires our being able to distinguish when one is in error from when one is correct. For example, an adequate theory of judgment might make reference to rules by which we agree that some claims are correct and some are not. Though he did not refer to the need for an account of how we may err in 'My early beliefs', Keynes put his finger on the matter directly when he recounted how debates among his friends during his youth were less often won by those who could offer good grounds for their views than by those 'who could speak with the greatest appearance of clear, undoubting conviction and could best use the accents of infallibility' (CWXb: 438).

Changes in Keynes's philosophical thinking

We can see that the emphasis of Keynes's self-criticism was on the nature of judgment. How, then, did he reinterpret individual judgment in his later philosophical thinking? A clue lies in his characterization of economics as a moral science. In writing to Roy Harrod on the latter's Presidential Address to Section F of the British Association, 'Scope and method of economics', Keynes said that economics deals with individuals' 'motives, expectations, psychological uncertainties' (CWXIVb: 300). Economic behaviour is complex and often unpredictable, and one accordingly 'has to be constantly on guard against treating the material as constant and homogeneous' (*ibid.*). This would seem to make economics an especially difficult subject, but Keynes also said that economics deals with 'introspection and values' (*ibid.*), and this suggests a means by which economists might investigate the complexity of economic behaviour that has implications for his view of judgment. I maintain that when Keynes refers to 'introspection and values' he means to say that we each, whether as economists or ordinary individuals, make assessments of other individuals' motives and behaviour by considering how we ourselves would act in similar situations. That is, we look into ourselves and rely on our own values in an attempt to make sense of why other individuals behave as they do.

Basically, if human behaviour is complex and variable in nature, then one of the best resources we have for understanding it is the understanding we have of our own behaviour. If this is true, economists would not be the only ones to rely on introspection and values in evaluating the actions of others. Ordinary individuals would equally rely on the method of comparing their own cases to those of others when trying to sort out why people act as they do. Of course, not all economic behaviour is highly unpredictable, and much of the time we may simply look to past experience in explaining how others will act. But when we consider such things as investment behaviour and the role of animal spirits in the business community, we are likely to find deeper reflection on the causes of economic behaviour a necessity.

What does this tell us about Keynes's conception of individual judgment? If people in the economy all engage in a process of consulting their own motives and values to judge those of others, then judgment is a highly interdependent affair. If individual A acts with an opinion of the intentions of individual B, while B also acts with an opinion of the intentions of A, then in a very real sense their respective individual judgments are interdependent. Keynes gave a vivid illustration of this type of interdependency in Chapter 12 of *The General Theory* when he described investment behaviour as being like a particular kind of newspaper beauty contest (CWVII: 156). The contest is one where the winner must guess who readers will find the most beautiful from a selection of photographs. That is, the winner of the contest is the one who can best judge what other people's opinions will be. Investment, Keynes tells us, is a process by which investors focus less on what the best investment is and more on what other investors will think the best investment is.

When we understand individual judgment as interdependent in this manner, nothing remains of Keynes's old concept of individual judgment as intuition. On that old view, each individual autonomously sees into the underlying nature of reality. On Keynes's new view, 'intuition' (if we were to continue using the old name for judgment) is neither autonomous nor concerned strictly with the underlying nature of reality (in economics, what today might be called 'the fundamentals'). Put more simply, intuition or judgment in Keynes's later philosophy is social. Moreover, it is social in a specific sense. Keynes is not saying 'society has a general influence on the thinking of individuals' (though he may well have thought this also to be true). Rather, Keynes treats judgment as social in virtue of a concrete interdependence of particular individuals' judgments, as when he refers to a particular collection of individuals making investments in a particular national economy at a particular point in time who influence one another in their thinking and decision-making.

This very concrete view of the judgments of a collection of individuals as interdependent stems from Keynes's awareness of the complexity and variability of human motivation. Because of the complexity and variability of human motivation, no two historical episodes are quite alike. Thus if we wish to understand economic behaviour, we must examine the intentions of individuals in particular historical circumstances. Again, the contrast with Keynes's youthful view of intuition could not be stronger. But perhaps more important for *The General Theory* is how this later view of judgment links up with Keynes's famous concept of radical uncertainty. Keynes's thinking, and Post Keynesian thinking (for example, Davidson 1994), are distinguishable from neoclassical synthesis Keynesianism, and also from New Keynesianism (see Rotheim 1998), in terms of Keynes's concept of radical uncertainty. Basically, the difference is that saying we are fundamentally uncertain about the future means that we do not know the probability distributions of events that are of interest to us. How, then, is this concept of uncertainty tied to Keynes's later view of judgment?

Most obviously, if economic behaviour is complex and variable, it will not be predictable, and we shall consequently not be able to know the probability distributions of future events. But Keynes's view of the judgment of individuals as interdependent adds something to this. If judgment is interdependent, then the judgments made by a collection of individuals may be generally indeterminate. We might put this sharply by saying that 'in Keynes's later philosophy ... uncertainty is ultimately a social relation' (Davis 1994b: 108). That is, what makes the future inaccessible to us from an economic point of view is the fact that our respective judgments about the future are contingent upon one another in a manner that reflects the social relationships between us. In regard to investment where uncertainty is significant, these social relationships reflect the historical organization of investment, where when Keynes was writing *The General Theory* this involved the separation of ownership and management and the rise of speculative behaviour on stock markets.

Another important concept in *The General Theory* that bears the imprint of Keynes's later view of judgment is the concept of convention. We saw above that Keynes contrasted rules and conventions with intuition in 'My early beliefs', and believed that rules and conventions were important to society. Yet conventions play a central role in Keynes's analysis of investment as well. In the face of the 'daily, even hourly, revaluations of existing investments carried out' on stock markets, 'we have tacitly agreed, as a rule, to fall back on what is, in truth, a *convention*. The essence of this convention ... lies in assuming that the existing state of affairs will continue indefinitely, except in so far as we have specific reasons to expect a change' (CWVII: 151–2). Individual judgment in this crucial domain of the economy thus also relies on rules and conventions. Keynes explains how this is so in terms of his analysis of average expectation.

Continuing with his treatment of judgment as interdependent, Keynes says that what constitutes a good or bad investment is 'governed by the average expectation of those who deal on the Stock Exchange as revealed by the price of shares, rather than by the genuine expectations of the professional entrepreneur' (*ibid.*: 151). That is, it is not the individual who autonomously judges the value of an investment in terms of its underlying fundamentals who sets the value of a stock in the market, but the individual who feels the pulse of the market, 'foreseeing changes in the conventional basis of valuation a short time ahead of the general public' (*ibid.*: 154), who sets the tone for the market, and guesses 'what average opinion expects average opinion to be' (*ibid.*: 156). Investments, then, have their values set conventionally in terms of the movement of average expectation. Investors 'fall back' on the assumption that 'the existing state of affairs', as average opinion records it, will 'continue indefinitely' or until 'we have specific reasons to expect a change', that is, until average opinion shifts.

More could be said about how Keynes's later philosophical thinking about judgment operates in *The General Theory*. However, not having the space to go into these matters in greater depth, I refer the reader to what I have written on the matter previously (Davis 1994b: esp. 120ff.). What can be said is that Keynes adopted a far more naturalistic account of knowledge and judgment in his later work, and this philosophical conception differs entirely from the neo-Platonism he originally adhered to under the influence of Moore. In general, Keynes replaced a conception of judgment as highly individual with one that was interdependent and social. This led him to see economic behaviour as dispositional, and permitted him to characterize it in the language of propensities.

Concluding remarks

It is tempting to look for philosophical reasoning in Keynes's later thinking that resembles the more academic philosophical reasoning found in his earlier thinking, and be disappointed in finding something quite different. Whereas Keynes's earlier philosophical thinking is set out explicitly as a philosophical commentary and development of G. E. Moore's philosophy, Keynes's later philosophical views do not appear as an extension or development of any philosophical literature. There is evidence, however, that Keynes was influenced by the later philosophical thinking of Ludwig Wittgenstein (see Davis 1996). Were this true, it might help us understand why Keynes appears to have retained his early *Treatise* commitment to seeing probability judgments as generally non-quantitative and comparative in nature. Wittgenstein emphasized that we need to attend to the way people use language. Keynes saw that people often express probability judgments in non-quantitative and comparative terms. Thus, while he gave up his early view of the meaning of probability, he saw no need to give up his early attention to the language of probability. But this must be left as a question for further research.

9 Probability and uncertainty in Keynes's *The General Theory*

Donald Gillies

The Post Keynesians and the problem

In the last two decades, a great deal of attention has been devoted to the question of probability and uncertainty in Keynes's *The General Theory* (CWVII) by a group often referred to as the 'Post Keynesians'. As I shall be making a good deal of use of the research of this group in the present chapter, I shall begin by saying a little in general terms about the group and its ideas.

After the Second World War, Keynesian economics became dominant in the British academic community, and British governments to a large extent followed the advice of Keynesian economists. Keynesian economics had a similarly important (even if not always quite so dominant) role in other advanced capitalist countries in the same period. During the 1970s, however, Keynesian economics came under increasing criticism from the monetarist school, and Keynesian economists began to lose both academic and political influence. In Britain, the election of Margaret Thatcher in 1979 signalled the end of the government's use of Keynesian policies, and the adoption instead of free market policies based on monetarist economic theory. Many academic economists went over to the new (or rather revived) free market ideas. However, some remained convinced of the value of Keynesian ideas in economics.

The remaining followers of Keynes were at this point faced with the unhappy situation that the academic and political influence of their ideas was declining, and that these ideas were being increasingly criticised as inadequate. The Post Keynesians reacted to this crisis in a way which has parallels in the behaviour of other intellectual schools at a time of difficulty. They argued that the Keynesian economics which had prevailed in the period 1945–75, and which was now increasingly being rejected, was not in fact the economics which Keynes himself had proposed in *The General Theory*, but rather a simplified and unsatisfactory version of what Keynes had said. They suggested that Keynes's approach could be revived by a return to Keynes's original ideas.

The object of the Post Keynesian attack was the standard textbook account of Keynesian economics based on Hicks's IS–LM diagram.

Skidelsky explains the origin of this kind of Keynesianism with characteristic clarity and historical erudition. He writes:

> The IS–LM diagram, first drawn by John Hicks in 1936, *is The General Theory* as it has been taught to economics students ever since: 384 pages of argument whittled down to four equations and two curves. Hicks, Harrod, Meade and Hansen in America, the leading constructors of 'IS–LM' Keynesianism, had a clear motive: to reconcile Keynesians and non-Keynesians, so that the ground for policy could be quickly cleared. These early theoretical models incorporated features which were not at all evident in the *magnum opus*, but which conformed more closely to orthodox theory. The constructors of these models also thought they were improving the original building.
>
> (Skidelsky 1992: 538)

A little later in a section significantly entitled 'Vision into algebra', Skidelsky writes:

> The mathematisation of the *General Theory* started immediately it was published but it was left to Hicks to map the mathematics on to a two-curve diagram which became the accepted form of the *General Theory*. His famous paper 'Mr. Keynes and the Classics: A Suggested Reinterpretation' was published in *Econometrica* in April 1937. What Hicks does is to turn Keynes's logical chain of reasoning designed to expose the causes which drive the economy towards a low employment trap into a generalised system of simultaneous equations, devoid of causal significance, with the behavioural characteristics of the propensities to be filled in according to assumption. The 'generalised' system has room for Keynes's 'special theory', but also, for example, for the Treasury view, which Keynes wrote the *General Theory* to refute.
>
> (*ibid.*: 611)

IS–LM Keynesianism does not include any reference to probability and uncertainty. But the Post Keynesians argue that probability and uncertainty were central to the real Keynes who wrote *A Treatise on Probability* in 1921, and who in *The General Theory* of 1936 made implicit use of probability in his theory of long-term expectation. The Post Keynesians have accordingly carried out a great deal of valuable historical research on the evolution of Keynes's ideas on probability, and his use of probability in *The General Theory*.

Post Keynesianism began in the 1980s as a reaction to the decline in the academic and political influence of post-Second World War IS–LM Keynesianism. Perhaps the first significant Post Keynesian book was the first volume of Skidelsky's masterly life of Keynes which appeared in 1983. This covers Keynes's life up to 1920, and discusses Keynes's early philosophical work on probability and induction – a topic which had been ignored for many years. Other Post Keynesian books that were to appear in the 1980s include Carabelli (1988), Fitzgibbons (1988) and O'Donnell (1989). In 1985, a collection of papers edited by Lawson and Pesaran appeared. This contains articles by Victoria Chick, Alexander and Sheila Dow, Tony Lawson and John Pheby. Somewhat younger Post Keynesians include Bateman (1987, 1988, 1996), Davis (1994b) and Runde (1994b, 1996). In what follows I shall make use of this Post Keynesian work on the reconstruction of Keynes's ideas.[1]

Let us turn now to Keynes's *The General Theory* of 1936, which I shall examine in conjunction with his 1937 *Quarterly Journal of Economics* (*QJE*) article, 'The general theory of employment', written to summarise and defend the earlier book. In these works Keynes argues that the *amount of investment* is the key factor in determining the performance of the economy as a whole. As we shall see, he regards it as the '*causa causans*' of 'the level of output and employment as a whole' (CWXIVa: 121). Let us start therefore with Keynes's analysis of investment. We shall consider two of the concepts which Keynes introduces in this connection, namely: *prospective yield* and *demand price of the investment*. Keynes defines these as follows:

> When a man buys an investment or capital-asset, he purchases the right to the series of prospective returns, which he expects to obtain from selling its output, after deducting the running expenses of obtaining that output, during the life of the asset. This series of annuities $Q_1, Q_2, \ldots Q_n$ it is convenient to call the *prospective yield* of the investment.
>
> (CWVII: 135)

> If Q_r is the prospective yield from an asset at time r, and d_r is the present value of £1 deferred r years *at the current rate of interest*, $\Sigma Q_r d_r$ is the demand price of the investment; and investment will be carried to the point where $\Sigma Q_r d_r$ becomes equal to the supply price of the investment as defined above. If, on the other hand, $\Sigma Q_r d_r$ falls short of the supply price, there will be no current investment in the asset in question.

(*ibid.*: 137)

So any decision to invest depends crucially on the quantity $\Sigma Q_r d_r$ (the demand price of the investment) which is the sum of the prospective annual yields discounted at the current rate of interest. But now the crucial problem arises, because the prospective yield $Q_1, Q_2, \ldots, Q_n$ of an investment is not known, and consequently $\Sigma Q_r d_r$ cannot be calculated. As Keynes puts it:

> The outstanding fact is the extreme precariousness of the basis of knowledge on which our estimates of prospective yield have to be made. Our knowledge of the factors which will govern the yield of an investment some years hence is usually very slight and often negligible. If we speak frankly, we have to admit that our basis of knowledge for estimating the yield ten years hence of a railway, a copper mine, a textile factory, the goodwill of a patent medicine, an Atlantic liner, a building in the City of London amounts to little and sometimes to nothing; or even five years hence.
>
> (*ibid*: 149–50)

Since the actual future yields are unknown, they must be replaced in calculating $\Sigma Q_r d_r$ to make an investment decision by expected yields. A decision to invest consequently depends on what Keynes calls *the state of long-term expectation* (the title of the famous Chapter 12 of *The General Theory*). Now the notions of expectation and of probability are interdefinable. If we take expectation as the starting point, we can define probabilities in terms of expectations, and vice versa.[2] If, then, Keynes is using the notion of expectation in its standard sense, he is implicitly operating with a concept of probability, and it is natural to ask what the interpretation of the probabilities involved should be. This then brings us to the fundamental question with which this chapter is concerned, namely: 'What is the most appropriate interpretation of probability in Keynes's *The General Theory*?' The Post Keynesians have devoted a great deal of attention to this problem, but, before we can consider their arguments in detail, it will be necessary to give a brief explanation of the various interpretations of probability.[3]

The logical, subjective and intersubjective interpretations of probability

Different versions of the logical interpretation of probability have been developed by different authors, but here, naturally, we will be concerned with Keynes's version as expounded in his 1921 work, *A Treatise on Probability* (CWVIII). In the case of deductive logic a conclusion is entailed by the premises, and is certain given those premises. Thus, if our premises are that all ravens are black, and George is a raven, it follows with certainty that George is black. But now let us consider an inductive, rather than deductive, case. Suppose our premises are the evidence (*e*, say) that several thousand ravens have been observed, and that they were all black. Suppose further that we are considering the hypothesis (*h*, say) that all ravens are black, or the prediction (*d*, say) that the next observed raven will be black. Hume argued, and this is in agreement with modern logic, that neither *h* nor *d* follow logically from *e*. Yet even though *e* does not entail either *h* or *d*, could we not say that *e partially entails h* and *d*, since *e* surely gives some support for these conclusions? This line of thought suggests that there might be a logical theory of partial entailment which generalises the ordinary theory of full entailment which is found in deductive logic. This, then, is the starting point of Keynes's approach to probability. He writes:

> Inasmuch as it is always assumed that we can sometimes judge directly that a conclusion *follows from* a premiss, it is no great extension of this assumption to suppose that we can sometimes recognise that a conclusion *partially follows from*, or stands in a relation of probability to a premiss.
>
> (CWVIII: 56)

So a probability is the degree of a partial entailment. Keynes further makes the assumption that if *e* partially entails *h* to degree *p*, then, given *e*, it is rational to believe *h* to degree *p*. For Keynes, probability is degree of *rational* belief *not* simply degree of belief. As he says,

> in the sense important to logic, probability is not subjective. It is not, that is to say, subject to human caprice. A proposition is not probable because we think it so. When once the facts are given which determine our knowledge, what is probable or improbable in these circumstances has been fixed objectively, and is independent of our opinion. The Theory of Probability is logical, therefore, because it is concerned with the degree of belief which it is *rational* to entertain in given conditions, and not merely with the actual beliefs of particular individuals, which may or may not be rational.
>
> (*ibid.*: 4)

Here Keynes speaks of probabilities as being fixed objectively, but he is not using objective to refer to things in the material world. He means objective in the Platonic sense, referring to something in a supposed Platonic world of abstract ideas.

The next question which might be asked regarding Keynes's approach is as follows: 'How do we obtain knowledge about this logical relation of probability?' Keynes's answer is that we get to know at least some probability relations by direct acquaintance or immediate logical intuition. As Keynes says: 'We pass from a knowledge of the proposition *a* to a knowledge about the proposition *b* by perceiving a logical relation between them. With this logical relation we have direct acquaintance' (*ibid.*: 13).

A problem which arises on this account is how we can ever assign numerical values to probabilities. Keynes indeed thinks that this is possible only in some cases, and writes on this point: 'In order that numerical measurement may be possible, we must be given a number of *equally* probable alternatives' (*ibid.*: 44). So in order to get numerical probabilities we have to be able to judge that a number of cases are equally probable and to enable us to make this judgement we need an *a priori* principle. This *a priori* principle is called by Keynes the 'Principle of Indifference', and he gives the following statement of it:

> The Principle of Indifference asserts that if there is no *known* reason for predicating of our subject one rather than another of several alternatives, then relatively to such knowledge the assertions of each of these alternatives have an equal probability.
>
> (*ibid.*: 45)

Unfortunately, the Principle of Indifference leads to a number of paradoxes. Keynes gives a full account of these in Chapter 4 of the *Treatise*, and makes an attempt to solve them. Yet is has to be said that his solution is far from satisfactory.

This concludes my brief account of Keynes's version of the logical theory of probability. Let us turn now to the subjective interpretation.

The subjective theory of probability was discovered independently and at about the same time by Frank Ramsey in England, and by Bruno de Finetti in Italy. Their two versions of the theory are broadly similar, though there are important differences, which are well described in Galavotti (1991). In what follows I shall concentrate mainly on Ramsey since his work is directly connected with that of Keynes.

Ramsey was a younger contemporary of Keynes at Cambridge. His fundamental paper introducing the subjective approach to probability was read to the Moral Sciences Club at Cambridge in 1926, and Ramsey begins the paper by criticising Keynes's views on probability. According to Keynes, there are logical relations of probability between pairs of propositions, and these can in some sense be perceived. Ramsey criticises this view as follows:

> But let us now return to a more fundamental criticism of Mr. Keynes' views, which is the obvious one that there really do not seem to be any such things as the probability relations he describes. He supposes that, at any rate in certain cases, they can be perceived; but speaking for myself I feel confident that this is not true. I do not perceive them, and if I am to be persuaded that they exist it must be by argument; moreover I shrewdly suspect that others do not perceive them either, because they are able to come to so very little agreement as to which of them relates any two given propositions.
>
> (Ramsey 1978: 63)

This is an interesting case of an argument which gains in strength from the nature of the person who proposes it. Had a less distinguished logician than Ramsey objected that he was unable to perceive any logical relations of probability, Keynes might have replied that this was merely a sign of logical incompetence, or logical blindness. Indeed, Keynes (CWVIII: 18) does say: 'Some men – indeed it is obviously the case – may have a greater power of logical intuition than others'. Ramsey, however, was such a brilliant mathematical logician that Keynes could not have claimed with plausibility that Ramsey was lacking in the capacity for logical intuition or perception – and Keynes did not in fact do so.

In the logical interpretation, the probability of h given e is identified with the rational degree of belief which someone, who had evidence e, would accord to h. This rational degree of belief is considered to be the same for all rational individuals. The subjective interpretation of probability abandons the assumption of rationality leading to consensus. According to the subjective theory, different individuals (Ms A, Mr B and Master C, say), although all perfectly reasonable and having the same evidence e, may yet have different degrees of belief in h. Probability is thus defined as the degree of belief of a particular individual, so that we should really not speak of *the* probability, but rather of Ms A's probability, Mr B's probability, or Master C's probability.

Now the mathematical theory of probability takes probabilities to be numbers in the interval $[0, 1]$. So, if the subjective theory is to be an adequate interpretation of the mathematical calculus, a way must be found of measuring the degree of belief of an individual that some event (E, say) will occur. Thus we want to be able to measure, for example, Mr B's degree of belief that it will rain tomorrow in London, that a particular political party will win the next election, and so on. How can this be done? Ramsey (1978: 74) argues: 'The old-established way of measuring a person's belief is to propose a bet, and see what are the lowest odds which he will accept. This method I regard as fundamentally sound …' Ramsey defends this betting approach as follows:

> this section … is based fundamentally on betting, but this will not seem unreasonable when it is seen that all our lives we are in a sense betting. Whenever we go to the station we are betting that a train will really run, and if we had not a sufficient degree of belief in this we should decline the bet and stay at home.
>
> (*ibid.*: 85)

The betting approach to probability can be made precise as follows. Let us imagine that Ms A (a psychologist) wants to measure the degree of belief of Mr B in some event E. To do so, she gets Mr B to agree to bet with her on E, under the following conditions. Mr B has to choose a number q (called his *betting quotient* on E), and then Ms A chooses the stake S. Mr B pays Ms A qS in exchange for S if E occurs. S can be positive or negative, but $[S]$ must be small in relation to Mr B's wealth. Under these circumstances q is taken to be a measure of Mr B's degree of belief in E.

If Mr B has to bet on a number of events $E_1, \dots , E_n$, his betting quotients are said to be *coherent* if and only if Ms A cannot choose stakes $S_1, \dots , S_n$ such that she wins whatever happens. If Ms A can choose stakes so that she wins whatever happens, she is said to have made a 'Dutch Book' against Mr B.

It is taken as obvious that Mr B will want his bets to be coherent, that is to say he will want to avoid the possibility of his losing whatever happens. Surprisingly, this condition is both necessary and sufficient for betting quotients to satisfy the axioms of probability. This, then, is the content of the Ramsey–De Finetti theorem:

A set of betting quotients is coherent if and only if they satisfy the axioms of probability.

This theorem gives a rigorous foundation to the subjective theory of probability. The chain of reasoning is close-knit and ingenious. The first general idea is to measure degrees of belief by betting. This is made precise by introducing betting quotients. What is known as the Dutch Book argument then shows that for betting quotients to be coherent, they must satisfy the axioms of probability and so can be regarded as probabilities.

Let us turn now to the intersubjective interpretation of probability.[4] The subjective theory is concerned with degrees of belief of particular individuals. However, this abstracts from the fact that many, if not most, of our beliefs are social in character. They are held in common by nearly all members of a social group, and a particular individual usually acquires them through social interaction with this group. If we accept Kuhn's (1962) analysis then this applies to many of the beliefs of scientists. According to Kuhn, the scientific experts working in a particular area nearly all accept a paradigm which contains a set of theories and factual propositions. These theories and propositions are thus believed by nearly all the members of this group of scientific experts. A new recruit to the group is trained to know and accept the paradigm as a condition for entry to the group. Much the same considerations apply to other social groups such as religious sects, political parties, and so on. These groups have common beliefs which an individual usually acquires through joining the group. It is actually quite difficult for individuals to resist accepting the dominant beliefs of a group of which they form a part, though of course dissidents and heretics do occur. One striking instance of this is that individuals kidnapped by a terrorist organisation do sometimes, like Patty Hearst, adopt the terrorists' beliefs. All this seems to indicate that, as well as the specific beliefs of a particular individual, there are the consensus beliefs of social groups. Indeed, the latter may be more fundamental than the former. What will be shown next is that these consensus beliefs can be treated as probabilities through an extension of the Dutch Book argument.

Earlier we imagined that Ms A (a psychologist) wanted to measure the degree of belief of Mr B in some event E. To do so, she gets Mr B to agree to bet with her on E, under the following conditions. Mr B has to choose a number q (his betting quotient on E), and then Ms A chooses the stake S. Mr B pays Ms A qS in exchange for S if E occurs. S can be positive or negative, but $[S]$ must be small in relation to Mr B's wealth. Under these circumstances q is taken to be a measure of Mr B's degree of belief in E.

In order to extend this to social groups, we can retain our psychologist Ms A, but we must replace Mr B with a set $\mathbf{B} = (B_1, B_2, \dots, B_n)$ of individuals. We then have the following theorem:

> Suppose Ms A is betting against $\mathbf{B} = (B_1, B_2, \dots, B_n)$ on event E. Suppose B_i chooses betting quotient q_i. Ms A will be able to choose stakes so that she gains money from $\mathbf{B}$ whatever happens *unless* $q_1 = q_2 = \dots = q_n$.

Informally, what the above theorem shows is the following. Let $\mathbf{B}$ be some social group. Then it is in the interest of $\mathbf{B}$ as a whole if its members agree, perhaps as a result of rational discussion, on a common betting quotient rather than each member of the group choosing his or her own betting quotient. If a group does in fact agree on a common betting quotient, this will be called the *intersubjective* or *consensus* probability of the social group. This type of probability can then be contrasted with the *subjective* or *personal* probability of a particular individual.

The Dutch Book argument used to introduce intersubjective probability shows that if the group agrees on a common betting quotient, then this protects its members from a cunning opponent betting against them. This, then, is a particular mathematical case of an old piece of folk wisdom, namely the claim that solidarity within a group protects it from an outside enemy. This point of view is expressed in many traditional maxims and stories. A more recent example is to be found in Kurosawa's film, *Seven Samurai*. In one particular scene, Kambei, the leader of the samurai, is urging the villagers to act together to repel the coming bandit attack. 'This is a rule of war', he says. 'Collective defence protects the individual. Individual defence destroys the individual.'

One helpful way of regarding the intersubjective interpretation of probability is to see it as intermediate between the logical interpretation of the early Keynes, and the subjective interpretation of his critic Ramsey. According to the early Keynes, there exists a single rational degree of belief in some conclusion c given evidence e. If this were really so, we should expect nearly all human beings to have this single rational degree of belief in *c* given *e*, since, after all, most human beings are rational. Yet in very many cases different individuals come to quite different conclusions, even though they have the same background knowledge and expertise in the relevant area, and even though they are all quite rational. A single rational degree of belief on which all rational human beings should agree seems to be a myth.

So much for the logical interpretation of probability; but the subjective view of probability does not seem to be entirely satisfactory either. Degree of belief is not an entirely personal or individual matter. We very often find an individual human being belonging to a group which shares a common outlook, has some degree of common interest and is able to reach a consensus as regards its beliefs. Obvious examples of such groups would be religious sects, political parties, or schools of thought regarding various scientific questions. For such groups, the concept of intersubjective probability seems to be the appropriate one. These groups may be small or large, but usually they fall short of embracing the whole of humanity. The intersubjective probability of such a group is thus intermediate between a degree of rational belief (the early Keynes) and a degree of subjective belief (Ramsey).

The three views that we have considered so far have one thing in common: the fact that they regard probability as a measure of human belief, whether it is degree of rational belief, degree of individual belief, or the degree of a consensus belief of a group. Such theories are called *epistemological* theories of probability, and they can be contrasted with *objective* theories of probability. Here, objective does not, as in Keynes, mean objective in the Platonic sense, but rather in the sense of belonging to the objective material or physical world. The probability of a radioactive atom disintegrating in a year is an example of an objective probability in this sense. It is an objective feature of the physical world, and does not depend on human beliefs. Such objective probabilities are to be found in the natural sciences in situations where we have a set of repeatable conditions.

This concludes my brief survey of some of the main interpretations of probability. Let us see now how these views might be applied to Keynes's economics.

Probability in Keynes's theory of long-term expectations

In his *Treatise* of 1921, Keynes advocated the logical interpretation of probability as degree of rational belief. Should we therefore adopt the natural supposition that he is implicitly using this logical interpretation of probability in *The General Theory*? Or are there reasons for thinking that Keynes changed his views on probability between 1921 and 1936? These questions have been the subject of a fascinating debate among the Post Keynesians. One point of view is the *continuity thesis*, that Keynes held much the same view of probability throughout his life. This thesis is advocated by (among others) Lawson (1985), Carabelli (1988) and O'Donnell (1989). Opposed to this is the *discontinuity thesis*, that Keynes changed his views on the interpretation of probability significantly between 1921 and 1936. This thesis is advocated by Bateman (1987, 1996) and Davis (1994b). I am a supporter of the discontinuity thesis, and will next present the main arguments in its favour.

As far as the interpretation of probability is concerned, a most important intellectual event took place between 1921 and 1936. As was noted in the previous section, Ramsey, in his 1926 paper 'Truth and probability', subjected Keynes's logical interpretation of probability to an extensive criticism. There is strong evidence that Keynes, who had the greatest respect for Ramsey, took this criticism very seriously and altered his views on probability in the light of Ramsey's objections.

Ramsey died in 1930 at the age of only 26, and in 1931 Keynes paid tribute to this remarkable Cambridge philosopher, mathematician and economist. This is what Keynes had to say about Ramsey's treatment of probability:

> Ramsey argues, as against the view which I had put forward, that probability is concerned not with objective relations between propositions but (in some sense) with degrees of belief, and he succeeds in showing that the calculus of probabilities simply amounts to a set of rules for ensuring that the system of degrees of belief which we hold shall be a *consistent* system. Thus the calculus of probabilities belongs to formal logic. But the basis of our degrees of belief – or the *a priori* probabilities, as they used to be called – is part of our human outfit, perhaps given us merely by natural selection, analogous to our perceptions and our memories rather than to formal logic. So far I yield to Ramsey – I think he is right. But in attempting to distinguish 'rational' degrees of belief from belief in general he was not yet, I think, quite successful.
>
> (CWXa: 338–9)

We see that Keynes was prepared to yield to Ramsey on a number of points, but yet did not agree with Ramsey about everything. Bateman, in his interesting 1987 article on 'Keynes's changing conception of probability', argues that Keynes did adopt the subjective interpretation of probability. After quoting the above passage from Keynes, he writes: 'While he [Keynes] had originally advocated an *objective epistemic* theory of probability in *A Treatise on Probability* he was now willing to accept a *subjective epistemic* theory' (Bateman 1987: 107).

I agree with Bateman that Keynes abandoned the logical interpretation of probability, but I shall argue that Keynes moved towards an inter-subjective epistemic theory rather than a subjective epistemic theory of the kind advocated by Ramsey. Intersubjective probability is in fact closer to Keynes's original position, for, as I argued in the previous section, the intersubjective probability of a group is intermediate between a degree of rational belief (the early Keynes) and a degree of subjective belief (Ramsey).

Before discussing intersubjective probability in this context, however, I shall present a further piece of evidence for the argument that Keynes did abandon the logical interpretation of probability in *The General Theory*. As we saw earlier, Keynes's version of the logical interpretation of probability makes use of what he called the Principle of Indifference. Admittedly, Keynes does give a full discussion of the paradoxes to which this Principle leads, though he is not very successful in resolving these paradoxes. Yet in *A Treatise on Probability* he still regards the Principle of Indifference as essential for probability theory, as the following remarks about it show:

> On the grounds both of its own intuitive plausibility and of that of some of the conclusions for which it is necessary, we are inevitably led towards this principle as a necessary basis for judgements of probability. In *some* sense, judgements of probability do seem to be based on equally balanced degrees of ignorance.
>
> (CWVIII: 94)

By contrast, in *The General Theory* Keynes wrote:

> Nor can we rationalise our behaviour by arguing that to a man in a state of ignorance errors in either direction are equally probable, so that there remains a mean actuarial expectation based on equi-probabilities. For it can easily be shown that the assumption of arithmetically equal probabilities based on a state of ignorance leads to absurdities.
>
> (CWVII: 152)

This amounts to a complete repudiation of the Principle of Indifference, and it is interesting to note that Keynes may here be echoing Ramsey, who wrote:

> To be able to turn the Principle of Indifference out of formal logic is a great advantage; for it is fairly clearly impossible to lay down purely logical conditions for its validity, as is attempted by Mr Keynes.
>
> (Ramsey 1978: 91)

All this establishes that Keynes did abandon his logical interpretation of probability in the light of Ramsey's criticisms. But what interpretation of probability is appropriate, therefore, for Keynes's use of expectation in *The General Theory*? I think we can obtain an answer to this question through an analysis of Keynes's views on long-term expectation, as set out in *The General Theory* and in his 1937 *QJE* article (CWXIVa).

In 1937, Keynes argues that our knowledge of the future yields of investments is 'uncertain' in a sense which he distinguishes from 'probable'. This is what he says:

> By 'uncertain' knowledge, let me explain, I do not mean merely to distinguish what is known for certain from what is only probable. The game of roulette is not subject, in this sense, to uncertainty; nor is the prospect of a Victory bond being drawn. Or, again, the expectation of life is only slightly uncertain. Even the weather is only moderately uncertain. The sense in which I am using the term is that in which the prospect of a European war is uncertain, or the price of copper and the rate of interest twenty years hence, or the obsolescence of a new invention, or the position of private wealth owners in the social system in 1970. About these matters there is no scientific basis on which to form any calculable probability whatever. We simply do not know. Nevertheless, the necessity for action and for decision compels us as practical men to do our best to overlook this awkward fact and to behave exactly as we should if we had behind us a good Benthamite calculation of a series of prospective advantages and disadvantages, each multiplied by its appropriate probability, waiting to be summed.
>
> (CWXIVa: 113–14)

Keynes here uses 'uncertain' in the same sense as Knight, who in 1921 had distinguished between risk and uncertainty. Knight describes this distinction as follows:

> The practical difference between the two categories, risk and uncertainty, is that in the former the distribution of the outcome in a group of instances is known (either through calculation *a priori* or from statistics of past experience), while in the case of uncertainty that is not true, the reason being in general that it is impossible to form a group of instances, because the situation dealt with is in a high degree unique.
>
> (Knight 1921: 233)

Keynes next asks, regarding situations of uncertainty in the above sense: 'How do we manage in such circumstances to behave in a manner which saves our faces as rational, economic men?' He answers this question by saying that we resort to 'a variety of techniques' of which the most important is the following:

> Knowing that our own individual judgement is worthless, we endeavour to fall back on the judgement of the rest of the world which is perhaps better informed. That is, we endeavour to conform with the behaviour of the majority or the average. The psychology of a society of individuals each of whom is endeavouring to copy the others leads to what we may strictly term a *conventional* judgement.
>
> (CWXIVa: 114)

Keynes's point is that because of a lack of information and because of the general uncertainty of the future, entrepreneurs cannot form a rational expectation, which then determines their investment decisions. As a result, their expectation is largely conventional, and because of this, it is subject to waves of optimism or pessimism. This is the general state of Keynes's famous 'animal spirits', which he describes as follows:

> there is the instability due to the characteristic of human nature that a large proportion of our positive activities depend on spontaneous optimism rather than on a mathematical expectation, whether moral or hedonistic or economic. Most, probably, of our decisions to do something positive, the full consequences of which will be drawn out over many days to come, can only be taken as a result of animal spirits – of a spontaneous urge to action rather than inaction, and not as the outcome of a weighted average of quantitative benefits multiplied by quantitative probabilities ... Thus if the animal spirits are dimmed and the spontaneous optimism falters, leaving us to depend on nothing but a mathematical expectation, enterprise will fade and die; – though fears of loss may have a basis no more reasonable than hopes of profit had before.
>
> (CWVII: 161–2)

Keynes does not postulate, as a strict follower of Ramsey might have done, that each entrepreneur forms his or her own individual expectation which differs from that of every other entrepreneur. On the contrary, the entrepreneurs imitate each other so that the group comes to have more or less the same expectation. However, this expectation is not based on a rational assessment, but depends on factors such as the state of the animal spirits. What we are dealing with is the intersubjective degree of belief of a group of investors, which, through a process of social interaction, reaches a consensus. Keynes's long-term expectation is the intersubjective expectation of a group of entrepreneurs, and implicitly involves the notion of intersubjective probability.

This view is reinforced by the way Keynes sees the role of expert professionals who deal in stock-market investments:

most of these persons are, in fact, largely concerned, not with making superior long-term forecasts of the probable yield of an investment over its whole life, but with foreseeing changes in the conventional basis of valuation a short time ahead of the general public. They are concerned, not with what an investment is really worth to a man who buys it 'for keeps', but with what the market will value it at, under the influence of mass psychology, three months or a year hence.

(ibid.: 154)

Although intersubjective probability is largely an explication of what Keynes says, I think that it does improve on Keynes's position at one point. Both Keynes and Knight seem to assume that uncertainty is a qualitative concept which cannot be quantified, but, if we use the method of betting quotients and the Dutch Book argument, we can quantify uncertainty and treat it using the standard mathematical theory of probability. To see this, let us consider two of Keynes's examples of uncertainty, namely 'the price of copper and the rate of interest twenty years hence' (CWXIVa: 113). Although it is obviously very uncertain what the rate of interest will be in twenty years' time, there is nothing to prevent us getting a particular individual, or a social group, to propose a betting quotient on this price lying in a specified interval in twenty years' time. Thus, by the standard Dutch Book procedure, we can introduce probability distributions for the rate of interest in twenty years' time. These probabilities will, however, be subjective (or intersubjective) and not objective. Thus we can say that uncertainty in the sense of Keynes and Knight can be handled using subjective (or intersubjective) probabilities based on betting; while Knight's risk corresponds to an objective probability.

This analysis in fact accords quite well with what Keynes and Knight themselves say. Keynes says about examples such as the rate of interest in twenty years' time: 'About these matters *there is no scientific basis* on which to form any calculable probability whatever' (*ibid.*, emphasis added). Certainly there is no scientific basis on which to form a calculable probability, and so we cannot have an objective probability, but there is nothing to prevent individuals (or groups) betting and so forming a subjective (or intersubjective) probability. Knight associates risk with situations in which 'the distribution of the outcome in a group of instances is known', and claims that uncertainty occurs when 'it is impossible to form a group of instances, because the situation dealt with is in a high degree unique' (Knight 1921: 233). This concurs exactly with the position that objective probabilities (corresponding to Knight's risks) should be associated with sets of repeatable conditions, while single events, not uniquely characterised by a set of repeatable conditions, can only be assigned probabilities in the sense of degrees of belief. Indeed, Knight does actually say:

> We can also employ the terms 'objective' and 'subjective' probability to designate the risk and uncertainty respectively, as these expressions are already in general use with a signification akin to that proposed.
>
> (*ibid.*)

Knight was writing in 1921 before Ramsey and De Finetti had developed the method of betting quotients for making subjective probabilities measurable, and the Dutch Book argument for handling these subjective probabilities using the standard mathematical theory of probability. It was thus natural for Knight to think of subjective probability in his sense, that is, uncertainty, as 'indeterminate, unmeasurable' (*ibid.*: 46). This is no longer necessary today.

Thus we can take subjective (or intersubjective) probability to correspond to the uncertainty of Keynes and Knight, and objective probability to correspond to Knight's risk. There are advantages in doing so, since it avoids the need to use any concepts which cannot be handled by the ordinary mathematical calculus of probability. One qualification is needed, however.[5] Knight's risk does not correspond to a situation in which an objective probability exists, but to one in which the value of this objective probability is known. There might be a case in which there is an objective probability whose value is not known, perhaps because of a lack of statistical data. Such a situation would be one of uncertainty in the sense of Knight and Keynes, that is to say, in our analysis, a situation in which use would have to be made of a subjective or intersubjective, but not objective, probability.

Some concluding remarks in favour of the Post Keynesians

I will conclude by observing that Keynes's 1937 *QJE* paper from which I have quoted quite extensively provides very strong evidence in favour of the Post Keynesian interpretation of Keynes's economics. Keynes states that the aim of the paper is to summarise the main ideas of his book, and to explain the principal ways in which his theory differs from the standard economics of his time. Keynes indeed characterises what he calls 'orthodox theory' or 'classical economic theory' as a view held in common by then recent authors such as Edgeworth and Pigou, and their predecessors such as Ricardo and Marshall. He then explains the first way in which he diverges from this tradition as follows:

> But these more recent writers like their predecessors were still dealing with a system in which the amount of the factors employed was given and the other relevant facts were known more or less for certain. This does not mean that they were dealing with a system in

which change was ruled out, or even one in which the disappointment of expectation was ruled out. But at any given time facts and
expectations were assumed to be given in a definite and calculable
form; and risks, of which, though admitted, not much notice was
taken, were supposed to be capable of an exact actuarial computa-
tion. The calculus of probability, though mention of it was kept in the
background, was supposed to be capable of reducing uncertainty to
the same calculable status as that of certainty itself ...

(CWXIVa: 112–13)

Keynes then goes on to observe that 'we have, as a rule, only the
vaguest idea of any but the most direct consequences of our acts' (*ibid.*:
113). This may not matter for most of our actions, but it is important for
the accumulation of wealth, which is concerned with a comparatively
distant, or even *indefinitely* distant future. Keynes concludes: 'Thus the
fact that our knowledge of the future is fluctuating, vague and uncertain,
renders wealth a peculiarly unsuitable subject for the methods of the
classical economic theory' (*ibid.*: 113).

All this gives strong support to the Post Keynesian interpretation.
When Keynes sets out to explain how his theory differs from that of the
orthodox theorists, the very first point which he emphasizes is that he
takes account of uncertainty which they fail to do. The Post Keynesians
are thus correct to emphasise the crucial importance of uncertainty in
Keynes's economics, and to criticise IS–LM Keynesianism for failing to
mention, let alone discuss, uncertainty.

Keynes devotes section II of his 1937 paper to the question of uncertainty, and it is only in section III that he mentions effective demand,
which he describes as 'my next difference from the traditional theory.'
(*ibid.*: 119). Moreover, in his treatment of effective demand, the issues
connected with uncertainty, far from being forgotten, are strongly
emphasised. Keynes divides effective demand into investment expenditure and consumption expenditure, but he then argues that it is
investment expenditure which is the crucial factor in determining the
performance of the system as a whole. This is because consumption
expenditure is a fairly simple function of aggregate income, whereas
investment expenditure is liable to violent fluctuations owing to uncertainty about the future. It is thus the considerations regarding
uncertainty which lead Keynes to regarding the level of investment as
playing the most important role in determining how well or badly the
economy as a whole functions. This is how he summarises the argument:

The theory can be summed up by saying that, given the psychology
of the public, the level of output and employment as a whole
depends on the amount of investment. I put it in this way, not
because this is the only factor on which aggregate output depends,

but because it is usual in a complex system to regard as the *causa causans* that factor which is most prone to sudden and wide fluctuation. More comprehensively, aggregate output depends on the propensity to hoard, on the policy of the monetary authority as it affects the quantity of money, on the state of confidence concerning the prospective yield of capital assets, on the propensity to spend and on the social factors which influence the level of the money wage. But of these several factors it is those which determine the rate of investment which are most unreliable, since it is they which are influenced by our views of the future about which we know so little.

This that I offer is, therefore, a theory of why output and employment are so liable to fluctuation.

(ibid.: 121)

So Keynes was not a Keynesian, though he may have been a Post Keynesian!

Notes

1   The term 'Post Keynesianism' is rather vague, and not everyone would use it in the way adopted here. Indeed, several of those whom I have included in this group might deny that they are Post Keynesians. I am certainly using the term 'Post Keynesian' in a broad sense to cover a number of authors with very different views on economics and politics. The right wing of the Post Keynesians is represented by Skidelsky who holds that Keynes's ideas, though very interesting and important historically, are no longer applicable in the changed conditions of today. The left wing of the group, on the other hand, favour an integration of Keynes with Marx, and very left-wing policies.

2   In *The General Theory*, Keynes does use the terms 'uncertain' and 'uncertainty' quite often. He also sometimes, though not often, uses the word 'probability'. Characteristically, however, he speaks of 'expectation' rather than 'probability'. Now in standard probability theory, expectation can be defined in terms of probability, and vice versa. Suppose, for example, that a random variable X can take on the values $a_1, a_2, \ldots, a_n$, with probabilities $p_1, p_2, \ldots, p_n$. Then the expectation of X, $E(X) = a_1 p_1 + a_2 p_2 + \ldots + a_n p_n$. Similar definitions can be given for random variables with more complicated distributions. Conversely, let A be an event. We can define the indicator of A by

$$Y(w) = 1 \text{ if } w \, \varepsilon \, A$$

$$Y(w) = 0 \text{ if } \neg \, (w \, \varepsilon \, A)$$

Then Y is a random variable, and the probability of A, $P(A) = E(Y)$. Indeed, one can develop probability by introducing expectation as the primitive concept that appears in the axioms, and defining probability in terms of expectation. For these reasons, I shall assume that when Keynes speaks of expectation, he is making an implicit reference to probability. However, it was suggested to me by Tomohide Suzuki that Keynes may be using expectation in a non-standard sense which is not definable in terms of probability. This suggestion leads to a different interpretation of Keynes's writings which seems to me worth exploring, but which I shall not consider further in the present chapter.

3   For more detailed accounts of the various interpretations, see Gillies (2000).
4   What follows is an informal sketch of the intersubjective interpretation of probability. A more detailed account with full proofs of the relevant theorems is contained in Gillies and Ietto-Gillies (1991). This is a joint paper written with my wife who is Professor of Applied Economics at South Bank University, London. The theory of intersubjective probability as applied to economics was worked out by the two of us together. An account of the theory can also be found in Gillies (2000: 169–80).
5   This point was made to me by Jon Williamson in an informal discussion.

10 No faith, no conversion

The evolution of Keynes's ideas on uncertainty under the influence of Johannes von Kries*

Guido Fioretti

Introduction

Keynes precipitated a revolution in economics, a deep and lasting one that is still ongoing. Like all intellectual revolutions, it did not arise out of a rehashing of old ideas. On the contrary, Keynes's revolution was a product of his genuine curiosity about the most diverse fields of scientific research. Novelty, in science as much as in technology, arises out of the combination of previously isolated ideas.

An important aspect of the story of the development of Keynes's ideas was his discovery of Johannes von Kries, a German logician and neurophysiologist who came to the idea that probabilities are in general non-comparable and non-numerical. Keynes was quite open about this source of inspiration but, at the time he was writing *A Treatise on Probability*, attempted to accommodate von Kries's non-numerical probabilities into an unsuitable philosophical framework, one which he later rejected.

Going back to von Kries is extremely useful when attempting to clarify the concept of non-numerical probability in *A Treatise on Probability* (CWVIII), as well as the continuities and discontinuities between the *Treatise* and *The General Theory of Employment, Interest and Money* (CWVII). The next section illustrates von Kries's vision, and the section after that examines how it was received by Keynes. The penultimate section attempts to distinguish what Keynes might have changed between 1921 and 1936 from what stayed unchanged. Finally, an attempt is made to distinguish what parts of his theory Keynes might have changed during this same period.

Johannes von Kries

Unlike most students of probability, who tend to be philosophers or mathematicians, von Kries was a practical scientist. He was a doctor, a professor of physiology at the University of Freiburg, who pioneered laboratory experiments on the nervous system and its connections with motor and sensory organs (von Kries 1901, 1923, 1925). And also unlike most students of probability theory, who think of probability in connection with games of chance, von Kries's interests in probability theory were associated with measuring the effectiveness of new drugs. Here our physician realised that, unlike those who were throwing dice and assumed that a die has six identical faces, his problem was that of defining the set of possible events.

How can we say that a drug has been effective against a certain disease? Can we say that a drug has been effective because patients die ten days later, or if in healing one disease it induces another? Should we categorise all variants of a disease under a single label, or should we distinguish them as separate? And how do we establish boundaries between diseases that share common symptoms?

Von Kries realised that there exists a kind of cognitive uncertainty in the process of the classification of empirical facts into 'events'. In 1886, he published a treatise on probability that had considerable resonance in German-speaking countries (von Kries 1886). In subsequent years, he published several papers of a more philosophical character (von Kries 1888, 1892, 1899) and, finally, a treatise on logic (von Kries 1916). This was followed by works on Goethe (von Kries 1924a) and Kant (von Kries 1924b) that linked his logic to the cornerstones of German culture.

There is no space, and possibly no need, to repeat the analysis of von Kries's philosophy that I have already published elsewhere (Fioretti 2001). What is important to bear in mind is that his first book (von Kries 1886) already contained a fundamental intuition, namely that probability judgments are based on analogies with past situations that can never be exactly the same as the one at hand. Thus, comparing qualitatively different settings impairs the possibility of numerical evaluation, just as pears cannot be summed with apples. Of course, in the case of games of chance, outcomes are reasonably invariant over time so that numerical comparisons and calculations are possible. But this is not a general case. In general, symptoms are never exactly the same, just as investment opportunities are never exactly the same.

Von Kries did concede that, for practical purposes, individuals may eventually produce a numerical evaluation of non-numerical probabilities; however, since such an evaluation is necessarily subjective, he considered it to be of little practical help. This subjective numerical evaluation would later be called a 'subjective probability' by Ramsey (1978) and De Finetti (1931), who added the idea of *forcing* individuals to express a numerical value. Had von Kries been confronted with contemporary subjective probability theory, he would likely have questioned the usefulness of translating non-numerical probabilities into numerical values, if their subjective character prevents us from knowing whether these values are correct.

Keynes made several references to von Kries in *A Treatise on Probability*, and even more in its initial version submitted as a fellowship dissertation at King's College, Cambridge (Keynes 1907, 1908). However, on the specific issue of the 'weight of the arguments' that support probability relations, Keynes referred to two articles by Meinong (1890) and Nitsche (1892). While both of these papers are reviews of von Kries's first book, both offer original ideas too.

Meinong wrote a favourable review in which he tried to express von Kries's ideas in terms of the usual setting of throwing dice. Von Kries's problem, he argued, arises if you are throwing an object that looks approximately like a die. If you are going to throw a broken die, or an otherwise irregular die, then the extent to which you can apply the usual assumption of equiprobable outcomes depends on how similar the broken die is to a regular die. However, he pointed out that judgments of similarity are necessarily subjective, and that qualitative features of the broken die are not easily measured by some objective magnitude.

Meinong accordingly proposed a second measure of uncertainty, besides probability. This second magnitude was intended to measure the extent of subjective evaluation that it is necessary to carry out in order to transform a non-numerical probability into a numerical one. In the terms of Meinong's example, this second magnitude would be a subjective evaluation of how similar a specific broken die is to an ideal, regular one.

Unlike Meinong's review, Nitsche's was critical in orientation. In fact, Nitsche did not even refer directly to von Kries's work but rather to Meinong's interpretation of it. Nitsche rejected Meinong's example of 'an object that looks approximately like a die' on the grounds that, in order to see how different this object is from a regular die, it is sufficient to throw it often enough and see how often each face comes up. In this way, von Kries's concern with novel situations and cognitive issues was forgotten and similarity judgments reduced to probability measurement.

Nitsche did retain Meinong's idea of a second magnitude in order to describe uncertainty, but he identified this magnitude with the dimension of the sample upon which probability is calculated. Simply put, the more often a die is thrown, the better one can ascertain how similar it is to an ideal, regular die.

Thus, one may reasonably ask *why* Keynes mentioned Nitsche as a source of inspiration. For Nitsche was an absolutely marginal figure, a scholar devoid of any originality whose acceptance of a second magnitude for measuring uncertainty actually had nothing to do with the idea of non-numerical, non-comparable probabilities.

The answer lies in the particular philosophical framework in which Keynes cast von Kries's work. As we shall see in the subsequent section, this led Keynes to express his notion of the 'weight of argument' in terms that include the traditional notion of sample size.

John Maynard Keynes

As a young man in Cambridge, Keynes was fascinated by Moore's neo-Platonist philosophy. His *A Treatise on Probability* reflects this neo-Platonic attitude, treating probabilities as objective entities that can be known by means of intuition, just like Platonic ideas.

Not necessarily linked to neo-Platonism, but necessary in order to enquire about probabilities that are conceived as objective entities, is Keynes's assumption of atomism. Throughout *A Treatise on Probability*, Keynes assumed that any manifestation of reality arises out of the combination of atomic components whose number may be infinite, but whose variety is finite. This assumption has important consequences for Keynes's ideas on analogy and induction, the mental processes that underlie von Kries's non-comparable and non-numerical probabilities.

Given the assumption of a finite number of qualities, Keynes could then proceed to treat analogy in terms of collecting instances that share common qualities. On this assumption, there is neither scope nor need to classify objects into mental categories that may differ among individuals. Rather, recognising an object means to identify certain of its qualities, while drawing an analogy between two objects means to identify a certain set of qualities that are common to both of them (CWVIII: 248). For instance, one may draw an analogy among water birds that are big and white, calling them 'swans'.

Induction, according to Keynes, arises out of a repetition of slightly different instances and the recognition of the analogies among them (*ibid.*: 242). Keynes distinguished between two types of induction. The first is what he called *universal induction*, where, for example, from observing a series of white swans one draws the conclusion that 'all swans are white' (*ibid.*: 244). The second is what he called *statistical induction*, or *inductive correlation*, where, for instance, from observing many white swans and some black swans one draws the conclusion that 'most swans are white' (*ibid.*: 245).

Keynes claimed that statistical induction yields probabilistic judgments, but he did not claim that universal induction yields certainty. On the contrary, universal inductions may also come in degrees of probability, depending on the number of instances that share common qualities, such as the number of swans that have been observed – in other words, depending on sample size (*ibid.*: 244).

In both cases, Keynes maintained that probabilities originating from different inductions may not be comparable with one another. This happens when the conditions and conclusions of one induction cannot be included in those of another. For instance, the probabilities of two inductions such as 'all swans are white' and 'all swans have a colour' can be compared with one another because 'being white' is a quality that is included in 'having a colour'. In contrast, the probabilities of 'all swans are white' and 'all swans are beaked' cannot be compared because 'being white' and 'having a beak' are non-comparable qualities.

Besides being non-comparable, probabilities can be non-numerical. This may happen because, although the number of qualities has been supposed to be finite, we may not know what they are. We may fear, for instance, that our inductions about swans may turn out to be wrong because of instances that we were not able to conceive of, such as unknown or novel subspecies. To the extent that qualitatively novel instances may appear, probabilities are not numerical. However, according to Keynes, finiteness of possible qualities permits constraining non-numerical probabilities within numerical lower and upper bounds (*ibid.*: 288).

Keynes's assumption of a limited variety of empirical experiences, to be obtained through the combination of a finite number of qualities, suggests the conclusion that the arguments that support probability statements are: (1) how many different qualities constitute the available instances; and (2) the number of instances of each different combination of qualities. In terms of the probability, say, of extracting a ball of a certain colour from an urn, the above issues correspond to: (1) how many different colours can be found in the urn; and (2) how many balls have been extracted.

Given Keynes's neo-Platonic vision of probability judgments, his notion of the 'weight of argument' must entail both issues. Weight is not the same as Meinong's second uncertainty magnitude because it includes sample size, and it is not the same as Nitsche's sample size because it includes the evaluation of qualitative differences. Keynesian 'weight' includes both aspects, as Runde (1990) has already recognised.

On the whole, it appears that Keynes did understand von Kries's ideas, but that he transposed them into an alien, misleading philosophical frame-work. Keynes, at least at the time he was writing *A Treatise on Probability*, was a neo-Platonist who conceived of probabilities as real objects appre-hended via pure intuition. Von Kries, on the contrary, considered probability relations as the outcome of mental processes. While both of them were purporting to advance a logical view of probability relations, they had opposing ideas about where probability relations came from.

History has proved von Kries to be right, not Keynes. The enormous development of cognitive sciences in recent decades has shown that many aspects of human cognition can be understood, and that von Kries's ideas were well ahead of their time. However, Keynes's proba-bility theory stands to show how much can be done without enquiring as to what happens in an individual's mind.

Continuities and discontinuities

Does *A Treatise on Probability* provide the eventual microeconomic founda-tions of *The General Theory of Employment, Interest and Money*, or did Keynes change his mind at some point in time between his earlier work and his practical activity as an economist? This is a much debated issue, one that is worth revisiting in the light of von Kries's influence upon Keynes. The ensuing discussion focuses mainly on Carabelli (1988), a representative of the camp that stresses the continuities in Keynes's thought between the two works, and Bateman (1996), a representative of the camp that stresses the differences between the young and the mature Keynes.

Bateman (1996) relates the evolution of Keynes's ideas to the rhetorical tools he eventually used in order to support them, first within academic debates and later in the wider arena of public discussions on economic policies. Concerning the genesis of *A Treatise on Probability*, Bateman tells a convincing story that centres on the Apostles, an exclusive society that Keynes joined in Cambridge.

Although the Apostles were committed proponents of Moore's neo-Platonism, they did not share Moore's acceptance of established rules of moral conduct. Many years later, Keynes would comment:

> We entirely repudiated a personal liability on us to obey general rules. We claimed the right to judge every individual case on its merits, and the wisdom, experience and self-control to do so success-fully. This was a very important part of our faith, violently and aggressively held, and for the outer world it was our most obvious and dangerous characteristic.
>
> (CWXb: 38)

Moore based his argument for following general rules of conduct on the grounds that those rules yield good results most of the time. This was a probabilistic argument, based on a frequentist idea of probability. By defining neo-Platonic probabilities that can be grasped by an act of intu-ition, Keynes opened the way for single individuals to bypass rules of conduct in order to pursue the higher ideals that they have been able to understand. Sometimes some people are better than average at under-standing what it is right to do. Thus, they should not be prevented from doing it.

Once it is assumed that probability relations are objective entities waiting to be grasped by those who are capable of doing so, atomism is a necessary assumption in order to provide a theory of induction. By assuming that reality is the combination of a finite number of qualities, Keynes was able to move induction away from the human mind towards an objective reality of atoms and molecules. Keynes retained von Kries's idea of non-numerical, non comparable probabilities, but he transposed them from the realm of mental processes to a supposedly objective neo-Platonic world.

This attitude changed. In 'My early beliefs' (CWXb), Keynes openly rejected the neo-Platonism of his youth, and the mature Keynes was much concerned with conventions and rules of conduct. Furthermore, his stand on atomism appears to have changed as well, between the original publication of the *Treatise* in 1921 and an essay on Edgeworth that he wrote in 1926:

> The physicists of the nineteenth century have reduced matter to the collisions and arrangements of particles, between which the ultimate qualitative differences are very few; and the Mendelian biologists are deriving the various qualities of men from the collisions and arrangements of chromosomes. In both cases the analogy with the perfect game of chance is really present; and the validity of some current modes of inference may depend on the assumption that it is to material of this kind that we are applying them. Here, though I have complained sometimes at their want of logic, I am in fundamental sympathy with the deep underlying conceptions of the statistical theory of the day. If the contemporary doctrines of biology and physics remain tenable, we may have a remarkable, if undeserved, justification of some of the methods of the traditional calculus of probabilities.
>
> (CWVIII: 468)

> The atomic hypothesis which has worked so splendidly in physics breaks down in psychics. We are faced at every turn with the problems of organic unity, of discreteness, of discontinuity – the whole is not equal to the sum of the parts, comparisons of quantity fail us, small changes produce large effects, the assumptions of a uniform and homogeneous continuum are not satisfied. Thus the results of Mathematical Psychics turn out to be derivative, not fundamental, indexes, not measurements, first approximations at the best; and fallible indexes, dubious approximations at that, with much doubt added as to what, if anything, they are indexes or approximations of.
>
> (CWXe: 262)

The interpretation of the above passages is to some extent controversial, because one can imagine that Keynes ascribed atomism to the natural sciences and organicism to the human sciences, or that he relegated organicism to individuals and considered societies as atomistic, or, finally, that Keynes wrote *A Treatise on Probability* with the purpose of working out an assumption that he did not actually believe (see Gerrard (1992) for a review). However, the most widespread impression is that, not only regarding neo-Platonism but as far as atomism is concerned as well, Keynes did change his mind between *A Treatise on Probability* and *The General Theory*.

Nonetheless, those who stress a fundamental continuity between *A Treatise on Probability* and *The General Theory* do have some good arguments. However, continuity must be sought at a deeper level of analysis.

First, one may observe that if in 1936 Keynes thought that *A Treatise on Probability* was completely wrong, then he would not have referred to it in a footnote of *The General Theory* in order to explain what he meant by 'very uncertain' (CWVII: 148). The fact that he did so suggests that, at least for certain purposes, he felt that *A Treatise on Probability* was still good.

In fact, the view expressed in *A Treatise on Probability* did allow non-numerical probabilities and, conceivably, hoarding and preference for liquidity when a numerical evaluation of prospective returns is not possible. According to the *Treatise*, numerical evaluation of probabilities is not possible when decision-makers do not have enough information about the qualities that constitute the possibilities that they envisage. Modern 'New Keynesians' know that many Keynesian results, including under-employment equilibria, may be reached by simply assuming imperfect information. Thus, the view expressed in *A Treatise on Probability* is actually not at odds with *The General Theory*. However, it is not sufficient in order to explain all of it, particularly not the fundamental concept of 'animal spirits'.

Secondly, and more importantly, Keynes never accepted the idea that *all* human reasoning is akin to logical calculus. Carabelli (1988: Ch. 8) argues convincingly that, throughout *A Treatise on Probability* and its previous versions (Keynes 1907, 1908, CWVIII), Keynes rejected the idea that algorithmic logic, as expressed by Russell and the early Wittgenstein, could in any sense represent the way in which humans think.

Keynes did not accept this idea as a young man, when he imagined that human beings apprehend probability relations by means of intuition. Neo-Platonism was, for him, a possible alternative to the calculating rationality of marginalists. Even when Keynes stressed how far he had moved from his 'early beliefs', he stressed that he was happy that he had grown up with them: 'we were amongst the first of our generation, perhaps alone amongst our generation, to escape from the Benthamite tradition' (CWXb).

With equal determination, the mature Keynes continued to reject the idea that human reasoning is akin to formal logic. Even in the famous passage where he accepted the idea that probabilities are subjective 'degrees of belief', he pleaded for a 'human logic' as distinct from the formal logic upon which probability calculus rests:

> Ramsey argues, as against the view I had put forward, that probability is concerned not with objective relations between propositions but (in

some sense) with degrees of belief, and he succeeds in showing that the calculus of probabilities simply amounts to a set of rules for ensuring that the system of degrees of belief which we hold shall be a *consistent* system. Thus the calculus of probabilities belongs to formal logic. But the basis of our degrees of belief – or the *a priori* probabilities, as they used to be called – is part of our human outfit, perhaps given us merely by natural selection, analogous to our perceptions and our memories rather than to formal logic. So far I yield to Ramsey – I think he is right. But in attempting to distinguish 'rational' degrees of belief from belief in general he was not yet, I think, quite successful. It is not getting to the bottom of the principle of induction merely to say that it is a useful mental habit. Yet in attempting to distinguish a 'human' logic from formal logic on the one hand and descriptive psychology on the other, Ramsey may have been pointing the way to the next field of study when formal logic has been put into good order and its highly limited scope properly defined.

(CWXa: 338–9)

Keynes's consistent opposition to the application of formal logic to human reasoning does not mean that he had a perfectly developed idea of the way in which the human mind actually works. So of course, there was no theory for him to remain consistent with here. As a young man, he thought that neo-Platonism was a viable alternative. As a mature man, he rejected neo-Platonism and pleaded for a logic to explain what psychology, at that time, merely described.

Keynes should not be regarded as a religious prophet. His story is neither that of a man who received Illumination and spent his life propagating Truth, nor is it a story of conversions and abjurations of previous creeds. Rather, Keynes was a serious scientist, one who followed one basic thread throughout his life. This thread consisted of refusing the idea that human beings think and act according to the prescriptions of formal logic, the probability calculus and utility maximisation. In his search for an alternative kind of logic, he approached and rejected many views but, in retrospect, we can say that he never came so close to the goal as when he met von Kries.

Von Kries was very much ahead of his time. He was a forerunner of *Gestalt* psychology, one who understood the operating principles of mental categories in a way that only began to surface in the cognitive sciences in the 1980s (Barsalou 1987; Lakoff 1987; Hampton 1993). On the contrary, formal logic gave rise to the Artificial Intelligence research programme of the 1950s and 1960s, now abandoned as a faithful account of the way the human mind actually works but still valuable for modelling certain features of high-level, conscious thinking.

Thus, Keynes was right. But he would have been even more so had he not distorted von Kries by imposing on him Moore's neo-Platonism.

Keynes after von Kries

Studying von Kries undoubtedly helps us to understand Keynes's seemingly awkward statements concerning non-numerical probabilities. Furthermore, it throws light on current models of 'fundamental' uncertainty (Fioretti 1998). However, von Kries is also a good starting point for improving on Keynes's thought, both with respect to individual as well as to collective behaviour.

Keynesian scholars have rightly emphasised the importance of 'animal spirits' for Keynes's economics. Animal spirits give rise to patterns of individual behaviour that appear 'irrational' if one looks upon them from the perspective of formal logic, the probability calculus and utility maximisation (Dow and Dow 1985; Winslow 1993a). Interestingly, Keynes's account of basic will is consistent with Freud's psychoanalysis, with which he is likely to have been acquainted (Winslow 1986b, 1992).

But following von Kries, animal spirits, just like any human motivator, could be understood in terms of idiosyncratic mental categories and causal maps. Ultimately, von Kries may act as a link between Keynesian economists and cognitive scientists. The cognitive sciences have undergone impressive developments since the 'connectionist revolution' of the 1980s, and these may yield a basis for a true microfoundation of Keynes's economics.

Prospects for improving our understanding of collective behaviour are even more exciting. Von Kries's account of the formation of probability judgments rests upon structures of information and cognitive processes of information classification, which represent a proper framework for investigating the possibilities for unemployment equilibria under alternative institutional arrangements. Keynes scholars have already hinted at opportunities for understanding conventions in terms of common knowledge and self-organisation (Dupuy 1989b), Wittgenstein's later views on 'language-games' (Davis 1996) and Hayek's concern with social constructs (Lawson 1996). Much more could be achieved by applying connectionist models to social interaction.

Note

* I wish to thank Alberto Baccini, Bradley Bateman, Anna Carabelli, Victoria Chick, Marco Dardi, Sheila Dow, Giorgio Rampa and Jochen Runde for encouragement and suggestions

Part III
Social ontology

11 The foundations of Keynes's economics

Ted Winslow

Introduction

Once again the functioning of financial markets is creating very serious problems for the world economy. This has led to a renewal of interest in the economics of Keynes.

There are, however, significant obstacles in the way of properly understanding and evaluating Keynes's economics. The development of economics in the sixty and more years since the publication of *The General Theory of Employment, Interest and Money* in 1936 has so entrenched the set of philosophical and psychological foundations from which Keynes escaped (CWVII: xxiii) that it has become practically impossible, particularly for those within economics, to conceive of, let alone properly understand and evaluate, an economics with different foundations. Keynes's economics, however, is an economics of just this kind. Both its philosophical and its psychological foundations differ radically from those now dominant.

What follows provides a summary account of these foundations. It is focused on their complex relation to Keynes's work on the philosophy of probability, some of the most important results of which are contained in *A Treatise on Probability* of 1921 (CWVIII). Its central interpretive thesis is that Keynes ultimately adopted the ontological hypothesis of 'organic unity' as the philosophical foundation both of his theory of induction and probability and of his economics. He combined these very different philosophical foundations with very different psychological foundations. This chapter's main interpretive thesis with respect to the latter is that Keynes attributes an important degree of irrationality to economic motivation and behaviour.

Philosophy

As we shall see, Keynes makes very significant use of ideas from *A Treatise on Probability* in his economics. Interpretation of this relation is complicated, however, by the fact that he later abandoned key aspects of the *Treatise*. In particular, he abandoned the idea of logical probability relations and the atomic hypothesis.

The foundation of rational degrees of belief

The *Treatise* had attempted to ground probability in directly perceivable logical probability relations (*ibid.*: Ch. 1). In his 1931 review of Frank Ramsey's *Foundations of Mathematics*, Keynes abandoned this approach. He substituted for it the idea that rational degrees of belief are 'useful mental habits' having their basis in something analogous to perception and memory rather than in formal logic. He adopted Ramsey's term, 'human logic', to designate the field of study concerned with the analysis of these habits. He rejected, however, Ramsey's attempt to elaborate the idea in terms of Charles Peirce's pragmatism.

> Thus he [Ramsey] was led to consider 'human logic' as distinguished from 'formal logic'. Formal logic is concerned with nothing but the rules of *consistent* thought. But in addition to this we have certain 'useful mental habits' for handling the material with which we are supplied by our perceptions and by our memory and perhaps in other ways, and so arriving at or towards truth; and the analysis of such habits is also a sort of logic. The application of these ideas to the logic of probability is very fruitful. Ramsey argues, as against the view that I had put forward, that probability is concerned not with objective relations between propositions but (in some sense) with degrees of belief, and he succeeds in showing that the calculus of probabilities simply amounts to a set of rules for ensuring that the system of degrees of belief which we hold shall be a *consistent* system. Thus the calculus of probabilities belongs to formal logic. But the basis of our degrees of belief – or the *a priori* probabilities, as they used to be called – is part of our human outfit, perhaps given us merely by natural selection, analogous to our perceptions and our memories rather than to formal logic. So far I yield to Ramsey – I think he is right. But in attempting to distinguish 'rational' degrees of belief from belief in general he was not yet, I think, quite successful. It is not getting to the bottom of the principle of induction merely to say that it is a useful mental habit.
>
> (CWXa: 338–9)[1]

This change left much of the rest of the *Treatise*'s treatment of probability intact. In particular, in locating the basis of degrees of belief in human rather than formal logic, Keynes retained the view that objective rational grounds were available for such beliefs. As Keynes's own account of the idea in the passage just quoted demonstrates,[2] Ramsey, by making human logic part of 'logic', meant to indicate that it was concerned with determining 'what we ought to believe', 'what it would be reasonable to believe':

> Let us therefore try to get an idea of a human logic which shall not attempt to be reducible to formal logic. Logic, we may agree, is concerned not with what men actually believe, but what they ought to believe, or what it would be reasonable to believe.
>
> (Ramsey 1978: 95)[3]

Keynes also retained the view that rational degrees of belief change with circumstances, that they can be non-numerical, and that they can be based on more or less complete evidence so that the *Treatise* concept of 'weight' remains relevant. I shall sketch below a theory of probability that grounds it in human logic while retaining these other aspects of Keynes's *Treatise* argument.

The 'inductive hypothesis'

The *Treatise* had attempted to ground universal and statistical induction in the hypotheses of 'atomism' and 'limited variety' (CWVIII: 468). Keynes had suggested somewhat tentatively there (*ibid.*: 290) that it was only if the 'universe of phenomena' was atomic that what he called the 'inductive hypothesis', the hypothesis that the facts or propositions with which an inductive argument is concerned belong to a *'finite* system' (*ibid.*: Ch. 22), could be justified. He gave reasons why the alternative ontological hypothesis, the hypothesis of 'organic unity', would, if true, make the inductive method useless (*ibid.*: 276–8). He endorsed (again somewhat tentatively) the following atomic view of the material of 'psychics' and 'physics': 'we do habitually assume, I think, that the size of the atomic unit is for mental events an individual consciousness, and for material events an object small in relation to our perceptions' (*ibid.*: 278).[4]

In his 1926 essay on Edgeworth, Keynes abandoned the atomic hypothesis as the appropriate basis for 'psychics':

> The atomic hypothesis which has worked so splendidly in physics breaks down in psychics. We are faced at every turn with the problems of organic unity, of discreteness, of discontinuity – the whole is not equal to the sum of the parts, comparisons of quantity fail us, small changes produce large effects, the assumptions of a uniform and homogeneous continuum are not satisfied.
>
> (CWXe: 262)

In his subsequent explicit writing on the methods of economics and in his implicit approach to method in his own economics, he adopts the hypothesis of organic unity.[5] He also continues, however, to make use of induction. *The General Theory of Employment, Interest and Money* is, obviously, a *general* theory. As we shall see, he also implicitly assumes that rational statistical induction is possible. Consequently, in abandoning the atomic hypothesis for the hypothesis of organic unity, he also abandoned his *Treatise* view that organic unity would make the inductive method useless.

There is a version of the hypothesis of organic unity that makes it compatible both with what Keynes called 'the inductive hypothesis' and with a human logic-based foundation for rational degrees of belief.

A. N. Whitehead on organic unity, induction and the frequency theory of probability

This version had been worked out by A. N. Whitehead in the form of his 'philosophy of organism', an ontology based on the hypothesis of 'organic unity' (Whitehead 1929). The defining concept of this hypothesis is 'internal relations'. Relations are 'internal' where the essential qualities of related individuals are the outcome of their relations. In contrast, the atomic hypothesis treats relations as 'external'; the essential qualities of individuals are assumed to be independent of their relations. Individuals conceived of in this way are 'atoms' in Keynes's *A Treatise on Probability* sense and their interdependence is 'atomic'.

In response to Keynes's *Treatise*, the arguments of which he had been familiar with since its 1908/1909 beginnings as a fellowship dissertation for King's College, Cambridge,[6] Whitehead argued (1948; see also 1929: 199–206) that the hypothesis of organic unity could be conceived so as to avoid the problems for induction that Keynes claimed it created. It could also, he argued, provide foundations for a 'frequency theory' of probability that could answer the questions Keynes had raised in the *Treatise* regarding Whitehead's version of that theory (CWVIII: 109–19). Moreover, all this could be justified by means of analysis of 'the material with which we are supplied by our perceptions and by our memory', that is, by means of what Keynes, following Ramsey, called 'human logic'.

The key concept in Whitehead's theory of induction and probability is 'real potentiality' (Whitehead 1929: 65), an aspect of his conception of reality as a system of internal relations. The present of each of us has this as an essential feature. It is the set of real possibilities constitutive of my present and future as created and constrained by my internal relations to everything else including my relations to everything past. It differs for different periods into the future. The possibilities that are open to me in the next second are fewer than those open to me in the next minute or the next day or the next year. Real potentiality is composed of the real possibilities for actualization within these periods. What will actually occur will depend on many things including my own decisions and actions.

Internal relations differ for each individual (Whitehead calls the specific location of a present individual, in the present system of internal relations that is the world now, that individual's 'standpoint'). Also, real potentiality changes as the present becomes past and new relations arise.

Whitehead claims that internal relations can be conceived so as to make real potentiality a 'finite system' in Keynes's *A Treatise on Probability* sense, that is, so as to satisfy what Keynes calls the 'inductive hypothesis' (see, for example, Whitehead 1948: 111). One aspect of the conception that accomplishes this is the assumption that the internal relations constituting real potentiality have differing degrees of stability. The more stable a given subset of these relations is, the more stable are the characteristics of real potentiality to which they give rise and the more possible it is to treat these characteristics as what Keynes calls 'given'.

Whitehead also claims that this conception of the individual as embedded in an organic unity productive of real potentiality as a finite system, this 'habitual idea', can be grounded in our direct experience of reality; it can be shown to describe accurately that reality. This grounding is provided by what amounts to 'human logic', by what Whitehead calls 'direct intuitive observation', a method having all those features of Ramsey's concept endorsed by Keynes in his review.[7]

The fact that the organic unity productive of real potentiality makes the latter a finite system also means that there is a basis for rational degrees of belief. This is provided by the 'truth frequencies' that characterize real potentiality. Such frequencies are the ontological foundation of Whitehead's frequency theory of probability.[8]

These frequencies change with changes in real potentiality so that, as in the theory of *A Treatise on Probability*, probabilities vary with circumstances. In addition, beliefs about them can be based on knowledge grounded in evidence derived from our direct experience of real potentiality. This knowledge can be more or less complete. Consequently, even though the frequencies that provide the ultimate basis for rational degrees of belief are themselves numerical, our knowledge of them may not be sufficient to produce actual numerical estimates; as in Keynes's original theory, rational degrees of belief can be non-numerical (Whitehead 1929: 201). For the same reason, the *Treatise* concept of 'weight' (CWVIII: Ch. 7), a measure of the completeness of the evidence on which rational degrees of belief are based, remains relevant. The weight associated with rational degrees of belief varies as additional evidence is acquired and as the frequencies themselves change with changes in real potentiality. The latter changes change weight by making some previously relevant evidence irrelevant.

As the distance into the future increases, rational forecasting becomes more and more difficult because fewer and fewer things can be treated as 'given'. This provides an ontological foundation for Keynes's claim that the long run is often 'fundamentally uncertain' in the sense that 'we simply do not know' and cannot know the long-run consequences of present decisions.

How does Keynes's economics reflect his adoption of the hypothesis of organic unity in 'psychics' and the theory of induction and probability derivable from it?

Philosophy and Keynes's economics

Keynes makes the hypothesis the foundation of his approach to economic modelling. He treats human nature as the product of circumstances and as changing with them. This ontological premise is combined with the psychological premise that there are 'insane and irrational springs of wickedness in most men' (CWXd: 447). Combined, these premises mean that the degree and form of the irrationality present in economic behaviour vary with the social context in which individuals develop and live.

Within capitalist economies, however, they are all variants of the general form of irrationality Keynes calls 'the essential characteristic of capitalism', namely, 'the dependence upon an intense appeal to the money-making and money-loving instincts of individuals as the main motive force of the economic machine' (CWIXb: 293). In 'Economic possibilities for our grandchildren', he looks forward to a time when the 'instinct of Avarice'[9] – 'the love of money as a possession' – that dominates capitalist motivation 'will be recognised for what it is, a somewhat disgusting morbidity, one of those semi-criminal, semi-pathological propensities which one hands over with a shudder to the specialists in mental disease' (CWIXe: 329).[10]

This psychological aspect of the foundations of Keynes's economics means that it is a mistake to interpret him as treating all economic behaviour as rational where 'rational' is interpreted in accordance with his philosophical treatment of rational degrees of belief in *A Treatise on Probability* and elsewhere. Keynes very explicitly and frequently claims that much economic belief and behaviour is not merely not rational in this sense, it is *irrational*. For instance, in *A Treatise on Money* he says of participants in financial markets that:

> the vast majority of those who are concerned with the buying and selling of securities know almost nothing whatever about what they are doing. They do not possess even the rudiments of what is

required for a valid judgment, and are the prey of hopes and fears easily aroused by transient events and as easily dispelled. This is one of the odd characteristics of the capitalist system under which we live, which, when we are dealing with the real world, is not to be overlooked.

(CWVI: 323)

Keynes does allow for some rational belief and behaviour, however. Explicitly (for example, CWVII: 383) and implicitly, he treats his own philosophical and economic beliefs – for example, his 'general theory of employment, interest and money' – as rational. He also allows for rational behaviour in his economics.[11] An important instance is rational 'speculation'. This illustrates the application of his philosophical conception of rational degrees of belief and rational behaviour to economics. Here, however, the application is to rationally forecasting the *irrational* behaviour of others. This is what Keynes means by rational speculation. It is 'the activity of forecasting the psychology of the market' (*ibid.*: 158). Given the influence of this psychology on prices in financial markets, it pays the 'wisest' participants in such markets 'to anticipate mob psychology rather than the real trend of events, and to ape unreason proleptically' (CWVI: 323).

Organic unity and economic modelling

In his essay on Marshall, Keynes picks out as demonstrating 'the profundity of his [Marshall's] insight into the true character of his subject in its highest and most useful developments' (CWXc: 188) Marshall's assumption that 'man himself is in a great measure a creature of circumstances and changes with them' (Marshall, as quoted in *ibid.*: 196).

Keynes ties this aspect of Marshall's approach to Marshall's critical view of certain uses of mathematical and statistical methods in economics. Marshall criticized those uses that overlook the fact that interdependence is organic. The fact of organic interdependence does not entirely rule out use of such methods; it does, however, severely restrict it. This is the philosophic basis for the contrast Keynes draws between the methods conventional in physics and those appropriate in economics (see, for example, *ibid.*: 186–7, CWXe: 260–2, CWVII: 297–8, CWXIVb: 295–7, 299–301).

In his criticisms of Tinbergen's early work in econometrics, for instance, Keynes insists that it is a mistake to attempt to construct economics on the basis of 'the pseudo-analogy with the physical sciences'. The approach of the latter involves a 'habit of mind', a kind of 'logic' (the kind studied in 'human logic'), 'directly counter to the habit of mind which is most important for an economist proper to acquire' (*ibid.*: 300). The main characteristic of the material of economics which makes atomism inappropriate is the lack of continuity in the data arising from the fact that the relation of individuals to the data is constantly changing, that is, from the fact of organic unity, of internal relations.[12]

Keynes repeatedly stresses this fact of organic unity in his discussions of the requirements for rational induction in economics. His treatment of this unity implicitly gives it the form that makes it consistent with the possibility of rational induction. In particular, he assumes factors can be divided into those which are 'semi-permanent or relatively constant' and those that are 'transitory or fluctuating':

> Put broadly, the most important condition ['for the inductive transition'] is that the environment in all relevant respects, other than the fluctuations in those factors of which we take particular account, should be uniform and homogeneous over a period of time.
>
> (CWXIVe: 316)

> Economics is a science of thinking in terms of models joined to the art of choosing models which are relevant to the contemporary world. It is compelled to be this, because, unlike the typical natural science, the material to which it is applied is, in too many respects, not homogeneous through time. The object of a model is to segregate the semi-permanent or relatively constant factors from those which are transitory or fluctuating so as to develop a logical way of thinking about the latter, and of understanding the time sequences to which they give rise in particular cases.
>
> (CWXIVb: 296–7)

This is Keynes's methodological approach in *The General Theory* (CWVII: 245–7). He uses the word 'given' to designate factors he intends to treat as relatively constant. These are, however, only *relatively* constant; over longer periods of time, allowance must be made for the possibility of changes in them. Analysis must take account of the fact that 'actual psychology and ways of behaving and deciding' change both cross-culturally and over time (CWXIII: 433). On the hypothesis of organic unity, such changes reflect changes in social relations, for example in family and work relations.

To apply the framework of Keynes's analysis to Japan, for instance, requires a profound knowledge not only of the actual facts of industry and trade in Japan but also of the relation of individuals in Japan to those facts, a relation determined by the culturally specific character of those individuals. In sharp contrast to the approach now dominant in economics, Keynes provides merely the 'bare bones' of an analysis, bones that require fleshing out to be made applicable to a particular set of facts in a particular time and place.[13]

Keynes's account of rational speculation illustrates his treatment of 'fundamental psychological factors' as irrational and as the product of organic unity. This account also illustrates his application of his final philosophical conception of probability and induction to his economics.

Rational speculation

In *The General Theory* (CWVII: 158), Keynes defines speculation as 'the activity of forecasting the psychology of the market'. He does not assume that all speculators are rational. He claims, for instance, that Wall Street is dominated by both speculation and irrationality, that is, that much speculation there is carried on irrationally. He also allows, however, for rational speculation.

In fact, in another definition of 'speculator', he narrows the meaning to rational speculation. In a memorandum of 8 May 1938 for the Estates Committee of King's College, Cambridge, on the outcome of his management, as Bursar, of the College's investment funds, Keynes defines the 'speculator' as 'one who runs risks of which he is aware' (CWXII: 109). This contrasts with the 'investor', the ordinary financial market participant, 'who runs risks of which he is unaware'. Implicit in this distinction is the idea that speculation in *The General Theory* sense can be rational, that it can be based on knowledge of 'risks'. Keynes introduces this definition to characterize his own investment policy as manager of the College funds.

How does the object of rational speculation, 'the psychology of the market', meet the requirements, spelled out in Keynes's explicit philosophical writings, for rational induction and forecasting embodying rational degrees of belief? Keynes's claim is that the psychology is irrational in a predictable way. As I pointed out above, in *A Treatise on Money*, having claimed, as we have seen, that 'the vast majority of those who are concerned with the buying and selling of securities know almost nothing whatever about what they are doing',[14] he goes on to claim that this means it will profit the 'wisest' participants in such markets to focus on rational speculation, that is, 'to anticipate mob psychology rather than the real trend of events, and to ape unreason proleptically' (CWVI: 323).

What we require philosophically for this possibility to exist is a 'real potentiality' of the kind outlined above. In Keynes's language, this is created in part by 'psychological factors' that can be treated as sufficiently stable to enable us to make limited generalizations about the behaviour issuing from them. For such factors to be rationally taken as stable, we must have grounds in our direct knowledge of their organic embeddedness for reasonably believing that the factors will be preserved into, and hence continue to govern behaviour in, the future we wish to forecast. Since such givenness is always strictly limited, rational forecasting of this kind will be restricted to a relatively short period into the future. Keynes claims that the forecasting involved in rational speculation is short run: 'so long as the crowd can be relied on to act in a certain way, even if it is misguided, it will be to the advantage of the better-informed professional to act in the same way – a short period ahead' (*ibid.*: 324). Rational speculators are not interested in 'distant events' because they 'have no intention of holding the securities long enough for the influence of distant events to have its effect' (*ibid.*: 323). In *The General Theory*, this short run is put at 'three months or a year hence' (CWVII: 155).[15]

So far as this short run is concerned, Keynes implicitly assumes that the 'real potentiality' associated with the psychology of financial markets has the character required for rational induction and prediction and for rational estimates of probabilities. In both *A Treatise on Money* and *The General Theory*, he implicitly claims that the inductive generalizations about 'unreason' on which rational speculation is based can be rationally grounded in experience.

In *A Treatise on Money*, Keynes says that 'speculators' (who make money by 'aping unreason proleptically') form their expectations 'on the basis of past experience of the trend of mob psychology' (CWVI: 323). This claim that in some circumstances 'the crowd can be relied on to act in a certain way', so that forecasts of 'mob psychology' can be rationally grounded in experience and made the basis for rational speculation, is repeated in *The General Theory*: 'The professional investor [the "specu-lator"] is forced to concern himself with the anticipation of impending changes, in the news or in the atmosphere, of the kind by which experi-ence shows that the mass psychology of the market is most influenced' (CWVII: 155).

A particular inductive generalization about mass psychology that Keynes employs both in his economics and in his own practice as a spec-ulator is that 'day-to-day fluctuations in the profits of existing investments, which are obviously of an ephemeral and non-significant character, tend to have an altogether excessive, and even an absurd, influence on the market' (*ibid.*: 153). Another, pointed to in a letter of 10 April 1940 to F. C. Scott, is that 'very few American investors buy any stock for the sake of something which is going to happen more than six months hence, even though its probability is exceedingly high; and it is out of taking advantage of this psychological peculiarity of theirs that most money is made' (CWXII: 78).

As this last quotation demonstrates, Keynes also assumes that rational speculation can be based on rational calculations of probability. It is possible to know that the probability 'of something which is going to happen more than six months hence ... is exceedingly high'. At times, Keynes claims that a particular outcome is close to certain. He says this, for instance, of the likelihood of a future fall of US interest rates in the early 1930s (CWXXI: 113, 319). In this case, the opportunity for certain profit arises in part from the fact that

> almost everyone who has any pretensions to being a sound or orthodox thinker on financial problems in New York probably has his brain stuffed with fallacies on this particular matter. So there is an opportunity for anyone, if there is anyone, who can think (or so it seems to me) scientifically straight on this issue.
>
> (*ibid.*: 320)

These probabilities change as real potentiality changes. This is the basis in philosophy and ontology for Keynes's advocacy of an 'active investment policy':[16]

> Particularly in these days, no one is so wise that he can foresee the future far ahead. Anyone who obstinately takes up the view that over the next twenty years the rate of interest is bound to fall, or is bound to rise, is going beyond the evidence. If he is to be wisely guided he must take a shorter view and be prepared constantly to change it as the tide of events ebbs and flows.
>
> (CWXII: 243)[17]

His discussions of rational investment policy constantly reiterate this point. In a letter of 7 June 1938 to F. C. Scott he says: 'The whole art [of investment policy] is to vary the centre of gravity of one's portfolio according to circumstances' (*ibid.*: 68).

We also find Keynes making use in this context of his *A Treatise on Probability* concept of 'weight'. Where weight – 'confidence' – is low, the appropriate strategy is to avoid taking a 'decided view'. Reporting to the Annual Meeting of the National Mutual Society in January 1926, Keynes, believing that in the long run interest rates would have to fall but concerned that the restoration of the Gold Standard at the pre-war parity would force a short-term increase to maintain external balance, claims:

> Success in the investment of insurance funds mainly depends on anticipating, so far as possible, the course of the rate of interest. Unforeseen fluctuation in this rate is the one factor which is capable of seriously upsetting our calculations. If only we knew for certain what the course of the rate of interest was going to be, whether high or low, we could act without hesitation. But as things are, it is partic-ularly difficult to take up a confident attitude.
>
> (*ibid.*: 144)

In a letter of 15 August 1934 to F. C. Scott (see also the 6 February 1942 letter; *ibid.*: 81–3), he invokes this idea of 'confidence' as completeness of the evidence on which rational degrees of belief are based to explain why he thinks 'it is a mistake to think that one limits one's risks by spreading too much between enterprises about which one knows little and has no reason for special confidence':

> As time goes on I get more and more convinced that the right method in investment is to put fairly large sums into enterprises which one thinks one knows something about and in the management of which one thoroughly believes. It is a mistake to think that one limits one's risks by spreading too much between enterprises about which one knows little and has no reason for special confidence. Obviously this principle ought not to be carried too far. The real limitation, however, on its application in practice is in my experience the small number of enterprises about which at any given time one feels in this way. One's knowledge and experience are definitely limited and there are seldom more than two or three enterprises at any given time in which I personally feel myself entitled to put *full confidence*.
>
> (*ibid.*: 57)

In Keynes's theory and practice of rational speculation, therefore, we find deployed the full array of concepts found in his mature philosophy of induction and probability. These include many aspects of the argument found in *A Treatise on Probability*. These aspects, however, are now anchored in the hypothesis of 'organic unity'.

Conclusion

I have argued that Keynes abandoned the two key foundational ideas of *A Treatise on Probability*: the atomic hypothesis and the idea of logical probability relations. He replaced these ideas with the hypothesis of organic unity, a hypothesis that provides the foundation for A. N. Whitehead's alternative theory of induction and probability. Whitehead claimed that this alternative could answer the questions which Keynes had raised in the *Treatise* both about the hypothesis and about Whitehead's frequency theory of probability. These changes in the foundations left much of the superstructure of Keynes's *Treatise* argument intact. In particular, the following aspects were preserved: an objective rational basis for induction and probability; the dependence of rational degrees of belief on relevant evidence; the variation of rational degrees of belief with variations in this evidence including variations in its ultimate source, 'real potentiality' and its 'truth frequencies'; the relevance of the *Treatise* concept of 'weight' as a measure of the completeness of the evidence; and the possibility that the amount of evidence available might be insufficient to ground numerical estimates so that rational estimates could be non-numerical. They also created a ground in ontology for Keynes's claim that, particularly with respect to the long-run consequences aimed at in the accumulation of wealth, the amount of relevant evidence is frequently so small that 'there is no scientific basis on which to form any calculable probability whatever. We simply do not know.'

The relation of these ideas to Keynes's economics is illustrated by the foundational role they play in his understanding of the methods of economics and by their implicit use in his treatment of rational 'speculation'. The latter illustration also demonstrates the key part played in Keynes's economics by the idea that the 'essential characteristic of capitalism' is the 'dependence upon an intense appeal to the money-making and money-loving instincts of individuals as the main motive force of the economic machine'. In 1930, Keynes prophesied that, in a more enlightened future when we would be able to afford to enquire more curiously into the 'true character' of this 'purposiveness' than was then 'safe', it would be seen to be 'one of those semi-criminal, semi-pathological propensities which one hands over with a shudder to the specialists in mental disease'.

The seventy years that have passed since Keynes made this prophecy have seen enormous improvements in our scientific and technical knowledge. Our continuing inability to make full and effective use of this knowledge to put 'the economic problem' behind us and get on with solving 'our real problems – the problems of life and of human relations, of creation and behaviour and religion' (CWIX: xviii) – has made the enquiry that Keynes looked forward to so many years ago a vital present necessity.

Throughout his life, Keynes urged that, whatever grounds there might be in the present for pessimism, we could and should always take heart from rational 'faith' in the 'optimistic hypothesis'. For him, as for many others, the highest expression of this faith was the Enlightenment faith in the ability of human reason ultimately to overcome all resistance, including the resistance anchored in our own irrational 'instincts'. It is this faith that informs the optimistic prophecy that concludes *The General Theory*:

> if the ideas are correct – an hypothesis on which the author himself must necessarily base what he writes – it would be a mistake, I predict, to dispute their potency over a period of time ... soon or late, it is ideas, not vested interests, which are dangerous for good or evil.
>
> (CWVII: 383–4)

Notes

1 In accepting important aspects of Ramsey's approach to 'everything else' (that is, everything outside the field of formal logic) including degrees of belief, Keynes is, with Ramsey, rejecting Wittgenstein's 'solution', which was 'to regard everything else as a sort of inspired nonsense, having great value indeed for the individual, but incapable of being exactly discussed' (CWXa: 338). This strikes me as fatal to attempts, of which there have been several (see, for example, Carabelli 1988; Coates 1996; Cottrell 1993), to find parallels between Keynes's mature philosophical views and Wittgenstein's.

2 Keynes describes human logic as 'a sort of logic' concerned with the analysis of certain 'useful mental habits' we have 'for handling the material with which we are supplied by our perceptions and by our memory and perhaps in other ways, *and so arriving at or towards truth*' (my emphasis).

3 The description of 'what men actually believe' differed from this; it was 'descriptive psychology' rather than human logic. Ramsey proposed a system based on betting for doing this. The interpretive literature on Keynes frequently ignores the fact that this system is a method of 'descriptive psychology' rather than of human logic. The mistaken implication is then drawn that human logic designates a subjective rather than an objective approach to probability. (Both sides of the interpretive debate over the implications of the paragraph just quoted make this error. See, *inter alia*, Bateman (1987), Davis (1994b), O'Donnell (1989) and Runde (1994b).) As I pointed out in the preceding note, however, Keynes well understood that by human logic Ramsey meant something different from descriptive psychology and, in particular, that he meant a field of study able to provide objective rational grounds for degrees of belief: 'in attempting to distinguish a "human" logic from formal logic on the one hand and descriptive psychology on the other, Ramsey may have been pointing the way to the next field of study when formal logic has been put into good order and its highly limited scope properly defined' (CWXa: 339).

4 The defining concept of this hypothesis is 'internal relations'. I explain what this means below.

5 Atomic individualism needs to be distinguished from individualism *per se*. Much writing on methodology, for example, on so-called 'methodological individualism', implicitly and mistakenly identifies individualism with atomic individualism. Keynes, though he abandoned atomic individualism, remained philosophically an 'individualist' in the sense of 'Paley's *dictum* that "although we speak of communities as of sentient beings and ascribe to them happiness and misery, desires, interests and passions, nothing really exists or feels but *individuals*" ' (CWXd: 449).

6 Seeking 'to understand how in fact the human mind can successfully set to work for the gradual definition of its habitual ideas' (1933: 145; see also 1929: 106), Whitehead finds the answer in 'logic in the broadest sense of that term – the logic of discovery' (Whitehead 1958: 67–71). This 'logic' locates rational grounds for adopting particular 'habitual ideas' in 'direct intuitive observation'.

7 'All knowledge is derived from, and verified by, direct intuitive observation. I accept this axiom of empiricism as stated in this general form' (Whitehead 1948: 177; see also 1929: 39, 1938: 112).

8 Real potentiality can be divided into a set of 'cases of equal probability'. For any particular proposition about the future whose probability we wish to estimate, some of these cases will be 'favourable', that is, in them the proposition will be true, and some will be 'unfavourable', that is, in these the proposition will be false. The probability of the proposition is its 'truth

frequency', the ratio of favourable to total cases in real potentiality divided into a set of cases of this kind (Whitehead 1929: 201–2).

9 This phrase appears in the material from Keynes's unpublished writings published in O'Donnell (1992: 807–12).

10 For detailed discussions of the psychological foundations of Keynes's economics, see Winslow (1986b, 1990, 1993c, 1995).

11 Typically, interpreters of Keynes's economics assume he attributes rationality in this sense to long-run expectations of future yield from capital assets. In my judgment this interpretation is mistaken. First, Keynes assumes long-run yields are 'fundamentally uncertain' (for example, CWXIVa: 113, CWXXIX: 294). They cannot be rationally predicted. As has been pointed out by Meeks (1991), the *Treatise* sets out the rational response to fundamental uncertainty. It is to accept that no foundation is available for rational forecasting and 'to allow caprice to determine us and to waste no time on the debate' (CWVIII: 32). Elsewhere (CWIX: xviii, CWXXVII: 445–6), Keynes adds to this acting on the 'optimistic hypothesis'. The rational ground for doing so is that collective action based on this 'faith' tends to be self-justifying.

In the case of fundamentally uncertain yields, however, Keynes assumes that most people are psychologically unable to face the fact of fundamental uncertainty. The reason he gives for this is that consciousness of the fact provokes paralysing anxiety. Most people therefore deal with the fact irrationally through *denial*. They employ irrational forecasting 'conventions' to predict what is in fact unpredictable.

12 Whitehead (1968: 105–7) provides a succinct account of the limitations placed on the use of any form of deductive reasoning that makes use of the logical idea of the 'variable' (for example, algebra) by the fact of internal relations. He does this in the context of disconnecting the methods of 'human logic' from 'deduction', that is, from formal logic. One important source of Marshall's acquaintance with the idea of internal relations and with its relevance for social theory, a source pointed to by Marshall himself in a passage in the *Principles* (Marshall 1961: vol. I, 762–4) stressing both the fact of internal social relations and its critical importance for method in economics, is Hegel. This gives one of the main senses in which, as Marshall says in the preface, Hegel's *Philosophy of History* can be said to be one of 'two kinds of influences' which 'have affected, more than any other, the substance of the views expressed in the present book' (Marshall 1961: vol. I, ix).

13 'Marshall … arrived very early at the point of view that the bare bones of economic theory are not worth much in themselves and do not carry one far in the direction of useful, practical conclusions. The whole point lies in applying them to the interpretation of current economic life. This requires a profound knowledge of the actual facts of industry and trade. But these, and the relation of individual men to them, are constantly and rapidly changing' (CWXc: 196). Whitehead (for example, 1967b: Ch. VI) emphasizes this same point and criticizes, as does Marshall, the approach of earlier economists such as Adam Smith for ignoring it.

14 This claim is repeated in *The General Theory*. Conventional forecasting practices are said to produce 'conventional valuations' which are 'the outcome of the mass psychology of a large number of ignorant individuals' (CWVII: 154).

15 At some point after January 1924 (the date of an Independent Investment Company prospectus which describes the company's investment policy as a 'credit cycling' policy (CWXII: 33)), Keynes made a significant change in his investment policy (*ibid.*: 100–1, 106–9). He moved from an approach based on 'credit cycling' to one based on 'intrinsic value'. The latter involved looking significantly farther ahead into the future than the former and, on this basis,

holding securities for longer periods of time. 'Intrinsic value' was discoverable by looking farther ahead than market psychology was able to look and in this way foreseeing future events which, when they occurred, would, given the conventional reaction of market psychology to them, produce a predictable effect on the market value of the security. The 'intrinsic value' policy remained, therefore, a policy of rational 'speculation'.

16 As I indicated in the previous note, Keynes changed his investment policy at some point after 1924 from a 'credit cycling' to an 'intrinsic value' policy. The latter involved holding securities for a longer period than the former. It was, however, still very much an 'active' investment policy.

17 In a discussion of a particular psychological phenomenon in American financial markets, Keynes points to the general principle of induction involved:

> the prejudice of investors and investing institutions in favour of bonds as being 'safe' and against common stocks as having, even the best of them, a 'speculative' flavour, has led to a relative over-valuation of bonds and an under-valuation of common stocks. It is dangerous, however, to apply to the future inductive arguments based on past experience, unless one can distinguish the broad reasons why past experience was what it was. Otherwise, there is a danger of expecting results in the future which could only follow from the special conditions which have existed in the United States during the past fifty years.
>
> (CWXII: 247–8)

12 Keynes's realist orientation

Tony Lawson

Introduction

In recent years an increasing number of economists have come to appreciate the relevance of ontology to a social science such as economics. By this I mean that they have recognized the importance of investigating the nature of social material or social being, and of taking their findings on this into account in determining methods of analysis efficacious with respect to social phenomena. Theories of the nature and structure of the material domain of reality are usually designated forms of (ontological) realism. My concern here is with the fashioning of realist theories for economics.

An obvious advantage of projects that engage thus in ontology is that frequently they are able both to pinpoint and also to transcend the errors of *a priori* (or arbitrarily) based programmes. One such *a priori* programme is the current (extraordinarily dominant) mainstream project in economics. There is no doubt that the latter is largely unsuccessful, of course, even on its own terms. It fails as an explanatory and/or predictive project and is riddled with theory/practice inconsistencies (see the evidence in Lawson (1997a)). Until recently, most commentators sought the explanation for this failure in that project's substantive theories (such as its theories of rationality or equilibrium). In the past few years, however, it has become clear to many that the central problems stem instead from its history of ontological neglect. In the absence of explicit ontological analysis, methods have been adopted by mainstream economists on some conventional or *a priori* basis quite inappropriate (as it turns out) for addressing social phenomena.

Specifically, methods of mainstream economics are chosen largely on the criterion that they facilitate formalistic modelling. This criterion is accepted for no better reason than that formalistic methods are perceived (erroneously as it happens) to form the basis of the successful natural sciences. This basis for adopting such methods is as justified in logic as is using a pneumatic drill to make a hole in a piece of paper just because it has proven successful at making a hole in the road. To make a hole in the paper we need to take account of the nature of paper. To fashion methods for social science we need to take account of the nature of social material.

To do this is to engage in ontology. Any theory of ontology so derived is a realist theory.

If in recent years there has been an increasing recognition, at least by some heterodox economists, both that (1) explicit ontological analysis is essential to fashioning a successful social science, just as (2) ontological neglect explains in some part the failures of modern economics, this recognition, however, is not altogether novel. I would suggest, in fact, that most of those who have made a lasting contribution to the subject of economics (as a successfully explanatory discipline) have adopted such an ontological orientation more or less explicitly, even if never making reference to 'ontology' as a specific category. I am thinking here of the likes of Hayek, Keynes, Marshall, Marx, Menger and Veblen, among others. In this chapter I want to focus upon Keynes. Let me call an explicit orientation to ontological issues such as I am identifying a *realist orientation*. I shall be imputing to Keynes such an orientation. I shall also suggest that although Keynes's substantive theories were continuously revised, his *realist orientation* remained paramount throughout his substantial writings.

My basic thesis, then, is precisely that Keynes continually engaged in ontology, and that this realist orientation marks a distinctive, enduring, as well as fundamental, aspect of his contribution. Now my specific brief here (my precise invitation from the editors) is to make connections between *A Treatise on Probability* and *The General Theory*. The special case of my thesis relevant here, then, is just that a realist orientation underpins, indeed is essential to, both these contributions.

However, my focus in this chapter has to be broader than these two works. In the first place, Keynes's realist orientation is not only in evidence before he started *A Treatise on Probability*, it also explains why he embarked on *A Treatise on Probability* at all. In the second place, the methodological orientation and thinking of Keynes at the time of writing *The General Theory* is not stated explicitly within that publication, but revealed in correspondence and reviews whose publication roughly coincided with it. Thus this suggested commonality of the two books in question, that is, Keynes's realist orientation, can be better recognized by way of also considering briefly some of his other writings of the relevant periods. Let me elaborate.

The early period

In 1903, during Keynes's first year of study in Cambridge, G. E. Moore's *Principia Ethica* was published. This book had a big effect on Keynes who wrote many (mostly still unpublished) philosophical papers in reaction to it. In essence, Moore put forward an ethical theory of 'being good' and a theory of moral behaviour or 'doing good'. Briefly stated, Moore advanced (1) the ethical theory that certain things

– for example (and especially), personal affection and aesthetic enjoyment – can be known to be good by intuition, and (2) the moral claim that right action or duty entails adopting those strategies which appear to bring about the greatest amount of universal good, both immediately and also over the future.

Keynes, in fact, took issue with Moore on both accounts, and even wondered if 'being good' and 'doing good', Moore's ethics and morality, could be reconciled one with the other. Here, though, I want merely to focus on Keynes's reaction to Moore's account of proper conduct, of 'doing good'. It turns upon how Moore supposes we can determine the set of actions that will bring about the greatest universal good. According to Moore, we cannot be sure which action is best in this sense. Rather, we must follow that which seems *probably* right in maximizing universal good. To determine which is 'probably right', two conditions must be met. First, the course of action must, as far as we can tell, be that which will produce the best result in the near future. Secondly, we must have certain knowledge that pursuing actions that are right as far as we can see produces a total good result over the indefinite future more often than not. On this basis Moore supposes that following general moral rules (like, 'do not kill') is to be recommended.

Ethics in relation to conduct

In an as yet still unpublished paper, 'Ethics in relation to conduct' (1904), Keynes questions in particular the second of these requirements. The problem identified by Keynes is that Moore's programme for moral conduct is premised on the relevance of a relative frequency theory of probability. In Keynes's view, the nature of reality, including the future, is such that a relative frequency basis for knowledge is unjustified. In the language of today, the relative frequency approach presupposes a closed system (see, for example, Lawson 1997a). Keynes in effect rejects the relevance of this as a general specification of the world in which we live. Here, then, we see Keynes's stance underpinned by ontological reasoning. As we would put it now, Keynes is recognizing that the world is open whereas Moore's strictures on conduct presuppose (for the relative frequency approach to be valid) that it is everywhere closed.

How, though, is moral conduct to proceed in an open system? This translates to the question of how to act in conditions of uncertainty, an issue that was to occupy Keynes over and again for the remainder of his career. At the time of replying to Moore, Keynes, as I say, was concerned with Moore's supposition that probability judgments could be achieved using the theory of (stable) relative frequencies. It was in rejecting this assumption and attempting to replace this theory of probability with a more grounded judgmental account that Keynes started work on what would eventually become his *A Treatise on Probability*.

A Treatise on Probability

My purpose here is not to outline, let alone defend, Keynes's theory of probability as set out in the *Treatise*. Rather, I merely want to indicate that, after rejecting Moore's recommendations on ontological grounds, despite never mentioning the category (and indeed despite even describing his own contribution as one to epistemology), Keynes sets out to ground his alternative in ontology. In this he adopts, in effect, what I am here referring to as a *realist orientation*.

Most obviously, in examining whether the inductive methods he is interested in can be justified, he seeks to determine the implicit ontological presuppositions of contemporary natural scientists. Here we can see that he is most unusual among economists in questioning the ontological presumptions of the methods of science. He writes:

> The kind of fundamental assumption about the character of material laws, on which scientists appear commonly to act, seems to me to be much less simple than the bare principle of uniformity. They appear to assume something much more like what mathematicians call the principle of the superposition of small effects, or, as I prefer to call it, in this connection, the *atomic* character of natural law. The system of the material universe must consist, if this kind of assumption is warranted, of bodies which we may term (without any implication as to their size being conveyed thereby) *legal atoms*, such that each of them exercises its own separate, independent, and invariable effect, a change of the total state being compounded of a number of separate changes each of which is solely due to a separate portion of the preceding state. We do not have an invariable relation between particular bodies, but nevertheless each has on the others its own separate and invariable effect, which does not change with changing circumstances, although, of course, the total effect may be changed to almost any extent if all the other accompanying causes are different. Each atom can, according to this theory, be treated as a separate cause and does not enter into different organic combinations in each of which it is regulated by different laws.
>
> (CWVIII: 276–7)

Interestingly, while drawing attention to this assumption of the atomic character of natural law, Keynes is simultaneously raising the logical possibility that not all natural phenomena need be atomic. To the extent that some are not, then clearly the methods of natural scientists that presuppose atomicity cannot be accepted as universally applicable:

> The scientist wishes, in fact, to assume that the occurrence of a phenomenon which has appeared as part of a more complex phenomenon, may be *some* reason for expecting it to be associated on

another occasion with part of the same complex. Yet if different wholes were subject to laws *quâ* wholes and not simply on account of and in proportion to the differences of their parts, knowledge of a part could not lead, it would seem, even to presumptive or probable knowledge as to its association with other parts. Given, on the other hand, a number of legally atomic units and the laws connecting them, it would be possible to deduce their effects *pro tanto* without an exhaustive knowledge of all the coexisting circumstances.

(*ibid.*: 277–8)

As I say, I am not here concerned with Keynes's explicit conclusions concerning method, merely the manner in which he reaches them. In this, ontology figures quite fundamentally, especially in his defence of his theory of induction.

Keynes, in fact, is concerned with identifying a set of conditions to validate the use of inductive methods, a set which encompasses, but does not reduce to, that subset which validates induction in the context of material causation. Keynes speculates that scientists have previously tended to restrict inductive methods to material causation on ontological grounds, that the reason scientists often hold 'that we ought to limit inductive methods to the content of the particular material universe in which we live, is, most probably, the fact that we can easily imagine a universe so constructed that such methods would be useless' (*ibid.*: 272). In pursuing a more general set of conditions Keynes, of course, is also concerned that the conditions thus specified are such that the probability calculus can be legitimately employed.

Keynes builds into his system an assumption of a *limitation of independent variety*. This assumption amounts to the restriction that the number of *ultimate constituents* or *indefinables* of the system, on the basis of which other members are 'generated', together with the *laws of necessary connection*, must be finite (*ibid*: 279–88). I shall not go into details here (but see Lawson 1989). For the pertinent point is clear: in his approach Keynes seeks at all times to ground method in the nature, structure or properties of the system to which the method in question (here induction) is to be applied. Keynes everywhere maintains, in effect, that a method can reasonably be adopted only if its implicit ontological presuppositions matched the nature of the material to which it is to be applied.

As a final indication of Keynes's persistent realist orientation at this time let me recall the observations and reflections with which Keynes concludes *A Treatise on Probability*:

The physicists of the nineteenth century have reduced matter to the collisions and arrangements of particles, between which the ultimate qualitative differences are very few; and the Mendelian biologists are deriving the various qualities of men from the collisions and arrangements of chromosomes. In both cases the analogy with the perfect game of chance is really present; and the validity of some current modes of inference may depend on the assumption that it is to material of this kind that we are applying them. Here, though I have sometimes complained at their want of logic, I am in fundamental sympathy with the deep underlying conceptions of the statistical theory of the day. If the contemporary doctrines of biology and physics remain tenable, we may have a remarkable, if undeserved, justification of some of the methods of the traditional calculus of probabilities. Professors of probability have been often and justly derided for arguing as if nature were an urn containing blacked and white balls in fixed proportions. Quetelet once declared in so many words – 'l'urne que nous interrogeons, c'est la nature'. But again in the history of science the methods of astrology may prove useful to the astronomer; and it may turn out to be true – reversing Quetelet's expression – that 'La nature que nous interrogeons, c'est une urne'.

(*ibid*.: 468)

Moving towards *The General Theory*

If ontological analysis is pervasive in, and indeed essential to, Keynes's reasoning in *A Treatise on Probability*, it also very much underpins his methodological conclusions thereafter. That is not to say that his ontological assessments are necessarily fixed over time, only that they figure repeatedly; ontological assessments remained significant for Keynes in conditioning his various positions on method.

We can note, first, that if in the early years of the twentieth century Keynes seems somewhat non-committal regarding the extent to which the material of the natural world can be regarded as atomic, by the mid-1920s he is reasonably definite in his view that social phenomena cannot be. Thus, in his 1926 biography of Edgeworth, Keynes writes:

The atomic hypothesis which has worked so splendidly in Physics breaks down in Psychics. We are faced at every turn with the problems of Organic Unity, of Discreteness, of Discontinuity – the whole is not equal to the sum of the parts, comparisons of quantity fail us, small changes produce large effects, the assumption of a uniform and homogeneous continuum are not satisfied ...

(CWXe: 286)

As is well known, *The General Theory of Employment, Interest and Money* is a text not on philosophy/methodology but on economics. It contains very little explicit methodological reflection. As such, Keynes's realist orientation must be mostly reconstructed. But this is easily achieved, as I can briefly (albeit only very briefly) indicate.

An obvious place on which to focus here is Chapter 12, concerned with the buying and selling of financial assets on the stock market in conditions of fundamental uncertainty. For this is immediately recognizable as remarkably similar in orientation to his earlier work in dealing with moral conduct under similar circumstances of fundamental uncertainty, the latter reflecting the openness of social reality. In Chapter 12, as is well known, Keynes seeks to identify those structures that make economic conduct possible. Specifically, Keynes identifies certain conventions and psychological dispositions among the major causes or conditions of action. The important point here, though, is that Keynes does not suppose that such factors can be analysed formalistically. A legitimate use of formalistic modelling presupposes a closed system, a ubiquity of event regularities. Always mindful that the world in effect is open, or so I want to suggest, this ontological assessment accounts for Keynes's recognition of the methodological limitations on this score, facing both (i) agents within the economy:

> We are merely reminding ourselves that human decisions affecting the future, whether personal or political or economic, cannot depend on strict mathematical expectation, since the basis for making such calculations does not exist; and that it is our innate urge to activity which makes the wheels go round, our rational selves choosing between the alternatives the best we are able, calculating where we can, but often falling back for our motive on whim or sentiment or chance.
>
> (CWVII: 163)

and also (ii) economists addressing the economy:

> Too large a proportion of recent 'mathematical' economics are merely concoctions, as imprecise as the initial assumptions they rest on, which allow the author to lose sight of the complexity and inter-dependencies of the real world in a maze of pretentious and unhelpful symbols.
>
> (*ibid.*: 298)

Defending my interpretation

At this point I should perhaps address a likely objection to the position that I am putting forward. It may well be accepted that the aspects of *The General Theory* to which I am pointing indicate that Keynes accepted the social world to be open (event regularities facilitating legitimate mathematical modelling are not ubiquitous) and structured (irreducible to the actual course of events). But the most I can claim to be demonstrating here, it may be said, is that an open system ontology is *implicit* in

Keynes's thinking. However, I suppose myself to be arguing something stronger: that Keynes maintained a *realist orientation*, that is, an *explicit* orientation to ontological analysis. Specifically, I am claiming to demonstrate that (unlike, say, modern mainstream economists) Keynes was aware of his ontological conception when fashioning substantive theories and methods, etc.

Now it is true that in indicating briefly how Keynes's comments in *The General Theory* reveal a commitment to an open world, I do not *thereby* establish that explicit ontological reflection informs Keynes's substantive theorizing and method. After all, it is just as easily shown that mainstream economics also (and like all methods and approaches, etc.) presupposes an implicit ontology of some kind – in the case of mainstream economics of atomism and closure (see Lawson 1997a). But I certainly do not want to argue thereby that this ontology of the mainstream *explicitly* informs their methods. On the contrary, I am arguing that they are forced into such implicit ontological commitments by ignoring explicit ontological analysis and by being guided, instead, by an *a priori* commitment to formalistic modelling, necessitating in turn a reliance upon the deductivist (closed system) explanatory method (again, see Lawson 1997a). How then do I justify the claim that Keynes's substantive contribution and method reflects his adopting explicitly a realist orientation? I offer three arguments for this.

First, at a time when the prevailing academic culture was (as indeed it remains) to fashion formalistic methods whatever the context, any alternative involving a commitment to an ontological conception not conducive to formalistic modelling is likely to have been explicitly formulated in at least some of its aspects. People do not usually swim against the tide unknowingly. Moreover, of course, in such rare cases where explicit methodological comment is found in *The General Theory*, Keynes does, as in the passage reproduced above, explicitly criticize the reliance upon mathematical economics for allowing its perpetrators to 'lose sight of the complexity and inter-dependencies of the real world'.

Secondly, as I have already mentioned, Keynes's manner of addressing the question of uncertainty – an essential element of *The General Theory* – parallels extremely closely his questioning and analysis of the basis of moral conduct in a situation of uncertainty in the early years of the twentieth century. And in this early period of his work, Keynes's ontological thinking is laid out explicitly.

Thirdly, although Keynes's method along with its implicit ontological presuppositions is mostly left implicit in *The General Theory*, his rejection of methods of closed-system modelling is made explicit in other contributions made at roughly the same time. It is especially clear, for example, in his assessment of the likely relevance of econometrics. Let me elaborate this claim.

In recent years, the turn to ontological analysis has shown that the relevance of economic, including econometric, modelling assumes the satisfaction of two conditions: extrinsic and intrinsic closure. The former is that the objects or individuals of analysis be effectively sealed off from non-identified potentially systematic influences on the relevant behaviour being studied/'explained'. The latter is that the objects or individuals of analysis be intrinsically stable and structured - thereby guaranteeing a unique outcome or response to external stimuli, that is, a single exit. These conditions are automatically satisfied if, for example, the objects or individuals of analysis act in a homogeneous environment and are atomistic in nature. And these are precisely the conditions that Keynes identifies as rendering econometrics of use. He rejects econometrics just because he assesses that to assume these conditions are satisfied would not be realistic: they are not part of an adequate ontology for the social realm.

The context in which Keynes makes this ontological assessment is a review of Tinbergen's early econometric work on business cycles. It is clear that fundamental to Keynes's thinking at the time is an assessment that the material of economics is of a nature such that the natural scientific practices and formulae in question are inappropriate to its analysis: 'unlike typical natural science, the material to which [economics] is applied is, in too many respects, not homogeneous through time' (CWXIVb: 296).

And this thinking, as I say, is at the heart of Keynes's assessment of the potential value of econometrics. In an initial response to the League of Nations' invitation to review Tinbergen's work, Keynes writes:

> There is first of all the central question of methodology – the logic of applying the method of multiple correlation to unanalysed economic material, which we know to be non-homogeneous through time. If we are dealing with the action of numerically measurable, independent forces, adequately analysed so that we were dealing with independent atomic factors and between them completely comprehensive, acting with fluctuating relative strength on material constant and homogeneous through time, we might be able to use the method of multiple correlation with some confidence for disentangling the laws of their action ... In fact we know that every one of these conditions is far from being satisfied by the economic material under investigation ... To proceed to some more detailed comments. The coefficients arrived at are apparently assumed to be constant for 10 years or for a larger period. Yet, surely we know that they are not constant. There is no reason at all why they should not be different every year.
>
> (CWXIVf: 285–6)

These sorts of comments are repeated throughout the late 1930s and come to a head in Keynes's eventual 1939 review of Tinbergen's book:

> Put broadly, the most important condition is that the environment in all relevant respects, other than the fluctuations in those factors of which we take particular account, should be uniform and homogeneous over a period of time. We cannot be sure that such conditions will persist in the future, even if we find them in the past. But if we find them in the past, we have at any rate some basis for an inductive argument.

and he adds

> [The] main *prima facie* objection to the application of the method of multiple correlation to complex economic problems lies in the apparent lack of any adequate degree of uniformity in the environment.
>
> (CWXIVe: 316)

Whatever the reader may think about the correctness of Keynes's arguments (and elsewhere I have argued that they are indeed valid; see Lawson (1989, 1997b)), it is clear that in making these assessments Keynes draws on the insights of social ontology. In short, throughout his life's contributions Keynes adopts what I am calling a realist orientation towards science in determining the adequacy of various methods and procedures for social scientific research.

Final comments and conclusion

An alternative way of putting the central contention of this brief chapter is that, in his reflections upon proper (and improper) scientific practice, Keynes sought throughout to avoid a particular fallacy that is committed by the majority of modern economists. This mistake, the *epistemic fallacy*, consists in the view that statements about being can be reduced to, or analysed solely in terms of, statements about knowledge, that matters of ontology can always be translated into epistemological terms. Hume encouraged such a position by using the category of experience to define the world – thus giving an epistemological category an ontological task. In some recent post-modernist writing such a task has been assigned to language or conversation or the text or some such, so that the error might be rephrased as the linguistic fallacy. In mainstream economics, the insistence on conceptualizing reality according to what can be treated using the formalistic procedures of deductivist reasoning (assumed to predominate in the natural sciences) encourages the label of formalistic fallacy.

Can we learn anything from this brief discussion of Keynes? Clearly, the position I want to encourage is that social science, including economics, follow his example and continually modify its methods and practices in the light of better understanding of social material, always remembering that our current state of knowledge is but a contingently valid, fallible set of insights on the path to a better understanding. Of course, put like this, the conclusion seems almost banal, as indicating an obviously desirable goal that no one would want to dispute. Yet seriously embraced, it entails that the overwhelming bulk of contemporary academic economics is open to serious question. It is precisely because of the nature of the modern situation, the all-pervasiveness of its unthinking approach to explanation, including its neglect of explicit ontology in particular, that the very simple point of this chapter warrants repeating, that the identified enduring aspect of Keynes's work deserves more explicit attention.

13 Keynes and transformation

Stephen P. Dunn[1]

Introduction

In his economic writings, Keynes was clearly challenging the Benthamite calculus that underpins much of orthodox economic analysis, placing particular emphasis on the often significant levels of uncertainty surrounding investment decisions. Under conditions of uncertainty decision-makers have to decide what to do on the basis of imagined images of what the future might look like, which raises the possibility that the future may be influenced by the actions of economic actors as guided by their imaginations. On the basis of this possibility some commentators have taken the view that Keynes's contributions endorse the view that social reality is transmutable, that it is not pre-programmed and that aspects of the economic future will in part be created by human action today and in the future (although this future need not be the one intended).

However, there has been little detailed work on the extent to which Keynes's conceptualisation of uncertainty is embedded in a vision of the competitive process as creative in the sense just indicated. Here I attempt to begin to fill this lacuna, arguing that while Keynes appears to have assumed that social reality is transmutable, he overemphasised the impact of activity on financial markets while underestimating the creative potential of capitalism. In the next section I consider briefly the philosophy of practice and action embedded in Keynes's *A Treatise on Probability* (CWVIII). This allows us to consider the link between Keynes's discussion of uncertainty and the notion of animal spirits and enterprise elaborated in *The General Theory* (CWVII) and thereafter, and to assess Keynes's view of the competitive process. This discussion is then further illuminated with reference to his musings on the social system and the processes of capitalism suggested by *The General Theory*. I conclude by noting that aspects of Keynes's discussion of the competitive process need to be further augmented by a philosophy of emergence and transmutability.

Probability as a guide to conduct

It is possible to view *A Treatise on Probability* as an attempt to extend the domain of rational judgment and action to situations of uncertainty. Keynes seeks to challenge and move beyond frequency theories of probability and 'to emphasise the existence of a *logical relation between two sets of propositions* in cases where it is not possible to argue demonstratively from one to the other' (CWVIII: 9). That is to say, Keynes considers the nature of judgments of probability in situations in which one is unable to assign probability ratios to future events, namely under conditions of uncertainty.[2]

According to Keynes, any conclusion or proposition a is related to a given premise or such available evidence h via a probability relation, which can be written as a/h. This probability relation can be thought of as warranting the 'objective' degree of belief that it is rational to hold in any judgment given current knowledge. Keynes then introduces the notion of the weight of argument, which refers to the amount of the relevant evidence on which a judgment of probability is based. Later, in *The General Theory* (CWVII: 148), Keynes suggests that weight of argument is directly related to the confidence that one has in using a probability judgment as a guide to conduct. As Runde (1990) notes, Keynes employs several different definitions of 'weight' in *A Treatise on Probability*, using it to refer either to the absolute amount, or the degree of completeness, of the relevant evidence, or to the balance between knowledge and ignorance. But the basic idea is that the discovery of additional relevant evidence h_1 augments the weight of argument and gives rise to a new probability relation a/hh_1 (and where the degree of belief warranted by a/hh_1 may be greater, lower or the same as the degree of belief warranted by a/h).[3] It is not necessary for probability relations, judgments or weight to correspond to numerical values or be pairwise comparable, on Keynes's theory, and thus extend the province of probability to the study of rational decision-making under uncertainty.

It should be apparent from this brief overview that Keynes's discussion primarily considers the rational grounds for acting in the absence of numerical probabilities rather than the psychology of action or the emergent novelty, creativity or reproducibility associated with the imagination and action. Keynes does not consider the emergent historical processes that shape and contextualise the decision to act. Yet, '[h]aving opted for the supremacy of reason, [one] rejects what conflicts with reason … [one cuts oneself off] from the most ascendant and superb of human faculties. Imagination, the source of novelty, the basis of men's claims, if they have one, to be makers and not mere executants of history, is exempted' (Shackle 1979: 44). For the Keynes of *A Treatise on Probability*, the question of how to act is approached from an ethical and philosophical perspective, and he does not consider the origins of action, nor does he offer considerations of how they may find conduits for expression in the realm of practical affairs. For this we must turn to his economic writings.

Uncertainty and animal spirits

Many commentators have claimed that the revolutionary essence of *The General Theory* is the role accorded to uncertainty. This, though, is misleading. Coddington has cogently summarised the role of uncertainty in *The General Theory*: 'it is not the fact of uncertainty that is important for Keynes's argument, *but rather how individuals are supposed to respond to the fact of uncertainty*' (1983: 53, emphasis added). In developing this aspect of his argument, Keynes begins by noting the salience of the passing of time:

> All production is for the purpose of ultimately satisfying a consumer. Time usually elapses, however – and sometimes much time – between the incurring of costs by the producer (with the consumer in view) and the purchase of the output by the ultimate consumer. Meanwhile the entrepreneur (including both the producer and the investor in this description) has to form the best expectations he can as to what the consumers will be prepared to pay when he is ready to supply them (directly or indirectly) after the elapse of what may be a lengthy period; and he has no choice but to be guided by these expectations, if he is to produce at all by processes which occupy time.
>
> (CWVII: 46)

Keynes divides these expectations, upon which business decisions depend, into two groups: long-term and short-term expectations. Short-term expectations refer to the expected revenue associated with a production run against the current capital stock, whereas long-term expectations refer to the prospective revenues gauged by estimating the consequences of adding to the capital stock (*ibid.*: 47). Accordingly, the volume of current and future investment depends upon the state of these forward-looking, long-term expectations as they impinge on the psychological propensities to act (*ibid.*: 148). The decision to invest depends upon the 'most probable forecast' that can be made and the 'confidence' in such conjectures, a fact that is pivotal to enterprise (*ibid.*: 149–50). Nevertheless, a salient and often ignored aspect of this discussion is that Keynes highlights the importance of the state of long-term expectations with respect to the evolution of the institutions of capitalism, such as the emergence of the joint-stock corporation and the rise of the stock market:

In former times, when enterprises were mainly owned by those who undertook them or by their friends and associates, investment depended on a sufficient supply of individuals of sanguine temperament and constructive impulses who embarked on business as a way of life, not really relying on a precise calculation of prospective profit. The affair was partly a lottery, though with the ultimate result largely governed by whether the abilities and character of the managers were above or below the average. Some would fail and some would succeed. But even after the event no one would know whether the average results in terms of the sums invested had exceeded, equalled or fallen short of the prevailing rate of interest; though, if we exclude the exploitation of natural resources and monopolies, it is probable that the actual average results of investments, even during periods of progress and prosperity, have disappointed the hopes which prompted them ... If human nature felt no temptation to take a chance, no satisfaction (profit apart) in constructing a factory, a railway, a mine or a farm, there might not be much investment merely as a result of cold calculation. Decisions to invest in private business of the old fashioned type were, however, decisions largely irrevocable, not only for the community as a whole, but also for the individual. With the separation between ownership and management which prevails to-day and with the development of organised investment markets, a new factor of great importance has entered in, which sometimes facilitates investment but sometimes adds greatly to the instability of the system.

(*ibid.*: 150–1)

Such passages are instructive in several respects. First, the view of the entrepreneur, being based upon 'sanguine temperament' and 'constructive impulses', appears to emphasise the creative and transmutable potential embedded within the competitive process. Secondly, the recognition of the emergence of the stock exchange appears to embed the discussion of uncertainty into a historical process. Thirdly, such institutional developments fundamentally change the nature of the investment process, so that 'certain classes of investment are governed by the average expectation of those who deal on the Stock Exchange as revealed in the price of shares, rather than by the genuine expectations of the professional entrepreneur' (*ibid.*: 151). However, the subsequent focus is on how people react to uncertainty, rather than on how the creative actions of some agents generate uncertainty for others, especially around the decision to invest.

Keynes next proceeds to link the problems of uncertainty to the decision to invest, noting that it is the 'precariousness [of this market valuation] which creates no small part of our contemporary problem of securing sufficient investment' (*ibid.*: 153). He considers the factors that accentuate this precariousness, such as the 'gradual increase in the proportion of the equity in the community's aggregate capital investment which is owned by persons who do not manage and have no special knowledge of the circumstances, either actual or prospective, of the business in question, [so that] the element of real knowledge in the valuation of investments by those who own them or contemplate purchasing them has seriously declined' which gives rise to a 'conventional valuation which is established as the outcome of the mass psychology of a large number of ignorant individuals' (*ibid.*: 154; see also CWVI: 323).

Nevertheless, there is 'one feature in particular which deserves our attention' – the role of experts. Keynes suggests that '[i]t might have been supposed that competition between expert professionals, possessing judgment and knowledge beyond that of the average private investor, would correct the vagaries of the ignorant individual left to himself' (CWVII: 154). From a perspective that recognises the transmutability of the economic process, we should expect to find that the subsequent passages, elaborating why this does not 'correct the vagaries of the ignorant individual left to himself', allude to notions of novelty, emergence, imagination or the nature of economic time, that is, a consideration of the fact that while experts may be able to discern correctly and interpret the information contained in the past (and the present) they cannot extrapolate this into the future. That is to say, from a perspective which embraces transmutability, all individual agents, *including expert professionals*, are to some extent ignorant of the available courses of action or of the extent of future states of the world because of the irreversible and open-ended nature of time, because the future has yet to be created, and not merely because of limitations in the processing abilities of economic agents (see Dunn 2001). A conception of the economic process which *a posteriori* recognises its transmutability means that the future cannot be known in its totality prior to its *creation*, regardless of the processing powers we impute to agents. It is for this reason that a uniquely correct valuation cannot be arrived at.

However, according to Keynes, one of the reasons why the future cannot be known in advance of its creation is that experts are forced to follow the short-termism of the herd – social convention dictates it:

> It is an inevitable result of an investment market organised along the lines described. For it is not sensible to pay 25 for an investment of which you believe the prospective yield to justify a value of 30, if you also believe that the market will value it at 20 three months hence.
>
> Thus the professional investor is forced to concern himself with the anticipation of impending changes.
>
> (CWVII: 155)

The nature of the stock market decrees that the professional expert investor is forced to follow the general market valuation because both the short-termism and ignorance of the stock market swamp reason, and not because professional investors cannot gauge the entrepreneurial and creative actions of individuals and firms.[4] Keynes's discussion focuses on the conventions of the stock market that preclude the professional investor from forming a more rational judgment:

> If the reader interjects that there must surely be large profits to be gained from the other players in the long run by a skilled individual who, unperturbed by the prevailing pastime, continues to purchase investments on the best genuine long-term expectations he can frame, he must be answered, first of all, that there are, indeed, such serious-minded individuals and that it makes a vast difference to an investment market whether or not they predominate in their influence over the game-players. But we must also add that there are several factors which jeopardise the predominance of such individuals in modern investment markets. Investment based on genuine long-term expectation is so difficult to-day as to be scarcely practicable.
>
> (*ibid*.: 156–7)

The problem is that institutions and social conventions conspire against reason. If the professional investor is 'successful, that will only confirm the general belief in his rashness; and if in the short term he is unsuccessful, which is very likely, he will not receive much mercy. Worldly wisdom teaches that it is better for reputation to fail conventionally than to succeed unconventionally' (*ibid*.: 158). Keynes's discussion clearly centres on the unintended consequences of the institutional shift being observed in capitalism. The rise of the joint-stock company and its associated institutions has given rise to a cadre of dilettante investors who are able to alter their investment portfolios quickly and without appreciable cost nor consideration of the consequences of their actions upon the wider community. It is the institutions of finance, rather than the incipient creativity of the entrepreneurial class, that generate instability and uncertainty.

Notwithstanding the precariousness generated by the febrile atmosphere of the stock exchange, however, there are further instabilities to be recognised; the fact that it is a 'characteristic of human nature that a large proportion of our positive activities depend on spontaneous optimism rather than on a mathematical expectation, whether moral or hedonistic or economic' (*ibid*.: 161). That is to say, given the uncertainties surrounding the future, investment is very much a matter of animal spirits – 'a spontaneous urge to action rather than inaction, and not as the outcome of a weighted average of quantitative benefits multiplied by quantitative probabilities' (*ibid*.). This again appears suggestive of a conception of the economic process which assumes transmutability, especially as this discussion seemingly encompasses the professional investor. Nevertheless, the causal sequence in Keynes is clear: it is because of the uncertain nature of the future that economic agents rely on their animal spirits, or fall back on convention. Moreover, the emergence of the stock exchange accentuates the precarious nature of such investment decisions. This is quite distinct from a creative view of the economic process. That is to say, we might have expected Keynes to argue that because of the animal spirits and novelty-inducing actions of agents (especially those concerned with investment), uncertainty is increased for other agents. The focus is on the *reaction* to unforeseen events, rather than how the process of accumulation generates uncertainty. Even though Keynes links the notion of animal spirits to the plunge into the abyss of the unknown, he does not make the link with the emergent processes of origination and fecundity which are fuelled by the competitive process.

To summarise, Keynes focuses on expectations as a *reaction* to new events, to new circumstances, to 'shifting and unreliable evidence' (*ibid.*: 315).[5] His emphasis is thus quite distinct from one which suggests that expectations provide the raw imagination to create a new future. Expectations in Keynes refer to the response to circumstance rather than the creation of circumstance. Arguably, both are important and should be part of the same general story (see Davidson 1996). Moreover, the precariousness of expectations in financial markets is founded on the 'uncontrollable and disobedient psychology of the business world' (CWVII: 317). This results in the associated suggestion that if this psychology could be tamed then the associated problems of a collapse in business confidence could be overcome. Indeed, this is the more general argument of *The General Theory*, which deserves further consideration.

Transformation and *The General Theory*

It should not be inferred from this discussion that I am arguing that Keynes was a theorist who assumed the future was immutable. Throughout *The General Theory*, and elsewhere, Keynes makes many pregnant suggestions as to the transmutability of the economic realm. Indeed, in *The General Theory*, Keynes develops a structured and differentiated social ontology. One can identify three different levels of transformation in *The General Theory*, focusing on the actions and influence of individuals, institutions and governments. *The General Theory* is a treatise devoted to changing the philosophies of governments and hence the institutional structures of the economy, especially as they impinge on the 'free' actions of individuals within the economy.

Keynes clearly rejects immutable, natural-law philosophy and embraces a view that agents, and groups of agents, can alter the rules of the game. For instance, Keynes warns us that although we oscillate around 'an intermediate position' below full employment and above that which would 'endanger life', we 'must not conclude that the mean position thus determined by "natural" tendencies, namely, by those tendencies which are likely to persist, failing measures expressly designed to correct them, is, therefore, established by laws of necessity ... [It] is a fact of observation concerning the world as it is or has been, and *not a necessary principle which cannot be changed'* (*ibid.*: 254, emphasis added). This clearly provides for an open, transformative view of the economic system.

Indeed, Keynes recognises the power of the individual, noting that a 'decision to consume or not to consume truly lies within the power of the individual; so does a decision to invest or not to invest. The amounts of aggregate income and of aggregate savings are the *results* of the free choice of individuals' (*ibid.*: 65). This is suggestive of a transmutable conceptualisation of the economic system, and especially the decision to invest. Similarly, Keynes recognises the role of decentralised entrepreneurship (*ibid.*: 380). Nevertheless, while Keynes's discussion is suggestive of a transformative conception of choice, there is a failure to explore how the emergent novelty associated with enterprise might generate uncertainty for other investors. There is a failure to link the transformative actions of agents to the emergence of uncertainty in the minds of other agents.

Equally, when restating *The General Theory*, Keynes notes the psychological propensities which 'limit the instability resulting from rapid changes in the prospective yields of capital assets due to sharp fluctuations in business psychology or to epoch-making inventions' (*ibid.*: 252). This allusion to epoch-making inventions also suggests that Keynes accepts the transmutability of the economic process. Nevertheless, such creative acts are not linked up to a discussion and recognition of the emergence and salience of uncertainty in a historical perspective. There is a failure to link such allusions to and suggestions of the creative and imaginative impulse associated with enterprise and the emergence of the salience of uncertainty throughout *The General Theory* and thereafter.

Moreover, such comments should be considered alongside Keynes's (*ibid.*: 372–84) identification of the propensity of capitalism to stagnate owing to the exhaustion of investment opportunities and a rising propensity to save (factors which embody the concomitant implication that there are notional limits to human demands). According to Keynes, in wealthy communities the propensity to invest is weaker, reflecting a lower propensity to consume and a capital richness (*ibid.*: 31). Keynes 'came to see [saving] as excessive in relation to the investment opportunity available in an "old" economy like Britain's' (Skidelsky 1992: 274). Keynes judged the economic problem to be largely solved with the near exhaustion of profitable ventures upon which enterprise could embark – a view that regarded enterprise as decreasingly important and valuable.

Keynes's (mature) views on the relationship between saving and the macroeconomic position were embedded in a static conception of the nature of the economic process. Keynes's discussion points to a view of enterprise that stresses the discovery of profitable opportunities rather than their creation. This seemingly points to the satiation of wants and capital, and not the manufacture of wants and the pervasive and invasive thrust of creatively destructive capital accumulation and the uncertainties that this generates (see Schumpeter 1942: 111).

For Keynes, the entrepreneurial function is linked to the stagnating vices of the accumulating elite. He fails to link the explosive energy of capitalism to the long-run 'pathological vices' of accumulation existing in historical time. Keynes's historical vision succeeds in playing down the creative nature of the competitive process and diminishes the impact of the 'new consumers' goods, the new methods of production or transportation, the new markets, the new forms of industrial organisation that capitalist enterprise creates' (*ibid.*: 83). As Plumptre (1983: 153) has commented, reflecting critically on Keynes's 'Economic possibilities for our grandchildren': 'society is not likely to run out of new wants as long as consumption is conspicuous and competitive'. Or, to put it another way, Keynes does not consider how firms engage in the creation of new wants and desires and attempt to mitigate uncertainties so as to preserve accumulation and to enable themselves to reproduce. That the creative aspect of the competitive process, and its connection with uncertainty, lie dormant in Keynes is perhaps symptomatic of the fact that he 'was less interested in processes than in outcomes' (Skidelsky 1992: 274).

All in all, Keynes's discussion in *The General Theory* (and in its subsequent defence) is a short-run snapshot of a dynamic long-run process. As Schumpeter (1954: 1175) observed of *The General Theory*, but which has now been forgotten, '[t]hose who look for the essence of capitalism in the phenomena that attend the incessant recreation of this apparatus and the incessant revolution that goes on within it must therefore be excused if they hold that Keynes's theory abstracts from the essence of the capitalist process'. But is it the case that elsewhere Keynes 'abstracts from the essence of the capitalist process'?

Transformation and the entrepreneur

It turns out that Keynes does on occasion elsewhere allude to the creativity and change induced by the entrepreneur. In his essay 'The end of laissez faire', he argues that '[m]any of the greatest economic evils of our time are the fruits of risk, uncertainty, and ignorance' (CWIXb: 291). Keynes's discussion is suggestive of a creative view of the economic process:

[i]t is because particular individuals, fortunate in situation or in abilities, are able to take advantage of uncertainty and ignorance, and also because for the same reason big business is often a lottery, that great inequalities of wealth come about; and these same factors are also the cause of unemployment of labour, or the disappointment of reasonable business expectations, and of the impairment of efficiency and production.

(*ibid.*)

This discussion appears to link the discussion of uncertainty to capitalism's incessant drive to introduce product innovations and technological revolutions. Moreover, such an interpretation links well with Keynes's rejection of simplistic market-based selection-of-the-fittest arguments (*ibid.*: 276, 282–3). If the future cannot be known in advance of its creation, then the market (or governments for that matter) cannot select and learn the optimal rules and routines that characterise the economic environment because *they are not yet there to be discovered.* However, a moment's reflection reveals that such an interpretation is contentious. To describe the economic process as approximating a lottery, in which individuals 'take advantage of uncertainty and ignorance', is quite distinct from a stress on the new products, new methods of organisation, new governments and new institutional structures that are originated within the processes of competition and history.

Likewise, in his review of H. G. Wells's *The World of William Clissold*, Keynes (CWIXc: 315–20) recognised the 'creative force and constructive will' of the elite, arguing that the force for change came from men of knowledge and power – the business tycoons and the scientists. For Keynes, it is the 'profiteer' who injects life into capitalism. Investment is an uncertain vocation: 'It is enterprise which builds and improves the world's possessions … [and] the engine which drives enterprise is … profit' (CWVI: 132). However, such creativity was most important in earlier times, during the dawn of 'individualistic' capitalism. At the turn of the twentieth century, however, Keynes was of the opinion that many of the previously profitable opportunities were nearing exhaustion; the entrepreneurial class had become degenerate, not least owing to the corrupting influence of avarice.

All in all, as Skidelsky (1992: 259) documents, Keynes, unlike Marshall, 'had little respect for the business vocation … Keynes ranked business life so low partly because he considered that the material goods produced by entrepreneurs had less ethical value than the intellectual and aesthetic goods produced by dons and artists, [and] partly because he despised the "love of money" as a motive for action'. In sharp contrast to, say, Schumpeter, Shackle, Marshall, or even Marx, Keynes seems to regard the entrepreneur as a necessary evil and far from heroic: 'What chiefly impressed Keynes about British businessmen was their stupidity and laziness. He was a firm believer in the three-generation cycle: the man of energy and imagination creates the business; the son coasts along; the grandson goes bankrupt' (*ibid.*). In his essay 'Am I a liberal?', Keynes (CWIXf: 327) argued that the transmission of wealth and power via the hereditary principle underscores the decadence and decay of 'individualistic' capitalism and the emergence of a socialised, routinised form of capitalism, epitomised by the joint-stock corporation. And while Keynes sometimes talks about the 'spirit of enterprise', this is not equal to a recognition of those activities of enterprise that induce change and uncertainty.

Overall, Keynes's vision of the capitalist process is 'one lurching forward by fits and starts, while opportunities for exceptional profit cause, briefly, the gambling spirit to swamp the counsels of prudence' (Skidelsky 1992: 335). Indeed, it is significant, although from our perspective unsurprising, that Keynes argued that the 'necessity of profit as a spur to effort … was greatly exaggerated' (quoted in *ibid.*: 267). Keynes's theoretical discussion stands in sharp contrast to Schumpeter (1942) who defended profit as a reward for risk-taking and uncertainty-bearing, and linked it up to the creative processes of accumulation. What Keynes 'underestimated was humanity's ingenuity in inventing ways to keep capital scarce' (Skidelsky 1992: 609). Keynes seeks to play down a heroic conceptualisation of the entrepreneurial function. His elitist orientation led him to regard entrepreneurs as a necessary evil who could contribute, not to civilisation, but to the possibility of civilisation.

Concluding comments

This chapter has briefly considered Keynes's conception of the economic process. Keynes's whole discussion, while suggestive of a transmutable conception of the economic process, does not seek to emphasise the emergent creativity associated with the process of accumulation that gives rise to uncertainty and reverberates through the state of long-term expectations. Nevertheless, it is clear that Keynes's discussion centres on the idiosyncrasies of financial markets and significantly underemphasises the creative potential of capitalism and its connection to the process of investment. Keynes neglects the essential element of capitalism: creative destruction – the 'opening up of new markets, foreign or domestic, and the organisational development from the craft shop and factory … that incessantly revolutionises the economic structure *from within*, incessantly destroying the old one, incessantly creating a new one' (Schumpeter 1942: 83). In *The General Theory* and thereafter, the competitive process is treated as essentially static, with the creative potential of capitalism underestimated.

Notes

1 I should like to thank Vicky Chick, Geoff Harcourt, Geoff Hodgson, John King, Mike Oliver, Tony Lawson, Lord Robert Skidelsky, Malcolm Sawyer, Ted Winslow and the participants of the Workshop on Realism and Economics held at Newnham College, Cambridge University, on 25 February 2002 for their comments on earlier versions of this work. The usual disclaimer applies.
2 Nevertheless, and as Lawson (1985: 913) has lamented, '[u]nfortunately Keynes nowhere explicitly defines uncertainty in *A Treatise on Probability*'.
3 The accretion of new knowledge or evidence does not invalidate the previous probability relation, but gives rise to a new one (see Lawson 1985; Runde 1990).
4 Keynes's whole philosophy of investment was governed by the principle of purchasing stock that he reasoned was under-priced 'relative to its intrinsic worth'. Indeed, it is clear that Keynes held an 'intrinsic values' approach to investment at some point after 1924 (CWXII: 57, 77, 81–2, 99, 101), which suggests that the discussion in *The General Theory* was an elaboration of Keynes's own investment philosophy.
5 But, as Schumpeter (1936: 793) pointed out, '[a]n expectation acquires explanatory value only if we are made to understand why people expect what they expect. Otherwise expectation is a mere *deus ex machina* that conceals problems instead of solving them.'

Part IV
Convention

14 On convention: Keynes, Lewis and the French School

Jörg Bibow, Paul Lewis and Jochen Runde

Introduction

The purpose of this chapter is to explore Keynes's later remarks on the nature of social conventions, and to consider how these relate to the widely accepted notion of convention proposed by the philosopher David Lewis (1969). We shall address the latter issue via the work of an important representative of the *Économie des conventions* in France (Dupuy 1989a), whose work draws on both Keynes and Lewis.[1]

Keynes on conventions

Conventions and conventional behaviour come to the fore in Keynes's writings on financial markets and particularly in Chapter 12 of *The General Theory*, where he discusses the instability of investors' beliefs about prospective yields on assets and how this is reflected in stock-market behaviour and valuations. Keynes asks how the daily, even hourly, revaluation of stocks occurs in practice, given that investors are generally unable to calculate numerically definite probabilities of the possible outcomes of their investment decisions. His answer runs as follows:

> In practice we have tacitly agreed, as a rule, to fall back on what is, in truth, a *convention*. The essence of this convention – though it does not, of course, work out quite so simply – lies in assuming that the existing state of affairs will continue indefinitely, except in so far as we have specific reasons to expect a change.
>
> (CWVII: 152)

Keynes elaborates on this answer in his subsequent 1937 *Quarterly Journal of Economics* (*QJE*) article:

> How do we manage in such circumstances [of significant uncertainty] to behave in a manner which saves our faces as rational, economic men? We have devised for the purpose a variety of techniques, of which much the most important are the three following:

(1) We assume that the present is a much more serviceable guide to the future than a candid examination of past experience would show it to have been hitherto. In other words we largely ignore the prospect of future changes about the actual character of which we know nothing.

(2) We assume that the *existing* state of opinion as expressed in prices and the character of existing output is based on a *correct* summing up of future prospects, so that we can accept it as such unless and until something new and relevant comes into the picture.

(3) Knowing that our own individual judgment is worthless, we endeavour to fall back on the judgment of the rest of the world which is perhaps better informed. That is, we endeavour to conform with the behaviour of the majority on average. The psychology of a society of individuals each of whom is endeavouring to copy the others leads to what we may strictly term a *conventional* judgment.

(CWXIVa: 114)

In the passage from *The General Theory* and in point (1) from the *QJE* article, Keynes seems to be thinking of convention as a *human practice* adopted by individual human actors, namely the technique of projecting 'the existing state of affairs' to achieve an image of what the future might look like (adjusted for the possible impact of events that we have specific reason to expect). Clearly there is nothing to restrict this technique to predicting social phenomena, as it might equally be applied to such things as predicting the weather or the outcome of a repeated experiment. Point (2) locates point (1) in the specific context of asset markets. In 'accepting' current valuations as a correct reflection of the market's assessment of future prospects here, investors choose to ignore the fact that they are basing their expectations on what is ultimately no more than current market opinion. Finally, technique (3) brings in deliberate mimetic behaviour, whereby market participants attempt to cope with the fact that they do not have a clear idea of what the future holds by consciously falling back on the judgment of others. Note that Keynes describes this technique as leading to a conventional *judgment* rather than leading to a convention *per se*.

Keynes maintains that the 'conventional method of calculation' (at least in the sense of (1) and (2) above) is compatible with a considerable degree of stability and continuity in our affairs *'so long as we can rely on the maintenance of the convention'*:

For if there exist organised investment markets and if we can rely on the maintenance of the convention, an investor can legitimately encourage himself with the idea that the only risk he runs is that of a genuine change in the news *over the near future*, as to the likelihood of which he can attempt to form his own judgment, and which is unlikely to be very large. For, assuming that the convention holds good, it is only these changes which can affect the value of his investment, and he need not lose his sleep merely because he has not any notion of what his investment will be worth ten years hence.

(CWVII: 152–3)

How, then, does Keynes account for what we have said that Chapter 12 of *The General Theory* is primarily about, namely the instability of stock markets? One source of instability, of course, is the continuous flow of news that feeds into market participants' ongoing reassessments of the state of the economy and prospective developments. But another source, according to Keynes, is the very techniques that he at the same time describes as being compatible with 'considerable stability and continuity in our affairs'. There are two aspects to this seemingly paradoxical position. The first is that beliefs formed on the basis of the assumption that the future will be much like the present, particularly where these beliefs extend over longer time-horizons, are typically based on information that is highly limited relative to what will become known with the passage of time. In the language of *A Treatise on Probability* (CWVIII), the 'evidential weight' of the information on which such judgments are based is low. In *The General Theory*, Keynes (CWVII: 148–54) suggests that the confidence investors have in their beliefs about the future varies directly with evidential weight, and that where evidential weight and confidence is low, these beliefs are susceptible to sharp and sudden changes in response to new information.

The second aspect is concerned with the mimetic behaviour that Keynes alludes to in describing technique (3) above, namely the practice of 'attempting to conform with the majority on average'. In particular, the liquidity provided by asset markets allows market participants to concern themselves, not with attempting to judge the probable long-term yield of an investment, but with attempting to profit from predicting 'changes in the conventional basis of valuation a short time ahead of the general public' (*ibid.*: 154). In normal times, behaviour of this kind may not be particularly disruptive, if it leads only to limited fluctuations around the prevailing conventional judgment. But where speculation becomes rife, stock-market prices may be driven sharply from their existing levels. Keynes illustrates the processes involved with his famous beauty contest example:

> professional investment may be likened to those newspaper competitions in which the competitors have to pick out the six prettiest faces from a hundred photographs, the prize being awarded to the competitor whose choice most nearly corresponds to the average preferences of the competitors as a whole; so that each competitor has to pick, not those faces which he himself finds prettiest, but those

which he thinks likeliest to catch the fancy of the other competitors, all of whom are looking at the problem from the same point of view. It is not a case of choosing those which, to the best of one's judgment, are really the prettiest, nor even those which average opinion genuinely thinks the prettiest. We have reached the third degree where we devote our intelligences to anticipating what average opinion expects the average opinion to be. And there are some, I believe, who practise the fourth, fifth and higher degrees.

(ibid.: 156)

In beauty contests of this kind it is irrelevant who is objectively the prettiest candidate. What matters is what the other contestants believe, and therefore what the other contestants believe the other contestants believe, and so on. Keynes's point is that similar regresses occur with respect to stock-market valuations, but with consequences that may be considerably more serious than the outcome of a beauty contest. It is not merely that share prices that are driven by self-fulfilling speculative play may lead to an element of arbitrariness in asset prices and resource allocations. It is that when the speculatively driven changes in the conventional judgment become dominant, this might involve serious, sustained disruptions in financial markets and the real economy (as we are now witnessing with the current overcapacity in the IT and telecom sectors after the boom of the 1990s).

To summarise, Keynes uses the term 'convention' to refer to different human practices or techniques used to cope with an uncertain future. The techniques described in points (1) and (2) above are both instances of simple inductive behaviour, with (2) referring to the particular case of asset markets. The technique described in point (3) involves something more than simple induction, since it entails market participants deliberately attempting to conform to the judgment of others (where this reliance is only implicit in point (2) insofar as stock prices reflect some aggregation of the views of market participants). The widespread adoption of these techniques in the context of stock markets leads to what Keynes calls a conventional judgment, as opposed to a convention *per se*. This conventional or market judgment is compatible with (and may even contribute to) the relative constancy of stock prices over time, provided that market participants feel that they can rely on existing valuations being maintained over the near future. But such stability is tenuous, being prone to disturbance both by 'changes in the news' and also by the activities of speculators attempting to anticipate changes in the mutually dependent beliefs of other market participants. Where the activities of speculators who attempt to profit from such changes in beliefs become dominant, existing valuations may be destabilised and lead to dramatic variations in prices.

Conventions as solutions to coordination problems

Perhaps the most widely accepted characterization of social conventions in the contemporary economics literature stems from David Lewis's influential book *Convention: A Philosophical Study* (Lewis 1969). Drawing heavily on an earlier landmark study by Thomas Schelling (1960), Lewis analyses conventions as 'salient' or 'focal point' solutions to coordination games with multiple (Nash) equilibria. The basic idea is best conveyed by example. Consider the game of 'Heads or Tails?', a simple coordination game in which two players who are unable to communicate have to choose between Heads and Tails on the toss of a fair coin. Both know that they will obtain a pay-off of 1 if they make the same choice and 0 otherwise. The game is depicted in Figure 14.1.

The players' interests coincide perfectly and the game has two Nash equilibria in pure strategies (Heads, Heads) and (Tails, Tails). Coordination is problematic, though, since the players cannot communicate and the perfect symmetry of the game offers no clues about whether to choose Heads or Tails. If the players were to choose randomly without regard to what the other is doing, they might achieve coordination simply by luck. Their expected pay-offs would then be 0.5. However, and as was noted by Schelling (1960), players in games of this kind often do rather better than this. In the present case, for example, most people achieve coordination by playing Heads. More generally, it appears that in many coordination games certain strategies 'suggest themselves' by virtue of analogies or associations of ideas that connect those strategies to the common experience, culture or psychology of the players. Schelling calls equilibria arising from choices of 'salient' strategies of this kind 'focal points'.

Lewis (1969) extends and formalizes Schelling's ideas by assuming that the players have *common knowledge* (CK) of both (1) the fact that the coordination problem has more than one possible solution, *and* (2) the

		Player 2	
		Heads	Tails
Player 1	Heads	1,1	0,0
	Tails	0,0	1,1

Pay-offs (Player 1, Player 2)

Figure 14.1

salient solution.[2] This is an important point for our purposes, since in Lewis's framework it is common knowledge of the salient solution that guarantees the stability of the convention. Each player's conviction that he or she should conform to (contribute to establishing) the convention of choosing Heads, in our example, is reinforced by his rehearsing the reasoning that the other player performs in deciding to conform to that convention.

The French School: *Économie des conventions*

The guiding theme in the writings of the French School is that people attempting to decide what to do in a situation, what value to assign to a variable, and so on, often do so by attempting to gauge and replicate what other people are doing or thinking in that same situation. Self-referential thinking, imitation and mimetic behaviour thus figure heavily in this literature, along with the influence of what Keynes and Lewis have to say about such phenomena.

In what follows we concentrate on a paper by Jean-Pierre Dupuy (1989a), a leading member of the French School, in which Lewis's and Keynes's ideas are discussed at some length.[3] The part of the paper in which Dupuy considers Keynes begins with a summary of Lewis's theory of conventions. Dupuy is drawn to Lewis's analysis because of the role it accords to what Dupuy calls 'specular' behaviour, 'the capacity of the human mind to put itself in the place of another and "see" the world from this other party's point of view' (*ibid*.: 41). In the game described above, for example, Player 1 attempts to put himself in Player 2's shoes to gain an idea of what Player 2 would do, while Player 2 attempts to put herself into Player 1's shoes to gain an idea of what Player 1 would do. But as both players know that each of them is engaging in specular behaviour of this kind, they would both have to make their assessments of what the other will do in the light of what the other expects them to do, and so on. What interests Dupuy is Lewis's demonstration that although this kind of specular regress is infinite, people are often able to coordinate their actions *because* they know that the others are trying to coordinate with them and because they are able to fix on a focal point. In these cases specularity is a stabilizing factor.

How does all this relate to what Keynes has to say about conventions? Clearly, Lewis and Keynes share an interest in the role of specular behaviour.[4] Yet in an earlier part of the paper in which Dupuy first introduces a version of the beauty contest example (albeit without reference to Keynes at that point) he suggests that players do *not* in fact engage in specular behaviour when playing it (*ibid*.: 51–2). Instead, they resort to what he calls 'common sense'.

Yet this is obviously not how the players in fact play this game. The socio-cultural group that they make up is immersed in a history, a tradition, a particular world and a particular form of common sense. Each individual has an implicit, unformulated and tacit knowledge of this world, and although this knowledge is not explicit, it is constitutive of the individual's social being. This common sense has been collectively created by individuals, but it nonetheless appears to them *as if* it were an objective reality wholly external to their own making and doing ... The 'natural' way to play is clearly for each player to consult his or her common sense, making a judgment without reference to what others might choose. The others are still present in this agent's individual choice, but it is *as if* their views had been crystallized into objects. Mediation by means of common sense makes it possible to obtain with null specularity what logic thought only an infinite specularity could obtain ... To the extent that the representations of common sense are, as Pascal said, like a 'second nature' and seem wholly self evident, we can admit that these beliefs are by the same stroke CK.

(*ibid.*)

Where actors are guided by common sense, according to Dupuy, they automatically satisfy the infinity of conditions required by the assumption of common knowledge *without* engaging in specular behaviour. In situations of this kind they adopt (what they believe to be) external or objective points of reference to guide their actions. Where actors lack such points of reference, there occurs what Dupuy terms a 'crisis of common sense', and it is at this point that they engage in specular behaviour, looking for clues about what those around them are thinking. Hence, from this perspective, specularity is symptomatic of *disorder*. This stands in stark contrast to Lewis's account, according to which specularity underpins the stability of conventions.

Dupuy comes on to Keynes later in the paper and begins by noting two points emphasized in *The General Theory*: (1) that financial markets are characterized by a radical form of uncertainty not reducible to probabilistic reasoning; and (2) that the only *rational* conduct in such a context is to imitate others on the grounds that '[if] I know nothing about the social context in which I find myself (as in the context of a panic), there is some chance that others may know something, and by imitating them, I may draw some advantage from their knowledge'. This kind of situation corresponds to what Dupuy calls a crisis of common sense, and Keynes's insight, in his view, was that the specular mechanisms that lead to the crisis are the same as those that help resolve it (*ibid.*: 57). Dupuy describes the emergence of a solution as follows:

Suppose that there are two subjects *A* and *B* who are engaged in reciprocal imitation. Now, let us imagine that a rumor makes *A* think that *B* desires (wants to purchase, longs for, etc.) an object, *O*. Henceforth *A* knows that he must desire in turn (or wish to but, or long for, etc.). Acting in keeping with this new-found desire, *A* designates to *B* that *O* is the object of his (*A*'s) desire. When *B* in turn shows interest in *O*, *A* sees this as proof that his initial hypothesis was right. Here we see the emergence of an objectivity or exteriority through the closure of a system in which all of the agents imitate each other reciprocally.

(*ibid.*: 58)

This process has two moments. In the first, actors engage in specular behaviour, each one scrutinizing the others for some sign of the coveted knowledge until 'everyone is precipitated in the same direction'. In the second, the emergent object – a price or set of prices perhaps – stabilizes and achieves an exteriority or objectivity that 'is achieved through a forgetting of the arbitrariness inherent in the very conditions of that object's genesis'. As Dupuy describes it, 'the unanimity that was responsible for its genesis projects the object outside the system of specularity for a certain period of time' (*ibid.*). Stock-market prices are thus portrayed as the outcome of what economists would describe as a pure bootstrapping process, that is, one in which they are the product solely of the mutually reinforcing and self-realizing beliefs of economic actors. The kind of specular process Dupuy has in mind, which may be initiated by the merest imaginings of one of the participants, leads up to the point at which the solution or emergent object is established, and which is in turn sustained by its new-found exteriority (ephemeral and illusive as this may be).

Conclusion: comparison and three questions

We have seen that Keynes has different things in mind when he talks about convention, namely various human practices or 'techniques' for making choices under conditions of uncertainty, ranging from simple induction to deliberately mimetic behaviour. The widespread adoption of such techniques in financial markets generates what Keynes calls a conventional judgment (and which, in providing the basis for new rounds of predictions, contributes to its reproduction). Only the third of the techniques that Keynes identifies in his 1937 *QJE* article unambiguously involves mimetic behaviour and speculative play in the sense of the French School. The French School is thus generalizing what is only one, albeit important, form of what Keynes calls conventional behaviour.

Dupuy's (1989a) paper identifies some important differences between Lewis and Keynes on the subject of social conventions. Lewis's analysis rests on the assumption of common knowledge of some focal point, external to the formal structure of the game, around which beliefs about the appropriate course of action can coalesce. Specularity is a stabilizing force here, the convention being established and sustained by common knowledge of the focal point. For Keynes, in contrast, widespread specularity is what occurs in the intervals of disorder that punctuate periods of stability. And what stabilizes the solution or conventional set of valuations, at least on Dupuy's reading of Keynes, is the 'unanimity' of market participants and their forgetting of the arbitrary process by which this unanimity was achieved. Once established, on this view, conventional valuations in the Keynesian sense block the play of specularity. Specular behaviour is thus something that arises at the point where common sense breaks down and which subsequently evaporates once a new set of conventional valuations is established.

The contrast between Lewis and Keynes is useful because it illuminates important aspects of Keynes's analysis. First, it throws into relief the fact that beauty contest-type regresses are characteristic of disequilibrium processes which are played out until a new stable set of valuations is (temporarily) attained. Secondly, it illustrates well how arbitrary conventional valuations may be in financial markets. And thirdly, it is consistent with the second of the techniques that Keynes describes in his 1937 *QJE* article, namely that of existing valuations forming part of the common-sense or taken-for-granted world of market participants that serves as a basis for the extrapolation of future valuations (that is, where specularity is absent). That said, the picture presented by the French School raises a number of questions of its own. Since these questions are indicative of the complexity of the subject of social conventions in financial markets, we shall close by raising three of them.

The first question concerns how specular processes crystallize as Keynesian common-sense conventions in the absence of any apparent focal point. According to Dupuy, conventions emerge at the point at which 'everyone is precipitated in the same direction' and market participants display 'unanimity'. But what exactly is it that market participants are supposed to be unanimous about? Is it existing prices, future prices or merely the direction of future price movements? Is it a single stock, each of a set of stocks or indeed even 'the market' itself? Dupuy does not say, and even if he did the questions would not end there. For example, suppose that market participants are unanimous that the price of some share will continue to rise over the medium term. As long as 'unanimity' prevails, in this situation, the price of the share will indeed continue to rise, as everyone would want to acquire the share in the expectation of capital gains. The trouble is that processes of self-fulfilling expectations of this kind *continue* rather than come to a halt so long as unanimity prevails and everyone is 'precipitated in the same direction'. What is required for the process to come to a halt and for the price to stabilize is the emergence of a diversity of opinion, for some market participants to break with the common view and move from the bull to the bear camp.

A second question, related to the first, is whether a share price that has been stable for some time does indeed reflect unanimity in the market that this is what the price should be. The problem here is that the idea that the market may display 'unanimity' on the value of a share runs counter to Keynes's remarks on the diversity of opinion on financial markets:

> It is interesting that the stability of the system and its sensitiveness to changes in the quantity of money should be so dependent on the existence of a *variety* of opinion about what is uncertain. Best of all that we should know the future. But if not, then, if we are to control the activity of the economic system by changing the quantity of money, it is important that opinions should differ. Thus this method of control is more precarious in the United States, where everyone tends to hold the same opinion at the same time, than in England where differences of opinion are more usual.
>
> (CWVII: 172)

In situations where there is a diversity of opinion about the course of future interest rates, there will also presumably be a diversity of opinion about the future movement of share prices (and presumably, therefore, about the basis of existing valuations). Of course, it is possible to argue that share prices only reflect the 'the average opinion' of the market at any point in time. But the idea that the ruling price of a share should correspond to some average of the values set on it by market participants is itself problematic. For example, it is quite straightforward to construct cases in which the price of a share lies well above the average of market participants' marginal willingness to pay for that share, an instance of the winner's curse (Miller 1977; Runde and Bibow 1998).

Our third and final question centres on why market participants should suddenly forget the arbitrary way in which the conventional or market judgment is formed once it has been established. In the stock-market boom of the mid- to late 1990s, for example, the popular media contained numerous warnings of the arbitrariness of market valuations and the possibility of a market bubble (Shiller 2000: 113–14). Even where stock prices stabilize after a prolonged period of price rises, this surely does not by itself entail market participants forgetting the possibly arbitrary way in which those prices were reached. And after all, it is an integral part of Keynes's account of speculative activity that speculators are aware that current valuations are often based on flimsy foundations, and are accordingly driven to attempt to profit from anticipating changes in conventional valuations.

Notes

1   See also Dupuy (1989a, 1994, forthcoming) and Orléan (1989).
2   A proposition or event is common knowledge if everyone knows it, everyone knows that everyone knows it, everyone knows that everyone knows that everyone knows it, and so on.
3   See also Dupuy (1994a, forthcoming).
4   The interpretations of Keynes offered by members of the French School tend to emphasize the mimetic aspect of stock-market behaviour that Keynes alludes to in point (3) above.

15 Keynesian convention
A textual note

Sohei Mizuhara[1]

Introduction

Although a considerable amount has been written on John Maynard Keynes's notion of convention, there is some disagreement about what he meant by the term. Among those who have discussed this problem,[2] John Davis has probably done most to elaborate the development of Keynes's thinking on the role of convention. But Davis's interpretation has been challenged in Runde's (1994c) commentary on Davis (1994a). It is worth examining this exchange in detail, as this helps to provide greater insight into the meaning of the concept. My purpose, then, is to propose an alternative interpretation of Keynes's views on convention, one that turns out to be closer to Runde's than it is to Davis's.

Keynes's definition of convention revisited

No one knows precisely what the future consequences of their actions will be. Future-oriented actions necessarily entail a time-horizon, their consequences occurring in the immediate as well as the more remote future. Keynes writes:

> Actually, however, we have, as a rule, only the vaguest idea of any but the most direct consequences of our acts. Sometimes we are not much concerned with their remoter consequences, even though time and chance make much of them. But sometimes we are intensely concerned with them, more so, occasionally, than with the immediate consequences. Now of all human activities which are affected by this remoter preoccupation, it happens that one of the most important is economic in character, namely, wealth. The whole object of the accumulation of wealth is to produce results, or potential results, at a comparatively distant, and sometimes at an *indefinitely* distant, date.
> (CWXIVa: 113)

As Keynes describes the matter in the above quotation, one of the most important economic activities dominated by 'this remoter preoccupation' is 'the accumulation of wealth' which results from past investment decisions. And it is this kind of decision that is the subject of Chapter 12 that is often cited from Keynes's most famous book, *The General Theory of Employment, Money and Interest*. In a formal analysis of the investment decision contained in the preceding chapter of this book, Keynes argues that the essential determinants of investment are the marginal efficiency of capital and the rate of interest. He defines the former as 'being equal to that rate of discount which would make the present value of the series of annuities given by the returns expected from the capital-asset during its life just equal to its supply price' (CWVII: 135). Whenever an entrepreneur considers buying a capital asset, he needs to form an expectation of the series of prospective yields from the asset over its whole life. It is when he judges the value of this series that his expectations enter into his decision whether or not to buy the capital asset. The marginal efficiency of capital is therefore 'of fundamental importance because it is mainly through this factor (much more than through the rate of interest) that the expectation of the future influences the present' (*ibid.*: 145). The marginal efficiency of capital is governed more by the prospective returns of a capital asset than by its current returns. Keynes emphasizes the importance of the role of expectations in analysing investment activity. It is therefore especially important to explore what determines the prospective returns of a capital asset, the analysis of which Keynes saw as requiring 'a different level of abstraction from most of [*The General Theory*]' (*ibid.*: 149).

Our knowledge of the future is unreliable and uncertain. Estimates of the prospective yields that may derive from a capital asset over its life will be the more vague and ambiguous the more distant those yields lie ahead in time. Investment decisions are heavily influenced by the fact that we know very little about what will happen in the future. Keynes assigns the expectations that entrepreneurs form about the possible outcomes of their decisions to one of two categories according to their time-horizon. The first category, which he called short-term expectation, relates to 'the price which a manufacturer can expect to get for his "finished" output at the time when he commits himself to starting the process which will produce it; output being "finished" (from the point of view of the manufacturer) when it is ready to be used or to be sold to a second party' (*ibid.*: 46). The second category, which he called long-term expectation, is connected with 'what the entrepreneur can hope to earn in the shape of future returns if he purchases (or, perhaps, manufactures) "finished" output as an addition to his capital equipment' (*ibid.*: 47). It is quite clear that investment decisions typically involve, and so focus on, remoter consequences than do short-term expectations. Long-term expectations are mainly associated with the returns on 'durable' (or investment) goods. Here we refer to a statement in respect of convention-following that appears in both Chapters 5 and 12 of *The General Theory*. Regarding short-term expectations in particular, Keynes writes:

it is sensible for producers to base their expectations on the assumption that the most recently realised results will continue, except in so far as there are definite reasons for expecting a change.

(ibid.: 51)

The behaviour described in the above quotation is almost identical to that which Keynes describes as a convention further on in Chapter 12 *(ibid.*: 152). It is clear from the preceding Chapter 5 quotation that Keynes believes that this type of convention will dominate short-term expectations, as defined above, which in turn determine the volume of output and employment in the economy.[3] In Chapter 12 , Keynes describes more fully why convention plays an important role in the determination of output in the presence of fundamental uncertainty about the outcomes of investment decisions. First, he restates his view of convention, as alluded to earlier in the book:

It is reasonable, therefore, to be guided to a considerable degree by the facts about which we feel somewhat confident, even though they may be less decisively relevant to the issue than other facts about which our knowledge is vague and scanty. For this reason the facts of the existing situation enter, in a sense disproportionately, into the formation of our long-term expectations; our usual practice being to take the existing situation and to project it into the future, modified only to the extent that we have more or less definite reasons for expecting a change.

(ibid.: 148)

In forming long-term expectations, what should necessarily be taken into consideration are, as Keynes clearly points out, essentially two factors (see *ibid.*: 147). The first is 'existing facts' that we can assume to be known more or less for certain. The second is future events that can only be forecasted with greater or less confidence. Both factors enter into estimations of the prospective yields of a capital asset in investment decisions. However, Keynes also mentions an important caveat, namely that existing conventions be maintained. Thus, fundamental uncertainty as an inescapable fact of our ordinary lives leads to a falling back on the conventions that 'the need for action compels us to adopt'. In general, the more time that elapses between the purchase of a capital asset by investors and the subsequent flow of returns, the more vague and ambiguous our knowledge about these returns will be. It is the absence of information about the future consequences associated with the purchase of any capital asset that compels investors to fall back on conventions when making their decisions. The description of convention provided by Keynes runs as follows:

In practice we have tacitly agreed, as a rule, to fall back on what is, in truth, a *convention*. The essence of this convention – though it does not, of course, work out quite so simply – lies in assuming that the existing state of affairs will continue indefinitely, except in so far as we have specific reasons to expect a change. This does not mean that we really believe that the existing state of affairs will continue indefinitely. We know from extensive experience that this is most unlikely. The actual results of an investment over a long term of years very seldom agree with the initial expectation.

(ibid.: 152)

It is important to recognize that Keynes is considering a special kind of market in the statement quoted above, namely an organized stock market. The stock market reflects the separation between ownership and management in the historical development of the capitalist business system. This separation leads to 'investment markets organized with a view to so-called "liquidity"', which in turn encourages market participants to be concerned, 'not with making superior long-term forecasts of the probable yield of an investment over its whole life, but with foreseeing changes in the conventional basis of valuation a short time ahead of the general public' *(ibid.*: 154). Consequently, the enhanced liquidity in such markets often exacerbates the precariousness of conventions and thereby adds greatly to the instability of the system. Keynes illustrates the problem of what happens when people try to 'guess better than the crowd how the crowd will behave' with his famous beauty contest example,[4] where everyone is seeking to establish 'what average opinion expects the average opinion to be'. What is important here is the specific manner in which individuals form their expectations in a stock market, that is, that their expectations are based on agents' assessments of other agents' expectations about the same event. Expectations formed in this way are properly characterized as intersubjective, and it is to this intersubjectivity that I now turn.

More on Keynes's conventions

John Davis (1994a, 1994b, 1994c) has written extensively on Keynes's thought on convention and has also criticized others' views on this subject. In this section I shall present Davis's position and then contrast it with the interpretation and extension of Keynes's and Davis's views offered by Runde (1994c). Let me begin with Davis's position, which is reflected in the following extracts:

these psychological propensities and attitudes [determining the level of output and employment as a whole] manifest themselves in varying degrees in different individuals, and thus it is more useful and more informative to say that Keynes's interest in conventions was ultimately directed toward explaining how conventions act to structure different individuals' psychological propensities and attitudes in relation to one another, or alternatively how conventions relate the degrees to which psychological propensities and attitudes operate across different individuals.

(Davis 1994b: 125)

[and h]ere it is necessary to emphasize only that a convention is a form of practical interaction between individuals, where average opinion exercises regulative effects on individual opinion while still accommodating judgment and action that departs from this central reference.

(*ibid*: 129)

We may thus explain the convention operating in connection with investment as a structure of expectations having average expectation as a central tendency for a diverse collection of bulls and bears' individual expectations.

(Davis 1994a: 240)

According to the perspective on the nature of convention that emerges in the above passages, when individual agents form their expectations regarding a future event about which they are uncertain, they should always look to other agents' expectations of the same event. In particular, Davis terms the conventions governing such interdependent expectations as a 'structure of expectations'. This term suggests that individual agents must consider the average expectation as the basis on which to form their own expectations. In this connection, the prospective yield, of course, reflects different individual expectations of prospective yields both above and below that average (Davis 1994b: 127). Nevertheless, individual agents' expectations are accordingly interdependent and socially embedded in character. The average expectation will continue so long as individual expectations do not change.

This idea of average expectation connects naturally with financial markets, which differ from other markets in terms of the time-horizon of the expectations of the agents involved. In stock markets, agents often interact with one another and follow each other's behaviour. These interactions lead to the intersubjective character of expectations.[5] This characteristic also introduces a quite specific kind of uncertainty, namely the kind that stems from the difficulty of 'anticipating the behaviour of others' (Runde 1991: 138).

Let us look now at Runde's interpretation of Keynes's remarks about convention, contrasting it with Davis's:

A key theme, here, is what [is] call[ed] 'specular behavior,' that agents form beliefs by putting themselves into each others' shoes in attempt to 'see' the situation from the others' perspective. ... I would nevertheless urge that although specularity may be important, especially in situations of extreme uncertainty, that it cannot provide the basis for a general theory of partial belief in Keynes's later writings. The issue turns in part on what a 'convention' is taken to be, which Davis defines very broadly as a 'structure of expectations'. I shall use the narrower definition of a convention as a self-sustaining regularity in the behavior of agents in a social group that has the following property: given that each agent expects the other members of the group to conform to it, it is in each agent's own interest to conform to it.

(Runde 1994c: 248)[6]

Runde asks whether or not this definition of convention accords with that of Keynes and Davis. For this purpose, he considers an important passage in which Keynes expands on his understanding of convention by identifying three techniques that agents adopt in order to save their 'faces as rational, economic men' in situations of radical uncertainty. The three techniques, which Keynes called 'a practical theory of the future', are as follows:

(1) We assume that the present is a much more serviceable guide to the future than a candid examination of past experience would show it to have been hitherto. In other words we largely ignore the prospect of future changes about the actual character of which we know nothing.

(2) We assume that the *existing* state of opinion as expressed in prices and the character of existing output is based on a *correct* summing up of future prospects, so that we can accept it as such unless and until something new and relevant comes into the picture.

(3) Knowing that our own individual judgment is worthless, we endeavour to fall back on the judgment of the rest of the world which is perhaps better informed. That is, we endeavour to conform with the behaviour of the majority or the average. The psychology of a society of individuals each of whom is endeavouring to copy the others leads to what we may strictly term a *conventional* judgment.

(CWXIVa: 114)

Runde insists that techniques (1) and (2) do not accord with his own or Davis's definition of convention. That is to say, while both involve substituting the existing state of affairs for an unknown future, neither of them involve the kind of interdependent judgement emphasized by

Davis[7] (and which Keynes explicitly regarded as one of 'the factors which accentuate [the] precariousness' of convention). Furthermore, these two techniques do not involve Runde's additional condition that each agent's copying of the others in a group ought to be in the interests of all of its members. By contrast, technique (3) refers only to a 'conventional judgement' that is founded on what Runde calls specular behaviour, but does not mention anything about Runde's restriction that it is in the interest of everyone to conform to the convention if everyone else is conforming to it.

To sum up, the interaction of the agents in a group is a necessary condition for the existence of a convention in Runde's sense, but this is not a sufficient condition because it must also be in the interest of each agent to follow the convention if everyone else does. Runde's definition of convention corresponds to case (3) above. How, then, does Runde's added restriction (namely the clause cited above that 'it is in each agent's interest to conform to [the convention]') tie in with Keynes's views on rational behaviour under uncertainty?[8] Answering this question requires an answer to a prior question: what kind of rationality did Keynes believe that agents might display under uncertainty? It is safe to say that the kind of rationality Keynes had in mind was not 'the extraordinary contraption of the Benthamite School'[9] adopted by orthodox economics, which he described as a 'pseudo-rationalistic' notion. At the same time, it is not easy to specify Keynes's concept of rationality because he described it differently at different places in his writings. But with respect to the concept of convention, Keynes clearly maintained that the dependence on the existing state of affairs as a guide to life with a view to acting under uncertainty is 'reasonable'.[10] Let us then interpret Keynes as defining rational behaviour under uncertainty as behaviour that is guided by reasons. One such reason is the assumption that the existing situation will provide a good guide to the future, except insofar as there are specific reasons to expect a change. In other words, as argued in *A Treatise on Probability*, basing our decisions on all the relevant information that is available at the time of decision is a reasonable way of behaving under uncertainty.[11] (In contrast to the position I am developing here, Davis maintains that 'whether or not conventional individual behaviour may be regarded as rational seems less important than explaining just how conventions create structures of socio-economic interaction' (Davis 1994a: 235), and he thereby passes over the issue of what Keynes may have understood by the term 'rationality'.)[12]

Runde explores the different kind of uncertainty faced by investors in connection with Keynes's discussion of convention. He divides Keynes's uncertainty into two broad categories: first, where agents suffer a complete absence of knowledge of probabilities; and secondly, where agents have a knowledge of probabilities but where the weight of evidence on which those probabilities are based is low ('probable knowledge is based on information which is, in some sense, slight' (Runde 1991: 131)).[13] This second category of uncertainty clearly reflects a special notion discussed in *A Treatise on Probability*, the weight of arguments.[14] There is a close connection in Keynes's thinking between situations in which evidential weight is low and conventional behaviour. Uncertainty in this sense dominates the decision-making of investors in *The General Theory*: as they commonly lack any information on the remoter consequences of their own activities, they are compelled to fall back on conventions. I conclude by saying that reliance on conventions in such circumstances is 'a barometer of the degree of our distrust' of our beliefs concerning the future.[15] The point is that this is the best that investors can do under such circumstances, and therefore that their opting to follow existing conventions is to this extent rational.

Concluding remarks

Keynes argued that human actors, especially investors, are compelled to fall back on convention when making decisions in the face of fundamental uncertainty. As we have seen, there are different interpretations of Keynes on the subject of convention and how he developed the practical implications of convention-following. These interpretations and implications might be developed still further, and it is to this end that I have considered the competing interpretations of Davis and Runde. I hope that the preceding analysis will provide some useful hints as to how the concept of Keynesian convention might be developed in future.

Notes

1 I am grateful to John Davis for the many suggestions that he made to deepen my understanding of Keynes's conventions. I am also grateful to Bruce Littleboy for his invaluable comments on an earlier draft. Of course, responsibility for any remaining errors is mine alone. Finally, I wish to thank Howard Vane and Masahara Oishi for improving my written English.
2 See, for example, Carabelli (1988: esp. Ch. 12), Davis (1994a, 1994b: esp. Ch. 5, 1994c, 1997, 1998), Dequech (1999a), Lawson (1993), Levine (1984), Littleboy (1990: esp. Ch. 9), Meeks (1991), O'Donnell (1991b) and Runde (1991, 1994c, 1997).
3 Gerrard (1997: 197) considers the short-term relation between convention and the level of economic activity as a whole in *The General Theory*. Runde (1991: 135, note 15) also points to this short-term relation.
4 It should be noted that Keynes (CWVII: 156) uses the beauty contest example to highlight the precariousness of conventions.
5 The intersubjectivity of expectations is a theme common to both Davis (1994a: 227, 241) and Runde (1991: 138).
6 Runde (1994c) attributes the term 'specularity' as used in this quotation to Dupuy (1989a) and Orléan (1989).
7 In a private letter, Davis points out an important difference between his and Runde's interpretation of Keynes's conception of convention: for Runde, it is 'a practice followed in situations of uncertainty regarding how expectations

are formed'; for Davis, it is 'a structure of interdependent expectations' in the same environment. Davis emphasizes that Runde leaves aside the question of how conventions are formed, while he himself prefers to solve this question.

8 Littleboy (1990: 34, 271) interprets Keynes's remarks about convention as implying some form of rationality on the part of those conforming to it. His statement, 'Agents learn that conformity avoids losses' (272), supports my regarding convention-following as rational.

9 See Keynes (CWXIVa: 124).

10 Here 'rationality' is treated as a synonym for 'reasonableness', a view also adopted by O'Donnell (1991a: 45). Keynes does not regard rationality and irrationality as being inevitably opposed to each other (*ibid.*: 40–5). Keynes's rationality has been interpreted in various ways. In the same letter mentioned in note 8, Davis seems to agree with my interpretation that Keynes identifies rationality with 'reasonableness'. In his comments on an earlier draft of this chapter, Littleboy suggests that the stability of conventions would depend upon conformity being in one's interests.

11 See also Keynes (CWVIII: 339–40).

12 Davis considers Keynes's views on rationality to be 'less important than explaining just how conventions create structures of socio-economic interaction', and this leads naturally to his question of 'why conforming and one's own interest need to be linked' (this point is also raised in the letter referred to in note 8). Instead, Davis emphasizes the importance of interdependent judgment in situations of fundamental uncertainty as the mechanism by which individual expectations are formed relative to the average. However, conforming with the behaviour of the average, which is the essence of interdependent judgment, is often very much in the individual agent's interests (see Orléan 1989).

13 See also Runde (1991: 130–5). Hoogduin (1987) also locates Keynes's uncertainty in the paucity of information. For Keynes's thoughts on information, see Mizuhara (1996).

14 Keynes (CWVIII: 77–85). For a discussion of the 'weight of arguments' concept, see Runde (1990).

15 This conclusion is a partial paraphrase of Keynes's statement that 'our desire to hold money as a store of wealth is a barometer of the degree of our distrust of our own calculations and conventions concerning the future' (CWXIVa: 116).

Part V
Methodology

16 Probability, uncertainty and convention

Economists' knowledge and the knowledge of economic actors

Sheila C. Dow

Introduction

This chapter focuses on the common foundations of Keynes's philosophy as applied to knowledge in general and the knowledge of economists in particular. *A Treatise on Probability* was addressed to the question of how we construct reasoned grounds for belief as the basis for action. The analysis followed from Keynes's understanding of the way the world is; it was only under specific, restrictive conditions that knowledge could be held with certainty. Because of the particular significance of uncertainty for the social world, rather than the physical world, the *Treatise* had direct implications for economic behaviour. But by the same token it had direct implications for the way in which economists understand their own knowledge systems. Probability, uncertainty and convention are all issues for economists as economists, that is, for their methodology.

In what follows, we start with the *Treatise* in order to identify the elements of Keynes's philosophy that carried forward into his economics and into his methodology. We then explore further how Keynes's methodology paralleled his understanding of economic actors and their knowledge. We conclude with a discussion of parallelism between economic methodology and the depiction of economic actors in economics more generally. The discussion is brought up to the present day, referring to current issues in economic methodology and in economics.

Probability and uncertainty in *A Treatise on Probability*

The *Treatise* is an exercise in philosophy. Specifically, it is a contribution to the theory of knowledge in the form of offering a logical foundation to probability. Keynes makes clear in the opening sentences of the *Treatise* the broad sense in which he is using the term probability:

> Part of our knowledge we obtain direct; and part by argument. The Theory of Probability is concerned with that part which we obtain by

argument, and it treats of the different degrees in which the results so obtained are conclusive or inconclusive.

(CWVIII: 3)

Probability is thus concerned with uncertain knowledge, and the theory of probability is concerned both with how we arrive at this knowledge and the status that knowledge has.

While the analysis that Keynes is about to build up is philosophical, he makes it clear in the next introductory paragraph that the application is general:

> *In metaphysics, in science, and in conduct,* most of the arguments, upon which we habitually base our rational beliefs, are admitted to be inconclusive in a greater or less degree. Thus for a philosophical treatment of these branches of knowledge, the study of probability is required.
>
> (*ibid.,* emphasis added)

Looking at the *Treatise* from the perspective of economics, therefore, we can expect guidance not only at a philosophical level, but also at the level of economic methodology (the rational behaviour of economists) and at the level of how we understand rational behaviour in the economy.

Keynes's analysis of probability tells us what constitutes rational grounds for belief in propositions, as economists and as economic actors, and thus provides a theory of rationality. Keynes's theory of probability is prescriptive in the sense that it specifies what is rational and what is not rational, and thus what is or is not a good guide for action:

> The importance of probability can only be derived from the judgment that it is *rational* to be guided by it in action; and a practical dependence on it can be justified by a judgment that in action we *ought* to act to take some account of it. It is for this reason that probability is to us the 'guide of life'.
>
> (*ibid.*: 356, emphasis in original)

But, just as Keynes's use of the term 'probability' is broader than the statistical sense we are more familiar with now, so he meant something much broader by 'rationality' than what we now associate with 'rational economic man'. Rationality under uncertainty, where arguments are inconclusive, differs fundamentally from rationality under certainty. Keynes included in the latter category certainty-equivalence, referring to circumstances which allowed probability to be measured on the basis of frequency distributions. So the conditions for uncertainty are therefore coterminous with unquantifiable probability.

Certainty and uncertainty, in Keynes's usage, stem not from a psychological state but from the logical foundations for knowledge of the proposition in question. Our knowledge is held with greater certainty the greater the logical justification for it. While we might imagine that Keynes had in mind here a distinction between subjective (un)certainty and objective (un)certainty, his account in the *Treatise* does not fit with such a dualistic reading (see further Carabelli 1988). In Chapter 2 he distinguishes between direct knowledge, which may be held with certainty, and indirect knowledge, which is arrived at by argument, given direct knowledge, and is held with some degree of uncertainty. The degree of uncertainty reflects the degree to which we have evidence of which we have direct knowledge.[1] But the primary propositions which constitute our direct knowledge, derived from observation, cannot be seen as objective. Our direct beliefs are the result of the 'contemplation' of our 'experience, understanding, and perception' (*ibid.*: 12). Furthermore, our indirect knowledge is derived from direct knowledge by means of argument.

> It is not always possible, however, to analyse the mental process in the case of indirect knowledge, or to say by the perception of *what* logical relation we have passed from the knowledge of one proposition to knowledge about another.
>
> (*ibid.*: 13, emphasis in original)

The logic of argument for Keynes is thus not classical logic, for which we need premises that we can take as true, but 'ordinary' logic, or 'human' logic, which generates knowledge under uncertainty, and benefits from the exercise of intuition.

Thus we see that, while Keynes's theory prescribes rational argument, the way in which he understands argument is founded on a theory of human nature. It is not *a priori* logic that is independent of human nature, but a logic that incorporates human capacities, particularly what Keynes refers to as intuition, or which David Hume (1978) before him had termed 'imagination'. Just as Keynes argues that our knowledge is built on experience, so his own theory of probability is built on experience. It is not surprising, therefore, that Keynes should offer his theory of probability as being relevant to all of philosophy, science and conduct.

Since Keynes's theory of probability drew on his understanding of how arguments are in practice constructed, his understanding of rationality according to ordinary logic is descriptive as well as prescriptive.[2] But, as Davis (1994b) argues, Keynes's understanding of the role of social convention in argument did not mature until his work in economics. While there have been different accounts of the route between the *Treatise* and *The General Theory*, there is a reasonable consensus as to the way in which we can now understand the content of Keynes's economics, as well as his methodology, in the light of the *Treatise*. Keynes made the connection explicit only briefly, and indeed the significance of the connection was not generally understood until recently. Explicit treatment of probability is replaced by explicit treatment of convention. We turn now to consider uncertainty and convention in *The General Theory*.

The General Theory on uncertainty and convention

The General Theory incorporates key features of human behaviour under uncertainty. This is most noticeable in Chapter 12, which deals with investment behaviour, but is also central to his theory of liquidity preference in Chapter 17. Both are central to *The General Theory* since investment is potentially the most volatile element of aggregate demand and since liquidity preference may be so high as to prevent the interest rate from falling to a level consistent with full employment.

While Chapter 11 of *The General Theory* analyses the investment decision as a rational comparison between the marginal efficiency of capital (which depends on its prospective yield) and the rate of interest, Chapter 12 delves more deeply into how the prospective yield is arrived at. Here we see the book's closest connection to *A Treatise on Probability*. Keynes emphasises 'the extreme precariousness of the basis of knowledge on which our estimates of prospective yield have to be made' (CWVII: 149). Investment decisions do not satisfy the conditions for prediction with certainty.[3] The uncertainty attached to our knowledge of the future reduces confidence in our predictions and places relatively more weight on knowledge about the present, about which we feel more confident. It is conventional, therefore, to extrapolate from the present even when we know that the present will not be replicated, even stochastically. It is also conventional, Keynes argues, to accept current market valuations as correct, that is, that current knowledge yields the best predictions. He then proceeds to analyse the particular conventions of stock-market behaviour, of which he had personal knowledge (see further CWXIVa).

Keynes has thus enriched the analysis of the *Treatise* as to how rational grounds for belief are established under uncertainty by exploring the social aspect of knowledge (see further Davis 1994b). In the *Treatise*, primary propositions based on experience yield statements as to probability that are more or less uncertain depending on the weight of evidence. In the absence of enough knowledge to yield certain predictions, action requires some basis in reason. How the predictions are arrived at depends partly on logic and partly on intuition. In *The General Theory*, Keynes points out the limitations of classical logic:

> Most, probably, of our decisions to do something positive, the full
> consequences of which will be drawn out over many days to come,
> can only be taken as a result of animal spirits – of a spontaneous urge

to action rather than inaction, and not as the outcome of a weighted average of quantitative benefits multiplied by quantitative probabilities.

(CWVII: 161)

We also see more clearly in *The General Theory* the role of social convention. This role is significant because, as Keynes points out, social conventions are arbitrary and thus precarious. They may change, with widespread consequences. One consequence of a downward revision in conventional judgment about future levels of asset prices is an increase in liquidity preference. An increase in the speculative demand for money follows from the kind of widespread change in expectation caused by change in conventional judgment, as distinct from individual expectations (which might be expected to balance out).

The theory of liquidity preference is founded more directly on the uncertainty of knowledge. Keynes's understanding of the role and significance of money is that it provides stable value under conditions of uncertainty. As such it is fundamentally important to the working of the economy as the denominator of contracts, as well as a store of value and the more conventional means of payment. The demand for money can change dramatically, not only when conventional judgment about asset values changes, but also when the confidence held in any such judgment alters. When uncertainty increases, so too does liquidity preference and thus the rate of interest, with real consequences for the economy.

While the foundation of *The General Theory* in the *Treatise* can be seen here in terms of Keynes's depiction of the behaviour of economic actors, it can also be seen in the methodology Keynes used to construct *The General Theory*. His philosophy is relevant to economists as well as to economic actors. Keynes's economics drew on his understanding of social systems as organic and open. There was little scope for certain knowledge about the future. It also drew on Keynes's experience of the economy, both directly as the Bursar of King's College, Cambridge, and indirectly as an economic adviser. The logic he employed was therefore ordinary logic, building knowledge, with reason, from a range of sources in a variety of ways. This contrasted with classical logic that requires a starting point in true premises and yields a unified analytical structure, as we find in general equilibrium theory.

The General Theory is not an easy book because of its pluralist methodology. Chapters 11 and 12 are indicative of the approach. Chapter 11 offers a quite formal analysis of investment demand, taking prospective yield of investment as given. But Chapter 12 then opens up the determination of prospective yield to scrutiny, requiring a discussion of decision-making under uncertainty as well as a discussion of the conventions and institutional arrangements for investment and its finance. The two chapters involve a segmentation of a complex whole in order to explore each part with methods appropriate to each. Furthermore, Keynes adopts different methods in order to address different audiences: given the limited scope for demonstrative argument, persuasion is central. His opening chapter is rather polemical, while the analysis of the labour market in Chapter 2 is designed to show formally how little needs to be changed in the neoclassical model to undermine the full-employment equilibrium result.

Unfortunately, Keynes was rarely explicit about his methodological views, but there has been considerable analysis of his methodology by others (see, for example, Chick 1983; Harcourt and Riach 1997: vol. II). Particularly since the pioneering work of Carabelli (1988) and O'Donnell (1989) it has become accepted that Keynes's methodology is grounded in the philosophy of the *Treatise*. Keynes's use of pluralism to build up arguments in different ways, his awareness of the significance of persuasion, his reservations about mathematical formalism, his reference to psychology and to social convention as essential elements of behaviour – all follow from his understanding of the real, social world as complex and evolving and incapable of yielding much in the way of certain knowledge. Furthermore, while the real social world is organic and open, it is both feasible and necessary to invoke *provisional* closure on parts of the system in order to build up specific theories.

It has been the misunderstanding of Keynes's closures as being definitive (as they would be in closed-system reasoning) that has led to much misunderstanding of his methodology. Thus, for example, while Keynes took the money supply as given for the purposes of argument in *The General Theory*, this was simply a device to allow analysis of other features of the money market; it certainly did not mean that Keynes thought the money supply was exogenous, that is, both fundamentally causal and uninfluenced by the private sector. It was only a provisional closure for the argument at hand.

While Keynes was rarely self-conscious about his methodology, there has been a tremendous growth since then of work on methodology which has made us much more aware of our behaviour as economists. At the same time there has been a considerable advance in the thinking about the rational behaviour of economic actors. The parallelism between economist and actor has thus been brought to the fore; we turn to this modern literature in the next section.

Parallelism in economics between economists and economic agents

It could be regarded as unremarkable that Keynes's methodology should parallel his understanding of the way in which economic actors acquire knowledge. Indeed, the same parallel may be found in those theories which are held by economists with certainty, which in turn depict economic actors as being certain of the knowledge they hold. Similarly, models may be stochastic which depict agents as having certainty-equivalence. These parallels derive from a closed-system ontology that yields certain knowledge, rather than Keynes's open-system ontology where knowledge is generally held with uncertainty.

But parallelism is not always present in economic theory and methodology. This is sometimSes due to an understanding of the economist's knowledge as having a different status from economic actors' knowledge. The economist-as-expert, along modernist lines, knows better than economic actors. In classical economics there was thus a strand of thought that saw economic theory as being normative, demonstrating how rational individuals *ought* to behave (see Drakopoulos 1991). Alternatively, Austrian theory is founded on the view that the individual has the best knowledge of her/his own situation and opportunities; the economist has inferior specific knowledge, and is thus not justified in advocating intervention in that situation other than to alter the general environment (see, for example, Hayek 1975).

It was the absence of parallelism in neoclassical synthesis macroeconomics that sparked off the rational expectations revolution. The charge was that individuals were being portrayed as making systematic errors, that is, as being irrational (unlike economists). The solution was to have economic actors' knowledge mirror exactly the knowledge of economists; thus they were portrayed as employing the same econometric models as economists. But Sargent in particular has recognised the logical difficulties with this account of actors' knowledge; he has been grappling without success so far with the problem of providing a sounder basis for symmetrical treatment of economists and economic actors (see Sent 1998). Others pursuing this goal include Evans and Honkapohja (2001) who analyse actors as engaging in adaptive learning when faced with the same kind of model uncertainty as economists.

But sometimes a lack of parallelism arises unintentionally, as in much of the model uncertainty literature (see, for example, ECB 2001). This topic has arisen from certainty-equivalence models being found inadequate by policy-makers, who then have to face up to their own uncertainty when trying to find a rational basis for action. The outcome is a large literature that offers guidelines for rational policy-making where it is not known which model is closest to the 'true' model. But in much of this literature economic actors themselves continue to be modelled in terms of certainty-equivalence. From a Keynesian perspective, this situation has arisen because of the confrontation between the modelling of a closed-system economy on the one hand, and the experience of policy-making in an open-system reality on the other. The outcome, within a methodology that puts such an emphasis on consistency (as defined within classical logic), can only be described as logically uncomfortable.[4]

In the meantime, the issue of parallelism between the knowledge of economists and that of economic actors has been treated in a variety of ways in the methodology literature. The sociology of scientific knowledge literature focuses on the sociology of scientific communities, and the part that plays in the type of knowledge generated. Institutionalists focus on the formal institutions and informal conventions operating within scientific communities. The rhetoric literature focuses on the means of persuasion used within scientific communities. Perspectives more normally applied to economic actors are thus being applied to economists themselves. However, even here the parallelism is not generally drawn out.

Where parallelism comes closest to being made explicit in these literatures is in the discussion of the issue of reflexivity as impinging on the economist's capacity to provide a descriptive account of economic theory (see Sent's (1998) use of the concept). Description is always coloured by some perspective, normally that of the author. Reflexivity also has profound implications for the content of economic theory; it colours the economist's understanding of the real world, undermining any notion of objective 'facts'. This argument comes very close to neo-Austrian methodological individualism, where the subjectivity of individual knowledge is central to the argument that economists do not have knowledge that is privileged over that of economic actors.

Conclusion

The reflexivity argument within the methodology literature can be quite destructive of theorising. But it has had echoes, in recent times, in the commonplace understanding among economic actors that we live in a world of spin and style rather than substance, where the scope for government intervention is highly constrained by lack of knowledge. In contrast, while Keynes understood very well the limitations on our understanding, as economists as much as economic actors, he set out to analyse how we nevertheless build up rational grounds for action, as we do. His starting point was realist, namely the existence of a real world, however poorly we understand it. Furthermore, what he did know about the real world, based on experience, was that it is complex and evolving, which explains the limitations of our understanding. In addition, he understood the problems for government of undertaking policy action when the outcome is uncertain (see O'Donnell 1989). But, just as individuals take action under uncertainty, when the rationality of classical logic would not justify it, so Keynes provided guidance for governments to take action under uncertainty.

Notes

1   The 'degree of evidence' is the weight of argument, which Keynes suggested could be given as either the absolute, or the relative, amount of evidence. See further Runde (1990) and Dow (1995).
2   It is characteristic of Keynes's thought that it does not fit into the dualisms of classical logic.
3   This point was elaborated by Shackle (1955) in terms of investment decisions as 'crucial experiments'.
4   Indeed, Blanchard and Fischer (1989: 505) use the expression 'not logically comfortable'.

17 Keynes

Economics as a branch of probable logic

Anna Carabelli

Introduction

Keynes belonged to the twentieth-century tradition of science. He was against determinism and the view of knowledge as based upon certainty and logical time. He believed that nineteenth-century positivist attempts to cast economics as a physical science were doomed to failure. And against the view that the methods of the physical sciences could be universally applied, he argued that there is no ready-made scientific procedure to be learned and applied everywhere. Instead, he maintained that economists must shape their methods to the specific characteristics of the economic problem and material they are tackling.

The primacy of theory over experience

Keynes's criticism of the application of the scientific method to political economy is rooted in his rejection of empiricist and historicist methods. This rejection dates back to his juvenile studies and was maintained throughout his life (Carabelli and De Vecchi 1999b). Keynes thought that the criticism of the classical economic theory had been primarily empiricist rather than rationalist or logical. The critics believed, according to Keynes, that mere observation was sufficient to show that economic facts did not conform to the orthodox classical conclusions:

> The heretics of today ... are deeply dissatisfied. They believe that common observation is enough to show that facts do not conform to the orthodox reasoning.
>
> (CWXIII: 488–9)

Keynes maintained that this approach was invalid methodologically. Underlying this criticism was his own epistemological approach to the relationship between theory and observation, developed in his *A Treatise on Probability*. Observation, according to Keynes, is theory-laden (CWVIII 231; Carabelli 1988: 69–71). How could observation raise doubt about something upon which it was grounded? Mere empirical criticism based upon observations of facts that conflicted with the conclusions of the theory was therefore useless as a critique of a theory. As a consequence, merely pointing out that economic facts (empirical events) did not conform to the orthodox reasoning was bound to be unsuccessful as a criticism.

Keynes departed from the heretics' empiricist method of criticism by maintaining that theory (or, better, logic) rather than mere observation was the proper way to raise doubts about a theory. Keynes included the German Economic School among the group of 'heretics'. In contrast with the theoretical attitude demonstrated by German thinkers in other disciplines (in this connection, it is worth mentioning Keynes's own intellectual deference to German logicians in *A Treatise on Probability*), he accused the historical school of being 'sceptical', 'realistic', content with historical facts and results, or of using 'empirical methods' and discarding 'formal analysis' (CWVII: xxv).

Keynes was also against 'inductive verifications' and explanations reduced to 'simple generalisations'. In this regard, it is interesting to consider his appreciation of the changes in Malthus's position on method. Whereas he considered Malthus's first work, *Essay on Population*, as initially *a priori* and philosophical in method, he regarded its later editions as moving towards mere empiricism. This represented Malthus's second phase, in which general principles, according to Keynes, were overwhelmed with 'inductive verifications' and reduced to 'simple generalisations' of facts (CWXf: 85–6). Finally, Keynes's interpretation of Malthus's more mature writings (particularly *An Investigation of the Cause of the Present High Price of Provisions* (1800) and his correspondence with Ricardo) introduces aspects which, in my view, tend to reflect Keynes's own approach more than Malthus's. In fact, the last part of Keynes's essay 'Robert Malthus: centenary allocution' (CWXf: 71–103, 104–8) is very similar in flavour to Keynes's well-known reinterpretation of Newton's method in his essay 'Newton, the man'. There, he stressed the mixture of formal thought and intuition necessary to 'understand' the 'complex confusion of the world of daily events', the 'unusual combination of keeping an open mind to the shifting picture of experience and of constantly applying to its interpretation the principle of formal thought', the grasping of 'what should be for an economist the relation of experience to theory' (*ibid.*: 88, 107–8; on Newton, see Keynes CWXg: 364; on Keynes's interpretation of Newton's method and the parallel with Keynes's own method, see Carabelli 1988: 109). Keynes maintained that the material with which economists work are not facts, events or things, but what individuals think they are, that is, the beliefs that individuals hold. As a consequence, he insisted on the primacy of the theory over mere empirical observations in explaining complex social phenomena.

From the onset of his career as an economist, Keynes openly rejected positivism in economics. Already in his 1912 economics lectures, when dealing with the causes of changes in the value of money, the forces that he identified as causes were not material ones, homogeneous bodies that were moved by the 'force' of classical mechanics, but the various reasons, beliefs and opinions of people (CWXII: 731).

In his discussion with Harrod, Keynes not only confirmed his early attitude, contrasting Harrod's explanation based on material causes with his own based on reasons, thereby openly manifesting his dislike for the analogy between economic behaviour and the mechanical movement of physical bodies, but went so far as to completely reverse the positivist application of the Newtonian method of physical sciences to economics. He wrote:

> Economics deals with motives, expectations, and psychological uncertainty. One has to be constantly on guard against treating the material as constant and homogeneous. It is as though the fall of the apple to the ground depended on the apple's motives, on whether it is worth while falling to the ground, and whether the ground wanted the apple to fall, and on mistaken calculations on the part of the apple as to how far it was from the centre of the earth.
>
> (CWXIVb: 300)

For Keynes, then, the material, or the object of economics, were the beliefs, the opinions of economic agents. Intentionality, motives and human agency, on this view, are the material of economics.

Keynes maintained that economics is not a natural science and that positivistic methods could not be applied to it. His discussion on the limits of the application of the atomic hypothesis within physical science itself appears in his early writings on probability, in addition to his non-positivist interpretation of Newton's method (Carabelli 1988: 100–102, 109). Furthermore, a very early reference to the 'mechanical theory' of physical science, with its distinction between primary and secondary qualities, can be found in his 'Miscellanea ethica':

> It is often supposed that in shape, size and motion the objects are like the sensations, and that in colour, taste, smell, heat and cold they are unlike. This is the mechanical theory of the external world.
>
> (Keynes 1905)

What, then, is economics for Keynes? The answer is that he regards economics as both a moral science and a branch of logic. It is a moral science insofar as it deals with ethical values and introspection (CWXIVb: 300). And it is at the same time a branch of logic, a way of thinking. It is fundamentally a method, which helps economists to draw conclusions, which are 'logically' correct, that is, to avoid falling into logical fallacies in reasoning.

In his Introduction to the *Series of Cambridge Economic Handbooks*, 1922–23, Keynes writes: 'The theory of economics does not furnish a body of settled conclusions immediately applicable to policy. It is a method rather than a doctrine, which helps its possessor to draw correct conclusions' (CWXII: 856). The passage throws further light on the continuity between *A Treatise on Probability* and Keynes's economic works. For in his discussion with Roy Harrod in 1938, that is, in his most mature and outspoken methodological manifesto, when he declared that 'economics is a branch of logic, a way of thinking', rather than a 'pseudo-natural science', Keynes only restated his early position (CWXIVb: 296).

Keynes's view of economic theory is thus of a method or logic, perhaps best described as an apparatus of probable reasoning. In Chapter 21 of *The General Theory*, he writes that the object of economic analysis is 'not to provide a machine, or method of blind manipulation, which will furnish an infallible answer, but to provide ourselves with an organised and orderly method of thinking out particular problems'. But, he adds, 'after we have reached a provisional conclusion by isolating the complicated factors one by one, we then have to go back on ourselves and allow, as well as we can, for the probable interactions of the factors among themselves'. He points out that 'this is the nature of economic thinking' and that we would be lost in the wood without abstract and logical reasoning: 'Any other way of applying our formal principles of thought (without which, however, we shall be lost in the wood) will lead us into error' (CWVII: 297).

The key point, according to Keynes, is that without logic, economists may lose themselves in the empirical or mathematical wood, as both econometricians, like Tinbergen and Colin Clark, and mathematical economists had done. The problem as he saw it is that the application of mathematical language – with its presuppositions of atomism – to economic material that is essentially non-mathematical gives rise to logical fallacies, one of them being the fallacy of *ignoratio elenchi* in classical economic theory (Carabelli 1991). Keynes's definition of mathematics as 'imprecise' in *The General Theory* means that the blind application of mathematics to economics, with its non-numerical, non-comparative and non-ordinal aspects, requires logical attention (CWVII: 298; Carabelli 1995).

How does the economist work?

In respect of economic method, Keynes held that social phenomena are known not by observation and experience, but by constructing abstract theoretical models from the elements found in our own thought. How does the economic scientist build his theoretical models? It should be noted that at the root of Keynes's approach is the conception of thought and the mind that he developed in his early logical writings. Keynes's view of the mind and his own epistemology are not based on an evolutionary psychology and are not in line with modern cognitivism.

As for the role of models in economics, Keynes wrote that to convert an abstract model into 'a quantitative formula' is to destroy its usefulness as an instrument of thought. In his letter to Roy Harrod of 16 July 1938, Keynes reiterated that economics is not a natural but a moral science:

> My dear Roy, I think we are a little bit at cross purposes. There is really nothing in your letter with which I disagree at all. Quite the contrary. I think it most important, for example, to investigate statistically the order of magnitude of the multiplier, and to discover the relative importance of the various facts which are theoretically possible. My point against Tinbergen is a different one. In chemistry and physics and other natural sciences the object of experiment is to fill in the actual values of the various quantities and factors appearing in an equation or a formula; and the work when done is once and for all. In economics that is not the case, and to convert a model into a quantitative formula is to destroy its usefulness as an instrument of thought. Tinbergen endeavours to work out the variable quantities in a particular case, or perhaps in the average of several particular cases, and he then suggests that the quantitative formula so obtained has general validity. Yet in fact, by filling in figures, which one can be quite sure will not apply next time, so far from increasing the value of his instrument, he has destroyed it. All the statisticians tend that way. Colin [Clark], for example, has recently persuaded himself that the propensity to consume in terms of money is constant at all phases of the credit cycle. He works out a figure for it and proposes to predict by using the result, regardless of the fact that his own investigations clearly show that it is not constant, in addition to the strong a priori reasons for regarding it as most unlikely that it can be so. The point needs emphasizing because the art of thinking in terms of models is a difficult – largely because it is an unaccustomed – practice. The pseudo-analogy with the physical sciences leads directly counter to the habit of mind which is most important for an economist proper to acquire ... But do not be reluctant to soil your hands, as you call it. I think it is most important. The specialist in the manufacture of models will not be successful unless he is constantly correcting his judgment by intimate and messy acquaintance with the facts to which his model has to be applied.
>
> (CWXIVb: 299–300)

The art of thinking in terms of models in economics requires careful attention to the notion of time. Keynes was less interested in the passage of time as a slow and evolutionary process, permanence, repetition, patterns, rules, and so on, than he was in rapid change, uniqueness, exceptions, and so on. In *A Treatise on Money* (published in 1930), his attention was devoted to the factors driving change, his view being that economic theory was supposed to explain temporary divergences of price levels:

> Students of the theory of credit cycle, and, indeed, of all those parts of economic theory which deal with short-period phenomena, have sometimes, by overlooking the temporary divergences between price levels which in the long run are likely to move together, assumed away the very facts which it is the task of such theory to investigate.
>
> (CWV: 66–7)

In 1938, when discussing Harrod's economic method, Keynes's stress was placed again on the study of change:

> The object of a model is to segregate the semi-permanent or relatively constant factors from those which are transitory ... so as to develop a logical way of thinking about the latter and of understanding the time sequences to which they give rise in particular cases.
>
> (CWXIVb: 296–7)

One may also recall Keynes's well-known statement advanced in *A Tract on Monetary Reform* that 'in the long run, we are all dead' (CWIV: 65). Economic theory is to be concerned mainly with the present and short-period situations. One has to abandon confidence in expecting the long-run self-adjusting order and equilibrium so cherished by positive and orthodox economics. In 1937, in the *New Statesman and Nation*, Keynes writes:

> We do not know what the future will bring, except that it will be quite different from anything we could predict. I have said, in another context that it is a disadvantage of 'the long run' that in the long run we are all dead. But I could have said equally well that it is a great advantage of 'the short run' that in the short run we are still alive. Life and history are made up of short runs.
>
> (CWXXVIII: 62)

In Chapter 18 of *The General Theory*, where Keynes offers a methodological description of his economic model, his distinction between given and independent factors is again based upon a notion of short-run change. His notion of independence is also connected with the notion of logical relevance and independence developed in *A Treatise on Probability*:

> The division of the determinants of the economic system into the two groups of given factors and independent variables is, of course, quite arbitrary from any absolute standpoint. The division must be made … so as to correspond on the one hand to the factors in which the changes seem to be so slow or so little relevant as to have only a small and comparatively negligible short-term influence on our *quaesitum*; and on the other hand to those factors in which the changes are found in practice to exercise a dominant influence on our *quaesitum* … in a study so complex as economics, in which we cannot hope to make completely accurate generalisations, [we hope to discover] the factors whose changes *mainly* determine our *quaesitum*.
>
> (CWVII: 247)

The recent suggestion that Keynes embraced a conventionalist approach in his economic theory and in his view of expectations appears totally unacceptable. Certainly, Keynes was not an empiricist: he strongly disliked descriptive realism. His idea of theory as an abstract method of reasoning left him sceptical of the introduction of numbers and empirical quantities. Keynes held that markets actually follow conventions and practical hypotheses for facing the future. But he also held that these conventions are market idols.

The theories of classical economics, no less than actual markets, are dominated by theoretical idols: the certainty hypothesis and the Benthamite calculus in particular. Keynes held, however, that a proper economic theory should not follow these idols and should actually go against market conventions, against practical hypotheses of the future and theoretical idols.

Logic vs. evolutionary epistemology: Keynes vs. Ramsey

Keynes accepted the idea of an 'approximate uniformity of human organs'. From quite early in his intellectual career he defended the idea that an individual's thinking could be explained in terms of a capacity to reason in a manner that is objective and logical, that is, reasonable. This is clear in Keynes's 1905 'Miscellanea ethica' paper, where he draws a distinction between what an individual can think and feel and what an individual ought to think and feel:

> It is plain that the idea and the emotion appropriate to any given sensation are partly dependent on the nature and past history of the individual who feels. This is obvious enough; we ought not to all have precisely similar states in similar physical circumstances; common sense and the commandments are agreed on that. But we can in many cases abstract that element which ought to vary from man to man. Assuming the approximate uniformity of human

organs, we can often say what, apart from peculiar circumstances, a man ought to think and feel – not indeed what he can think and feel – that will always depend upon his nature and his past.

(Keynes 1905)

Thus although Keynes allowed a role for both psychological and subjective influences on individual judgment, he also supposed that one could say what an individual should reasonably think and feel on the grounds that there exists an 'approximate uniformity of human organs'.

This notion of a common mind and thought underlies Keynes's thinking in *A Treatise on Probability*. There, Keynes asserts that 'logic investigates the rational principles of valid thought' which form the basis for rational belief. While probability judgments do possess a subjective dimension insofar as the premises that form the basis of probability judgments will vary from individual to individual, this should not obscure the objective and logical character of probability (CWVIII: 18). Keynes's probability is logical. Probability, for him, is neither an empirical frequency of events nor a mere psychological or subjective attitude:

> But in the sense important to logic, probability is not subjective. It is not, that is to say, subject to human caprice. A proposition is not probable because we think it so. When once the facts are given which determine our knowledge, what is probable or improbable in the circumstances has been fixed objectively, and is independent of our opinion. The theory of probability is logical, therefore, because it is concerned with the degree of belief which it is rational to entertain in given conditions, and not merely with the actual beliefs of particular individuals, which may or may not be rational.
>
> (*ibid.*: 4)

In his famous critique of *A Treatise on Probability*, Frank Ramsey threw doubt on the existence of the logical probability relations on which Keynes's theory of probability is founded. Keynes admitted that there was something to Ramsey's complaint, and allowed that the basis of our degrees of belief, rather than corresponding to objective logical relations, may be part of our human outfit, perhaps given to us by natural selection (and therefore to be explained by evolutionary empirical psychology). But Keynes clearly continued to adhere to the contrast drawn in *A Treatise on Probability* between actual beliefs on the one hand and reasonable beliefs on the other. He insisted that Ramsey's account of probabilities as mere subjective and psychological attitudes was lacking in an important regard, that is, reasonableness:

> Ramsey argues, as against the view which I put forward, that probability is concerned not with objective relations between propositions

but (in some sense) with degrees of belief, and he succeeds in showing that the calculus of probabilities simply amounts to a set of rules for ensuring that the system of degrees of belief which we hold shall be a consistent system. Thus the calculus of probabilities belongs to formal logic. But the basis of our degrees of belief – or the a priori probabilities, as they used to be called – is part of our human outfit, perhaps given to us merely by natural selection, analogous to our perceptions and our memories rather than to formal logic. So far I yield to Ramsey – I think he is right. But in attempting to distinguish 'rational' degrees of belief from belief in general he was not yet, I think, quite successful. It is not getting to the bottom of the principle of induction merely to say it is a useful mental habit.

(CWXa: 338–9)

As Keynes continued to insist that our probabilities are not reducible to individual subjective beliefs or to empirical-psychological habits, his surrender to Ramsey was quite limited. Furthermore, it had no consequences for his own later view on economic expectations manifested in *The General Theory*.

Expectations, reason and rules

Keynes's conception of the mind and thought is reflected in his view on individuals' economic expectations and actions in a changing world. At the root of his economic theory is the rejection of the assumption of complete knowledge and the need for a theory of partial knowledge.

For Keynes, individuals have the capacity to form genuine and reasonable judgments concerning the future. To form expectations and act reasonably they follow their own judgment based on the information available to them, rather than falling back on the wisdom of tradition or empirical habits (abstract rules as manifested in patterns of behaviour formed through experience, habits and practices). It is true that in actual markets, individuals may attempt to cope with their ignorance of the future by imitating those whom they regard as having been more successful in pursuing their aims. But imitation cannot be a general rule for individual behaviour. Keynes was hopeful that public institutions as well as individuals would display the capacity for independent judgment. Public institutions do not help the process of coordination of individual plans by enforcing existing acquired habits and the average opinion of the market. There is a strong connection between the system of abstract rules of conduct, the conformist behaviour of individuals and public institutions, and the emergence of conventions in society. Conventions do not guarantee the coordination of individual plans of action, nor stability, because conventions may change unexpectedly and abruptly in time. As a consequence, the system of abstract rules of conduct cannot evolve without sudden and violent ruptures. For Keynes, conventions are extremely fragile.

Although Keynes was criticised for despising rules, his attitude towards tradition was in fact extremely respectful. He thought that conventions and conventional expectations play a significant role in our actual life. But, for him, the respect for tradition is not binding: it does not mean giving up reforms. Moreover, conventions are not genuine guides for action, but only artificial and practical means by which we rationalise our behaviour in cases of total ignorance. In his economics, Keynes distinguished between conventional and reasonable expectations. He attributed a positive role to our actual limited, yet positive, knowledge regarding the immediate future and ignored the paralysing effect of the ignorance of the remote future. For him, there exists the possibility for individuals to form reasonable judgments, which guide their actions in conditions of limited knowledge. Reasonable expectations are not grounded upon abstract rules of conduct or mathematical calculations, but on probability in his sense of *a priori*, that is, logical, probability.

It is true that in some situations it is impossible to form reasonable judgments about what may happen in the more distant future because we have no sound information available to us even regarding the present and the immediate future. In these cases – but only in these cases of total ignorance – Keynes suggests following conventional rules. In *The General Theory*, Keynes writes that if we have no knowledge on which to base our judgments, then it is reasonable to follow practical hypotheses to face an uncertain future. For example, we have no known evidence of or reasons for changes in the rate of interest twenty years hence. In this case, then, conventional expectations come into play. While reasonable expectations are grounded on *a priori* logical probabilities, that is, upon real, albeit limited, knowledge, conventional expectations are practical responses to the existence of total ignorance and uncertainty. While probability, for Keynes, is grounded upon knowledge, conventions and common knowledge are grounded upon the opinion of the majority of the market in the way represented by the well-known beauty contest example. Keynes would have listed Hayek's expectations among his own conventional expectations, as they are grounded upon habits, routines and imitation (Carabelli and De Vecchi 1999a, 1999b, 2001). He would have agreed with Hayek that imitation is a practical guide for action, but that it is reasonable to follow it only in situations of total ignorance. When no knowledge is available, the best thing to do is to refrain from acting. If you are compelled to act, then the best thing to do is to follow conventions. Keynes held that, in actual markets, agents are normally guided by conventional expectations. But he would have objected that these conventions are the 'idols' of the market place and give rise to negative social consequences (like financial instability and unemployment). Thus, as a rule, individuals and public institutions in particular should not follow them. According to Keynes, the individual has to consider each case on its own merits and by a personal autonomous judgment independent of traditional judgment, that is, independent of the judgment of the majority or of the most common opinion. This can be done by taking advantage of all the limited knowledge available to us. The importance attributed by Keynes to exceptions, in contrast to that which he attributed to rules, is one of the fundamental keys to understanding the difference between Keynes and Hayek on the theory of human action. As regards public institutions, Keynes's aim is to contrast conventions in order to avoid the negative social consequences of the market. The market ought not to lay down the rules of right and reasonable action, but our own judgment, based on the real, albeit partial, knowledge that we have.

Part VI
Looking ahead

18 The terminology of uncertainty in economics and the philosophy of an active role for government policies

Paul Davidson

Introduction

There are two significantly different concepts of uncertainty in economics: the classical and the Keynesian. The ability of economists to explain the importance of money, liquidity and the existence of persistent unemployment in a market economy depends on which of these two concepts of uncertainty the analyst uses.

Decision-making in economics

The economy is a process in historical time. Time is something that prevents everything from happening at once. The production of commodities takes time, and the consumption of goods, especially durables, takes considerable time. Economics is the study of how households and enterprises make decisions regarding production and consumption when the outcome (pay-off) of today's decision occurs at a significantly later date.

Any study of the behaviour of economic decision-makers, therefore, requires the analyst to make some assumption regarding what today's decision-makers 'know' about future outcomes. Because economists are split into two major theoretical camps about the meaning of uncertainty regarding future outcomes and therefore what decision-makers know about the future, these groups provide differing explanations of economic problems and their policy solutions. (Moreover, within the classical group there are schisms reflecting differing epistemological assumptions about what individual decision-makers 'know' about the presumed immutable external economic reality.)

Understanding the differences between the classical and the Keynesian concepts of uncertainty is essential to understanding the basic philosophical differences between economists on the need for a positive role for government and active economic policies to cure socially undesirable episodes in the economic system.

The absence of uncertainty in nineteenth-century classical economics

Ricardo (1817), the father of nineteenth-century classical economics, assumed a world of perfect certainty. On this view, all households and businesses were assumed to possess a full and correct knowledge of a presumed pre-programmed external economic reality that governed all past, present and future economic outcomes. The external economic environment was assumed to be *immutable* in the sense that it was not susceptible to change induced by human action. The path of the economy, like the path of the planets under Newton's celestial mechanics, was regarded as determined by timeless natural laws.

Economic decision-makers were assumed to have complete knowledge of these laws. Accordingly, while pursuing their respective goals of utility maximization and profit maximization, households and enterprises never make errors in their spending choices among all the goods available in the competitive market place. These 'economic agents' always spend everything they have earned on things with the highest 'known' future pay-off in terms of utility for households and profits for businesses. Accordingly, within the capacity of the economy to produce, there could never be a lack of demand for the products of industry or for workers who wanted to work. In this manner, classical economics justified a *laissez-faire* philosophy for the economic system. No government action could ensure a higher pay-off than the decisions of individuals with complete knowledge of the pay-off of each of their decisions made in free markets.

Uncertainty in today's orthodox economics

In the early twentieth century, classical economists tended to substitute the notion of probabilistic risk premia and 'certainty-equivalents' for the perfect knowledge assumption of earlier classical Ricardian theory. Risk premia provided uncertainty allowances that reflect the difference between the estimated value of some future outcome with an objective (frequency distribution) probability of less than unity and that same outcome with a probability of one.

By the 1970s, this classical risk analysis had evolved into what economists call the New Classical Theory of 'rational expectations', where individuals make decisions based on subjective probability distributions that are presumed to be the same as the immutable objective probability distributions that govern all current and future economic outcomes (Lucas 1972).

Today's orthodox economists interpret uncertainty in economics as synonymous with the knowledge of objective probability distributions (Lucas and Sargent 1981; Machina 1987) that govern future events. These economists who impose 'rational expectations' on the agents in their models are postulating that the governing, objective probability distributions are, in essence, known to all persons making economic decisions today. The standard deviations of these functions are the quantitative measure of uncertainty.

This device of labelling statistically reliable estimates of probabilistic risk (the standard deviation) as uncertainty permits orthodox economists to preserve intact most of the analysis that had been developed under the earlier nineteenth-century perfect knowledge assumption. While rejecting the perfect knowledge model, orthodox economists still accept, as a universal truth, the existence of a predetermined reality (similar to Newton's celestial mechanics) that can be fully described by unchanging objective conditional probability functions that are fully known by the decision-makers in one's model. Unlike the perfect certainty model, however, conflating the concept of uncertainty with probabilistic risk permits the analyst to state that individual decision-makers can make an occasional erroneous choice (in the short run) just as a single sample mean can differ from the true universe value. The assumption that people with rational expectations already 'know' the objective probabilities assures correct choices on average for those 'fittest' decision-makers who have survived in the Darwinian world of free markets. Again, the policy implication is that no government bureaucrat can make better decisions regarding resource use than those determined by rational individuals in free markets.

In orthodox economics where the standard deviation measures uncertainty, economic data are typically viewed as part of time series realizations generated by ergodic stochastic processes. In fact, Nobel Prize-winner Paul Samuelson, a self-proclaimed neoclassical synthesis Keynesian, has made the acceptance of the ergodic axiom of classical economics the *sine qua non* of the scientific method in economics (Samuelson 1969). Mainstream economists, since the Second World War, have followed Samuelson's (1947) *Foundations of Economic Analysis* and required the ergodic axiom for what they claim is a 'hard-headed' scientific analysis of economic problems devoid of politics and value judgments.

Uncertainty and ergodic stochastic processes

Why do Samuelson and the mainstream orthodoxy regard the ergodic axiom as a necessary attribute of scientific investigation? Logically, to make statistically reliable forecasts about future economic events, today's decision-makers should obtain and analyse sample data from the future. Since that is impossible, the presumption that all economic values are the outcome of ergodic stochastic processes permits the analyst to assert that the outcome at any future date is the statistical shadow of past and current market data. Accordingly, future outcomes can be discovered by analysing available past and present market data.

A realization of a stochastic process is a sample value of a multidimensional variable over a period of time, that is, a single time series. A stochastic process makes a universe of such time series. *Time statistics* refer to statistical averages (for example, the mean, standard deviation) calculated from a single fixed realization over an indefinite time space. *Space statistics*, on the other hand, refer to a fixed point of time and are formed over the universe of realizations (that is, they are statistics obtained from cross-sectional data).

If the stochastic process is *ergodic*, then for an infinite realization the time statistics and the space statistics will coincide. For finite realizations of ergodic processes, time and space statistics coincide except for random errors. Consequently, time and space statistics tend to converge (with the probability of unity) as the number of observations increase. If an ergodic economic environment is assumed to generate all economic outcomes, then statistics calculated from past time series or cross-sectional data are reliable estimates of the space statistics that will occur at any future date, that is, statistical analysis of past market data is assumed to provide reliable statistical information regarding any outcome on any future date.

All 'scientific' mainstream macroeconomic theories impose the ergodic axiom as an essential building block in the model. This implies that economic relationships are timeless or ahistoric 'natural' laws.[1] The historical dates when observations are collected do not affect the estimates of the statistical time and space averages. Accordingly, the classical presumption that decision-makers possess rational expectations implies that people in one's model have processed information embedded in past and present market data to form statistical averages (or decision weights) that reliably forecast the future. Or as Sargent (1993: 3), one of the leaders of the rational expectations school, states, 'rational expectations models impute much *more* knowledge to the agents within the model (who use the *equilibrium* probability distributions) ... than is possessed by an econometrician, who faces estimation and inference problems that the agents in the model have somehow solved'.

By using the standard deviation of objective probabilistic distribution as the measurement of uncertainty, rational expectations theory assumes that, on average, the actions fostered by these expectations are precisely those that would be forthcoming in a perfectly certain world – at least in the long run.

In recent years, partly in reaction to the rational expectations hypothesis, some mainstream economists have raised questions regarding the use of such stochastic concepts to define uncertainty. For example, Nobel Prize-winner R. M. Solow (1985: 328) has stated that 'economics is a social science ... much of what we observe cannot be treated as the realization of a stationary stochastic process without straining credulity'. Since stationary is a necessary but not sufficient condition for ergodicity,

Solow's statement implies that only the very gullible would ever believe that most important macroeconomic processes are ergodic. Nevertheless, since Solow considers himself to be a scientist in the Samuelson mould, the theoretical analysis for which he won the Nobel Prize requires the ergodic axiom as a fundamental building block.

Distinguishing between uncertainty and probabilistic risk

Beginning with Knight's (1921) seminal work, some economists have drawn a distinction between 'true' uncertainty and probabilistic risk, where the latter is calculable based on past frequency distributions and is, therefore, conceptually insurable, while uncertainty is neither calculable nor insurable.

John Maynard Keynes (CWVII) launched a revolution in economics. Keynes explicitly developed a 'general theory' as an alternative to classical theory. Keynes argued that the difference between probabilistic risk and uncertainty had important implications for understanding (a) the operations of a market-oriented entrepreneurial economy and (b) the positive, active role of government in influencing market outcomes through deliberate legislative policies.

In Keynes's (CWVII) analysis, whenever the full consequences of today's *crucial* economic decisions occur in the future, uncertainty would prevail and economic behaviour could not be described as an 'outcome of a weighted average of quantitative benefits multiplied by quantitative probabilities'.

This emphasis on the cruciality of some economic decisions implies that some other economic decisions may be of a more routine nature. One method of distinguishing between routine (and therefore conventional) decision-making processes and crucial decision-making processes would be to distinguish between situations where ergodic circumstances might prevail, and situations where non-ergodic circumstances are likely. *Decisions made under ergodic circumstances would be associated with routine decisions, while all crucial economic decisions would be associated with a non-ergodic environment.*

Unlike today's econometrically trained economists, Keynes did not use the language of stochastic processes in developing his concept of uncertainty. Consequently, Keynes's lexicon did not specifically identify non-ergodic processes as a necessary and sufficient condition underlying his concept of uncertainty. Keynes (CWXIVa: 114) simply described uncertainty as occurring when there is no 'scientific' basis to form any calculable probability. Nevertheless, in criticizing Tinbergen's use of econometric analysis, Keynes argued that Tinbergen's 'method' was not applicable to important economic data because 'the economic environment is not homogeneous over a period of time' (CWXIVc: 308). This criticism involving a non-homogeneous economic environment over time is equivalent to stating that economic time series are not stationary. Since non-stationary is a sufficient but not a necessary condition for non-ergodicity, it is clear that if Keynes were alive today he would accept his 1937 emphasis on uncertainty as the important distinguishing characteristic of his general theory vis-à-vis classical theory, namely that he associated important economic variables as being realized in a non-ergodic environment.

With the development of ergodic theory and stochastic process analysis since Keynes wrote, it is possible to interpret Keynes's concept of uncertainty in terms of this statistical concept of non-ergodic processes. In their scientific lexicon, it is also possible to explain to mainstream economists who believe themselves to be 'hard-headed' scientists the important conceptual difference between decisions made under non-ergodic (uncertain) conditions and those made under ergodic (probabilistic risk) situations.

Keynes's general-theory approach recognized that decision-makers 'know' that in some crucial economic dimensions the future is uncertain and cannot be reliably predicted on the basis of any statistical analysis of past evidence. Though Keynes did not know of, or use, stochastic terminology, the absence of ergodic conditions is a necessary and sufficient condition for the existence of Keynesian uncertainty in the real world. In a non-ergodic environment, even if agents had the capacity to obtain and process statistically past and current market data, such calculations do not, and cannot, provide a statistically reliable basis for forecasting the probability distributions, if any exist, that will govern outcomes at any specific date in the future. According to Keynes (CWXIVa: 114), '[a]bout these [future] matters there is no scientific basis to form any calculable [future] probability whatever. We simply do not know.' And in a world where decision-makers know that we cannot reliably predict the future, when fear of the uncertain future grows, putting one's unused claims on resources in liquid assets is similar to navigating one's boat to a safe harbour before the storm breaks.

Keynes's concept of uncertainty, therefore, reflects the fact that the future is *transmutable* or creative in the sense that future economic outcomes may be permanently changed in nature and substance by the actions today of individuals, groups (for example, unions, cartels) and/or governments, often in ways not even perceived by the creators of change. (It is also possible that changes that are not predetermined can occur even without any deliberate human economic action.)

This non-ergodic view of modelling uncertainty has been described by Nobel Prize-winner Sir John Hicks (1977: vii) as a situation where people in the model 'do not know what is going to happen and know that they do not know what is going to happen. As in history!' Hicks (1979: 113) declared: 'I am bold enough to conclude from these considerations that the usefulness of "statistical" or "stochastic" methods in economics is a good deal less than is now conventionally supposed.' Although in his published papers Hicks used non-stochastic deterministic models, Hicks (*ibid.*: 113n) associated uncertainty and Keynes's liquidity analysis with a violation of the classical ordering axiom, and in a private letter to me he indicated that he should have labelled his 'own point of view as nonergodic'.[2]

To summarize, following Samuelson, mainstream economic theory imposes the ergodic axiom for its 'scientific' approach. Requiring this ergodic axiom (or the equivalent ordering axiom in non-stochastic models) as a basis for scientific analysis dictates a *laissez-faire* policy philosophy by assumption. On the other hand, if one invokes Keynes's concept of uncertainty as involving a non-ergodic environment, then, logically, there can be a positive role for government in deliberately using monetary policy, and, if that fails, fiscal policy, to encourage the full employment of resources and promote economic growth.

Keynes's uncertainty concept and the search for microfoundations in orthodox economic theory

The microfoundations of macroeconomics concerns orthodox economists' attempts to specify macroeconomic relationships solely as based on the classical axiom-based theoretical analysis of individual (micro-)maximizing behaviour. All logical systems, however, are drawn from a set of premises or axioms and therefore contain no more information than the premises taken collectively imply. All orthodox microeconomic models are derived from Samuelson's *Foundations* (1947) where all decision-makers know all possible future outcomes, or from Samuelson's (1969) insistence that the ergodic hypothesis be imposed so as to permit probabilistic risk to represent uncertainty regarding future outcomes. Keynes's concept of uncertainty is scorned as non-scientific hand-waving. Consequently, what passes as the microfoundations of macroeconomics in orthodox theory is logically inconsistent with Keynes's macroeconomic general theory explaining employment, interest and money.

The result has been a continuing debate between Post Keynesian followers of Keynes and all mainstream theorists – including not only classical theorists but also those who call themselves Neoclassical Synthesis (Old) Keynesians and New Keynesians – over the relevant policy prescriptions for solving the macroeconomic problems of the real world.

Savage's (1954) expected utility theory (EUT) is a case in point involving orthodox microfoundations. EUT is *the* fundamental micro-model used by today's mainstream theorists in analysing how households and firms make decisions. The first postulate underlying

Savage's EUT framework is the *ordering axiom*, that is, the presumption that there exists a finite set of acts (each defined as a mapping from states to consequences) and that each agent can make a *complete* and transitive preference ordering of *all* possible acts. Savage characterizes the process of arriving at this ordering as 'Look before you leap'.[3]

Following Savage, orthodox economists use EUT to model decision-makers as valuing the possible acts open to them in terms of the probability-weighted sum of the utility of the consequences of each act (and where the relevant probabilities are the probabilities of each possible 'state of the world' that condition the consequences of each act). Unlike most economists who have adopted EUT as the micro-theoretical foundation of all economic theory, Savage recognizes that his 'Look before you leap' ordering analysis is *not* a general theory of decision-making for, though it deals with subjective probability distributions, it does not explicitly deal with uncertainty *per se*.

Savage recognizes that 'a person may not know the consequences of the acts open to him in each state of the world. He might be … ignorant' and hence might want to leave his options open. In the real world, income earners keep their options open by holding savings in the form of liquid assets. Thus Keynes's analysis of the demand for liquidity is an essential part of any explanation of why and how decision-makers keep options open.

Savage characterizes the leaving options open decision as 'You can cross that bridge when you come to it'. Savage admits that the latter is often a more accurate description of the human economic predicament than the 'Look before you leap' EUT analysis. When decision-makers fear the future because they cannot foresee the outcome, they will want to wait before making a decision. Such a situation involves Keynes's concept of uncertainty which may violate Savage's ordering axiom.

Since EUT requires the ordering axiom (or the ergodic axiom in stochastic models), mainstream utility maximizing theory is useful only when the analyst, as Savage puts it, 'attack[s] relatively simple problems of decision by artificially confining attention to so small a world that the "Look before you leap" principle can be applied', that is, where Keynes's uncertainty concept is not relevant and where only routine (non-crucial) decisions are involved. Savage warns that EUT is 'practical [only] in suitably limited domains … At the same time, the behavior of people is often at variance with the theory. The departure is sometimes flagrant … the "Look before you leap" principle is preposterous if carried to extremes.' Yet when today's mainstream economic theorists treat uncertainty in economics as synonymous with a probability measure, the behaviour they describe flagrantly departs from the behaviour that determines employment in a money-using market economy.

If, as Savage recognizes, in some areas of economic activity the ability of humans to form a complete preference ordering regarding all potential consequences of all actions is not possible, then EUT cannot provide a useful explanation of the behaviour of decision-makers in these areas. It is here that Keynes's uncertainty concept becomes paramount.

In the mainstream (ergodic) theory, where all probabilities are conceptually calculable, there is never a need, at least in the long run, to keep options open. People will therefore spend all they earn and there can never be a lack of effective demand to prevent the system from reaching full employment. On the other hand, when households and firms 'know that they do not know', as Hicks has noted, then decision-makers cannot rationally order all future consequences associated with any possible choice made today. In these circumstances, decision-makers may wish to defer indefinitely making Savage's 'Look before you leap' decisions. When people believe the future is uncertain in the sense of Keynes, they prefer to leave their options open, that is, to cross that bridge when, and if, they come to it. Holding one's savings in the form of liquid assets permits the holder to leave his/her options open. Whenever households and business managers believe they cannot predict the future with any degree of *a priori* or statistically reliable probability, then Savage's ordering axiom is violated. Hicks (1979) has associated a transgression of Savage's ordering axiom with Keynes's long-term 'liquidity' concept. For Keynes, it is the existence of an uncertain future that makes a long-run demand for liquidity (money) a ubiquitous fact of life. The ability to save one's income in the form of money and other liquid assets (that is, securities traded on organized markets) permits households and firms to keep their options open by not having to spend all their earned income on the products of industry, even in the long run.

As long as income-earning decision-makers have this option of demanding liquidity rather than the products of industry, then a *laissez-faire* market system cannot ensure that people's total market demand for goods and services will be sufficient to make it profitable for firms to employ fully all who want to work. In fact, as long as there is a fear of the future, it is highly unlikely, in the absence of active government policy, that full employment can ever be achieved.

The notion of a demand for *long-term* liquidity can only be justified in a world of Keynes's (non-ergodic) uncertainty. This desire for long-term liquidity is incompatible with both Savage's ordering axiom and Samuelson's ergodic hypothesis as a requirement for an economic science. Only Keynes's concept of non-ergodic uncertainty in economics provides a logical explanation of the phenomenon of persistent unemployment that occurs in market economies in the real world that we inhabit. Only Keynes's concept of uncertainty can justify an active positive role for government policies to assure full employment when questions of liquidity are important.

Conclusion

This chapter has argued that the terminology that one chooses for the purpose of defining concepts such as uncertainty can affect (or reflect) one's philosophy as to the appropriate role of government in economics. This should lead us to designing economic policies with a paraphrase of Reinhold Neibuhr's famous 'Serenity Prayer' in mind: God give us the grace to accept with serenity the things that cannot, and should not, be changed (routine decisions made in ergodic situations), courage to change the things that should be changed (crucial decisions in non-ergodic circumstances) and the wisdom to distinguish the one from the other.

Notes

1   Even if the model-builder permits the possibility of 'a change in regime', that is, a change in the objective probability distributions at some time in the future, the assumption of rational expectations implies that the people in one's model 'know' the objective probabilities of the regime change happening at any specific future date. As Sargent (1993: 27) noted, under the rational expectations hypothesis, at the initial instant, the probability of any regime changes in the future is known by the agents who already 'take this possibility into account'.
2   After reading my paper on rational expectations (Davidson 1982–83), in a private letter to me (dated 12 February 1983) Hicks wrote: 'I have just been reading your RE [rational expectations] paper ... I do like it very much. I have never been through that RE literature ... but I had just enough of it to be put off by the smell of it. You have now *rationalized* my suspicions, and have shown me that I missed a chance of labelling my own point of view as *nonergodic*. One needs a name like that to ram a point home' (emphasis in original).
3   Remember, Hicks associated uncertainty with the violation of this ordering axiom.

19 Keynesian uncertainty
What do we know?

Bill Gerrard

Introduction

The importance of the theme of uncertainty in Keynes's writings has long been recognised by what Coddington (1976) called his 'fundamentalist' followers. Two early exponents of the centrality of uncertainty to Keynes's thought are Robinson (1964) and Shackle (1967). Both argued that Keynes rejected the probability calculus as a means of understanding economic behaviour under conditions of uncertainty, citing as the two key pieces of textual evidence Chapter 12 in *The General Theory of Employment, Interest and Money* (CWVII) and his 1937 *Quarterly Journal of Economics* article (CWXIVa). However, Shackle and Robinson and other early Keynesian fundamentalists tended to present Keynes's arguments as largely negative, destructive of mainstream theorising. Keynes was not interpreted as offering a constructive alternative approach to developing a theory of economic behaviour under uncertainty.

The latter part of the 1980s witnessed the emergence of a 'new' Keynesian fundamentalism with contributions by Lawson (1985), Carabelli (1988), O'Donnell (1989) and several other Keynesian scholars. These new interpretations of Keynes sought to explore the links between Keynes's later observations on uncertainty in *The General Theory* and his earlier writings, especially *A Treatise on Probability* (CWVIII). Many of these contributions were primarily concerned with 'scholastic' issues of textual interpretation and debating the historical, philosophical and methodological implications of Keynes's writings on uncertainty and related themes. Rather less attention was paid to attempting to exploit the theoretical and empirical relevance of Keynes's constructive contributions to probability theory.

The objective of the present chapter is to attempt to fill this gap, to show how Keynes's writings on probability may be so exploited. More specifically, it will (1) attempt to show that Keynes provides the basis of a general theory of economic behaviour under uncertainty and (2) explore how he applied this theory to understanding the determinants of investment and the operation of the stock market. The basic argument is that Keynes has provided the outline of a theory of the effects of *fundamental uncertainty* on economic behaviour, in stark contrast to the characteristic assumption of mainstream economic theory that agents possess perfect or near perfect knowledge of the consequences of their actions.

The structure of the chapter is as follows. The next section provides an account of the logical theory of probability proposed in Keynes's *A Treatise on Probability* with a consideration of his own criticisms of that theory in subsequent writings. The following section shows how he attempted to operationalise the logical theory of probability in Chapter 12 of *The General Theory* on the state of long-term expectation. It is argued that Keynes's analysis provides the foundations for the development of a Keynesian general theory of economic behaviour under uncertainty that encompasses the more restrictive mainstream approaches. The next section considers Keynes's application of his practical theory of economic behaviour under uncertainty to the analysis of the investment decisions of firms. The key role that Keynes assigned to the stock market as the source of conventional valuations under conditions of fundamental uncertainty is discussed. Finally, there is a summary and some conclusions.

Keynes on probability

In *A Treatise on Probability*, Keynes proposed a logical theory of probability. Keynes considered the probability relation to take the following form:

$$p = a/h$$

where p is the probability of some proposition a given the available evidence h. The probability relation corresponds to the degree of belief that it is rational to hold in a proposition on the basis of the available evidence. The logical theory of probability represents an epistemic approach to probability in which the probability relation reflects a person's strength of belief in proposition a given h. Keynes nevertheless presents the probability relation as objective, a matter of logic and independent of individual subjective evaluations. In this respect, the logical theory is a normative theory, a theory of the degree of belief that individuals ought to hold in any proposition given the available information. A key concept in *A Treatise on Probability* is that of the weight of argument. Keynes defined the weight of argument as follows:

$$V = V(a/h)$$

The weight of argument, V, is a measure of the amount of evidence, h, on which the proposition, a, is based. If additional relevant evidence, h_1, is obtained, then the weight of argument increases:

$$V(a/hh_1) > V(a/h)$$

There is no unidirectional association between probability and weight of argument. Additional relevant evidence may increase, decrease, or leave unaltered the rational degree of belief in the proposition. Keynes considered the weight of argument as bearing on the extent to which people should feel justified in using the relevant probability as a guide to conduct, but he believed that it is difficult to represent this in a strict formal relationship.

> The question appears to me to be highly perplexing, and it is difficult to say much that is useful about it. But the degree of completeness of the information upon which a probability is based does seem to be relevant, as well as the actual magnitude of the probability, in making practical decisions.
>
> (CWVIII: 345)

Despite the practical importance that Keynes attached to the concept, he did not define the weight of argument consistently throughout the *Treatise*. As Runde (1990) has argued, Keynes variously defined the weight of argument as (1) the absolute amount of relevant evidence, (2) the degree of completeness of the evidence, and (3) the balance of absolute amounts of relevant knowledge and relevant ignorance, on which a probability is based. The latter two definitions measure evidence relative to ignorance. The differences between the three definitions are not merely a matter of semantics. They differ in their operational implications. Whereas an increase in the amount of relevant evidence necessarily increases weight under definition (1), it does not necessarily imply so under definitions (2) and (3). Indeed, if additional relevant evidence indicates that there is considerably more ignorance than previously believed, then under definitions (2) and (3) the weight of argument may be reduced.

A Treatise on Probability is primarily concerned with the development of the rules of logic as applied to the probability relation. As such, the emphasis is on abstract issues of probability theory rather than the explanation of human behaviour. However, as his discussion of the weight of argument indicates, Keynes did consider the practical relevance of the logical theory of probability. In particular, in Chapter 26 of the *Treatise*, 'The application of probability to conduct', Keynes analysed the usefulness of the doctrine of mathematical expectation as a guide to human conduct. In terms of this doctrine, the choice between alternative courses of action depends on both probability and the 'goodness' of outcomes, an alternative being evaluated in terms of its goodness weighted by its probability:

$$E = pA$$

where E is the mathematical expectation, p is the rational degree of belief and A is the amount of goodness that might be attained if the course of action is chosen.

Keynes made four criticisms of the doctrine of mathematical expecta-tion. First, goodness is assumed to be numerically measurable and arithmetically additive. This requires that goodness is atomic in char-acter (that is, divisible into separate and independent constituent units) or at most only partly organic (that is, non-divisible). Keynes subse-quently became increasingly sceptical of the validity of the atomic assumption for social phenomena (see Brown-Collier 1985). Secondly, mathematical expectation requires that probabilities must be numeri-cally measurable, whereas Keynes considered that most probabilities cannot be measured and may even be non-comparable or non-existent. Thirdly, the doctrine of mathematical expectation does not allow the weight of argument to influence the choice of action. Finally, Keynes also criticised the doctrine of mathematical expectation for taking no account of the expected loss (what Keynes termed 'risk') attached to the choice of any course of action. (See Gerrard (1995) for further discussion of Keynes's concept of risk and its application to the resolution of the St Petersburg Paradox.)

According to Keynes, then, the doctrine of mathematical expectation is inadequate as an explanation of human behaviour under conditions of uncertainty. He argued for the need to develop a more general theory of behaviour under uncertainty. Such a theory would involve at least four determinants of the choice between alternative courses of action: (1) degree of goodness, (2) probability, (3) weight, and (4) risk. Keynes explored the possibility of using a more complicated function of proba-bility that incorporated weight and risk effects, suggesting a 'conventional coefficient' c defined as:

$$c = 2pw \, (1 + q)(1 + w)$$

where p is the probability, w is the weight of the available evidence and q ($= 1 - p$) is the risk. The conventional coefficient ranges from unity when there is full information ($w = 1$) and full belief ($p = 1$) to zero when there is no evidence ($w = 0$) and no degree of belief ($p = 0$). Keynes considered using the conventional expectation, cA, as the general theory of behaviour under uncertainty. However, he concluded that it is unlikely to be useful to formulate the conventional coefficient in a precise mathematical form, given the implied uniformity of behaviour and the problems of measuring goodness, probability and weight.

After the publication of *A Treatise on Probability* in 1921, Keynes's thought continued to evolve. In particular, he became more concerned with the practical understanding of decision-making. He sought to encompass his earlier, more rationalistic and academic thought within a more psychological and practical framework. *The General Theory* exempli-fies Keynes's more practical approach. There are two key pieces of textual evidence showing the transition in the principal orientation of

Keynes's thought between the *Treatise* and *The General Theory*. The first is the letter that Keynes wrote in 1926 to Urban, the translator of the German edition of *A Treatise on Probability*. In this letter, Keynes expressed his growing dissatisfaction with the *Treatise*. He believed that the ultimate theory of probability may differ considerably from the logical theory of probability and would not be surprised if the ultimate theory of probability is found to be some form of frequency theory. Keynes felt that progress in understanding probability required the further development of the partly psychological subject of vague knowledge.

The second piece of textual evidence is Keynes's 1931 review of Ramsey's *Foundations of Mathematics* (CWXa). Ramsey was critical of Keynes's logical theory of probability and rejected the notions of objective and non-numerical probabilities. Ramsey developed a subjectivist approach to probability in which probabilities take the form of degrees of belief quantified through a betting method. Ramsey's approach formed the basis of the subjective expected utility (SEU) model that has become the foundation of the modern economic theory of decision-making under uncertainty. Keynes accepted Ramsey's distinction between formal logic and human logic. Formal logic consists of the set of rules of consistent thought whereas human logic comprises useful mental habits. The probability calculus represents a consistent system of degrees of belief and as such is a matter of formal logic. The core of Keynes's *A Treatise on Probability* had been concerned with the elaboration of a formal logic of probability. Keynes accepted Ramsey's criticism that the basis of the degrees of belief is part of our human logic and not within the province of formal logic. But Keynes believed that Ramsey did not have an adequate theory of induction and hence had not succeeded in distinguishing rational degrees of belief. In Keynes's view, it was not sufficient to describe induction as a useful mental habit: its usefulness needed to be explained. Keynes considered Ramsey to have clarified the limitations of the logical theory of probability and to have pointed the way towards the next area of enquiry, namely the psychological and practical aspects of human behaviour under uncertainty.

There has been much controversy in the 'new' Keynesian fundamentalist research programme over the degree to which Keynes retained his early beliefs in his later work. (See the contributions by Carabelli, Bateman, Davis, Fioretti, Gillies, Runde and Winslow in this volume, and Gerrard (1992) for a survey of the 'continuity-or-change' debate.) The interpretation adopted here is that of dynamic continuity in Keynes's thought. Keynes did not reject his early beliefs. Rather, he sought to encompass his logical theory of probability within a more general framework as he became more concerned with the richness of human experience and the vagueness of human knowledge. Keynes came to recognise that purely logical analyses of human behaviour are likely to be inadequate for understanding practical decision-making when agents are faced with fundamental uncertainty. The transition from *A Treatise on Probability* to *The General Theory* represented the generalisation, not rejection, of Keynes's early thought on probability and uncertainty.

Keynes on long-term expectations

A crucial distinction is drawn in *The General Theory* between short-term expectations and long-term expectations. Short-term expectations are defined by Keynes as 'the amount of proceeds which the entrepreneurs expect to receive from the corresponding output' (CWVII: 24). Short-term expectations are relevant for the pricing and output decisions of firms. They are subject to a gradual and continuous process of revision in the light of actual market outcomes. Mistaken short-term expectations can lead to output and employment diverging temporarily from their equilibrium levels. Hence Keynes classified short-term expectational errors as one possible cause of frictional unemployment. Crucially, short-term expectations do not cause involuntary unemployment.

Long-term expectations affect the investment decisions of firms. Long-term expectations concern the prospective yields that firms expect to earn over the life of a capital investment project. The prospective yield together with the supply price of capital determine the expected (monetary) rate of return on a capital investment, defined by Keynes as the marginal efficiency of capital. (It is important to note that Keynes's concept of the marginal efficiency of capital is a monetary phenomenon, relating to the expected monetary flows to be generated by an investment, and, as such, is quite distinct from the neoclassical concept of marginal productivity of capital and the associated logical problems highlighted by the capital controversy.) Firms will consider undertaking those capital projects for which the marginal efficiency of capital exceeds the prevailing rate of interest. Hence the aggregate level of investment in the economy depends crucially on the state of long-term expectations. Given the principle of effective demand and its corollary that the aggregate level of investment determines the equilibrium levels of output and employment, it follows that the state of long-term expectations is a fundamental determinant of involuntary unemployment. Consequently, Keynes's discussion of the state of long-term expectations is central to *The General Theory*.

Keynes considered the state of long-term expectations to consist of two components: the most probable forecast and the state of confidence. The most probable forecast is the best (that is, highest degree of belief) estimate of the future outcome. Keynes's concept of the most probable forecast has a close connection with the maximum likelihood approach developed by Fisher to which Keynes had made an important contribution in a paper entitled 'The principal averages and the laws of error which lead to them', published in 1911 and subsequently incorporated into *A Treatise on Probability*. (See Conniffe (1992) for a discussion of Keynes's contribution to the development of the maximum likelihood approach.) In his 1911 paper, Keynes discussed the appropriateness of alternative principal averages – the arithmetic mean, the geometric mean, the harmonic mean and the median – given the shape of the probability distribution (that is, the law of error). A key implication of this analysis is that the most probable forecast is not necessarily the mathematical expectation (that is, the arithmetic mean) of a set of alternative future outcomes. The arithmetic mean may be appropriate for the normal bell-shaped probability distribution but not necessarily so for other, non-normal distributions.

The second component of the state of long-term expectations is the state of confidence. Keynes (CWVII: 148) defined the state of confidence as 'how highly we rate the likelihood of our best forecast turning out quite wrong'. The state of confidence is weak 'if we expect large changes but are very uncertain as to what precise form these changes will take'. In a footnote, Keynes explained that by 'very uncertain' he did not mean 'very improbable' and he referred back to his discussion of weight of argument in Chapter 6 of *A Treatise on Probability*. Also, the definition of the state of confidence echoes Keynes's discussion of risk in Chapter 26 of the *Treatise*.

Keynes's discussion of the state of long-term expectations in *The General Theory* can be seen as attempt to construct a practical theory of economic behaviour under uncertainty based on the logical theory of probability developed in *A Treatise on Probability*. The links between *The General Theory* and the *Treatise* are explicitly acknowledged by Keynes in the footnote on uncertainty and weight. In the *Treatise*, Keynes had developed a logical theory of probability. But Keynes had recognised that probability alone is insufficient as a guide to action. The weight of argument and the associated risk of any course of action are also key factors affecting actual choices. The recognition of the limits to the practical relevance of probability calculations is at the foundation of Keynes's concept of the state of long-term expectations. The most probable forecast depends on the degrees of belief attached to alternative estimates of future outcomes. The state of confidence depends on the evaluation of the evidential basis for these degrees of belief. Thus, whereas the most probable forecast represents the practical expression of the probability relation, the state of confidence represents the practical expression of the weight of argument (as well as the risk of loss). The propensity for firms to undertake investment projects depends crucially on the state of confidence. If the evidential basis is weak, so that firms are very uncertain and the state of confidence is low, the propensity to invest is low even though the marginal efficiency of capital is calculated to exceed the rate of interest.

Hence Keynes's practical policy conclusion that a merely monetary policy of lowering the rate of interest is likely to be ineffective if the state of confidence is low.

The practical relevance of the distinction between probability and weight of argument is not limited to the state of confidence. The distinction is also crucial for Keynes's concepts of risk premium and liquidity premium discussed later in *The General Theory* (CWVII: 240) as well as in a letter that Keynes wrote to Hugh Townsend in December 1938. The risk premium is associated with probability and is expected to be rewarded by an increased reward at the end of the period. In contrast, the liquidity premium is associated with the weight of argument and depends on the state of confidence. Unlike the risk premium, the liquidity premium is not expected to be rewarded by tangible income at the end of the period. Rather, it represents the payment for an increased sense of comfort and confidence during the period.

Keynes's analysis of the practical relevance of probability and weight of argument to actual decision-making provides the basis for the development of a Keynesian general theory of economic behaviour under uncertainty that can encompass the more restrictive mainstream approaches. Mainstream approaches to decision-making under uncertainty have focused almost exclusively on choice situations characterised by well-defined probability distributions. Mainstream theorists have variously used epistemic and aleatory justifications for the assumption of a well-defined probability distribution. Some adopt a subjectivist epistemic approach and follow Ramsey in asserting that all probabilities can be measured numerically. Others take an aleatory approach, assuming that the choice situation is replicative with a known set of relative frequencies. Keynes's analysis of behaviour under uncertainty moves beyond mainstream approaches in two ways. First, Keynes considered probabilities to be non-numerical for the most part, often non-comparable, and that there are situations in which it is not possible to form a probability judgment at all. Hence probability distributions are mostly ill-defined (or fuzzy) in varying degrees; well-defined probability distributions are a special limiting case. Secondly, Keynes stressed the importance of the amount of available relevant evidence to actual behaviour. A lack of available evidence may be reflected in fuzzy probability distributions. But even if the evidential basis can support a set of numerical probabilities and the calculation of a mathematical expectation, the recognition of the limited nature of the evidence may have an important impact on the decision outcome. This can be termed the Keynesian uncertainty hypothesis: the propensity to act on an expectation depends on the credence of the probabilities underpinning it, where credence reflects an assessment of the adequacy or otherwise of the available relevant evidence. The mainstream focus on well-defined probability distributions neglects the possibility that the assessment of the adequacy of the available evidence may affect economic behaviour.

Keynes's approach suggests that choice situations should be classified with respect to two dimensions: probabilities themselves and the degree of credence in those probabilities, where such credence reflects the adequacy of the evidence on which those probabilities are based (effectively, Keynes's concept of weight of argument). Probability and credence provide two separate but interconnected channels by which the available evidence is brought to bear on the decision.

The classification of choice situations is presented graphically in Figure 19.1. Mainstream economic theory has concentrated on choice situations with well-defined probability distributions and in which the agents are assumed, at least implicitly, to possess all relevant information. Knight (1921) described such situations as situations of risk. Following Ellsberg (1961), mainstream economic theory has moved beyond the consideration of situations of risk to analyse ambiguous choices. Ambiguity refers to cases of repeated trials in which there is incomplete information of the long-run relative frequencies. Although ambiguity involves some inadequacy of the evidential base, the degree of credence remains high given the repeated-trial nature of the choice situation. Keynes's analysis of long-term expectations can be seen as generalising the theory of economic behaviour to deal with cases of fundamental uncertainty in which choices are unique and the evidential base is very limited. It is Keynes's contention that, under conditions of fundamental uncertainty, economic behaviour depends not only on the most probable forecast derived from the probability distribution but also

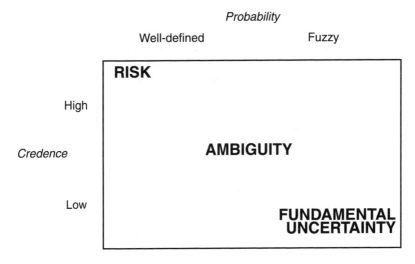

Figure 19.1

on the state of confidence reflecting the credence attached to the evidential base.

Keynes on investment and the stock market

Keynes's analysis of the state of long-term expectations suggests that there are three different aspects to the investment decision of firms: the rational aspect, the creative aspect, and the active aspect. The rational aspect of the investment decision is the calculation of whether a specific capital project can be expected to yield a sufficient rate of return. Keynes formalised the rational aspect of the investment decision as the calculation of the marginal efficiency of capital. This calculation depends crucially on the state of long-term expectations, specifically the most probable forecast of the prospective yield of the capital project. A second aspect of the investment decision is the creative aspect. Investment is not only a matter of calculation; it also involves imagination. Investment is a process of change through which firms seek to improve their future business performance. Investment provides an opportunity for a firm to alter its competitive environment creatively by renewing or expanding its productive capacity, introducing new production techniques and developing new product lines. The possible future consequences created by an investment must be first imagined before being quantified and the marginal efficiency of capital calculated.

However, creativity and rationality alone will not lead to the actual realisation of potential investment opportunities. Firms must act if the imagined and calculated returns are to be achieved. This is the third aspect of the investment decision. Understanding the factors influencing the propensity to act is crucial to the analysis of the investment decision. Keynes provided considerable insight into the propensity to act. One key group of factors is the personal characteristics of the individual decision-makers. In particular, Keynes highlighted the importance of the state of confidence, the assessment by individuals of the adequacy of the evidential base on which their decisions are to be made. Beyond the epistemic aspect of the propensity to act, Keynes also stressed the role of animal spirits – 'a spontaneous urge to action rather than inaction' (CWVII: 161). Investment plans will only be implemented if the calculated expected return is adequate and backed by sufficient confidence and a strong urge to action: 'individual initiative will only be adequate when reasonable calculation is supplemented and supported by animal spirits' (*ibid.*: 162).

Although personal factors such as the state of confidence and animal spirits are important factors affecting the implementation of investment plans, Keynes also suggested that the propensity to act would depend on the nature of the firm as an organisation and its competitive environment. The importance of these organisational and environmental factors in Keynes's analysis is discussed by Marchionatti (1998). Marchionatti suggests that the strength of animal spirits is affected by the age of the firm and the degree of competitive pressure.

According to Keynes, the 'outstanding fact' of the investment decision is 'the extreme precariousness of the basis of knowledge on which our estimates of prospective yield have to be made' (CWVII: 149). According to Keynes, the recognition of the extreme precariousness of the base of knowledge affects the investment decision through the state of confidence. This behavioural pattern is characteristic of situations of fundamental uncertainty in which 'knowledge of the factors which will govern the yield of an investment some years hence is usually very slight and often negligible' (*ibid*.). Fundamental uncertainty creates the potential for instability in the economic system, but Keynes argued that generally stability prevails because the state of long-term expectations tends to be stable. The stability of long-term expectations is generated by the conventional response to fundamental uncertainty. Faced with a lack of knowledge about prospective yields, Keynes believed that investors rely on valuations based on the conventional assumption that '... the existing state of affairs will continue indefinitely, except in so far as we have specific reasons to expect a change' (*ibid*.: 152). According to Keynes, the stock market is the source of these conventional valuations. Hence the key role assigned by Keynes to the stock market in his analysis of the investment decision.

Keynes's analysis of the stock market in Chapter 12 of *The General Theory* has been largely neglected by Keynesian scholars other than as a source of further textual evidence of the importance that Keynes attached to conventional behaviour. The substance of Keynes's analysis of the stock market has been typically viewed as a digression. Few have considered Keynes as constructing a theory of stock-market behaviour. One important exception is Pratten (1993) who argues that Keynes provides seven propositions on stock-market behaviour:

1 It is difficult or impossible to forecast long-term yields on investments.
2 Investors assume that the current state of affairs will continue except if there are definite reasons to expect change.
3 Investors assume that existing prices correctly reflect future prospects.
4 Investors endeavour to conform with the behaviour of the majority.
5 Professional investors are concerned with forecasting changes in the conventional valuations, not with superior forecasting of prospective yields.
6 Conventions can impart stability rather than volatility but the stability is precarious.
7 Instability increases with the proportion of ignorant individuals.

Keynes's analysis of stock-market behaviour suggests that it is important to distinguish between three types of market participants: business entrepreneurs, professional speculators and the general public. Business entrepreneurs possess specialist information on the future prospects for their own businesses. This specialist information may be private or publicly available. Professional speculators have access only to publicly available information. The expertise of professional speculators lies in their knowledge of the stock market and ability to forecast changes in market psychology. Professional speculators are able to filter newly available information (that is, the 'news') to determine which information is relevant for market valuations of individual businesses. The general public also has access only to publicly available information but, unlike the professional speculators, does not have the expertise to determine the relevance of specific pieces of information. Hence the general public accepts the prevailing market valuations as the best estimate of prospective yields and uses price movements as a signal of market-relevant news that has led to a re-evaluation of prospective yields. The relative ignorance of the general public and, as a consequence, its slowness to react to relevant news creates profitable opportunities for professional speculators to anticipate future market movements. Thus the conventional valuation of future business prospects generated by the stock market is the outcome of a complex process of information dissemination and evaluation involving groups of market participants with different information and different interpretative frameworks. In contrast to current mainstream economic theory such as the efficient-market hypothesis and the random-walk theory of share price movements, Keynes did not consider stock-market valuations to be fundamental valuations. Under conditions of fundamental uncertainty, the knowledge of the factors affecting prospective yields is too limited to be able to provide a fundamental valuation. In the absence of fundamental valuations, agents rely on the conventional valuations determined by the stock market. These conventional valuations provide the best available estimate of prospective yields, in the sense that they represent the collective market assessment of all currently available information. But individuals are aware of the precariousness of conventional valuations and hence the propensity to act on these valuations depends on the state of confidence, animal spirits, and other organisational and environmental factors.

Summary and conclusions

A constant theme that runs throughout Keynes's writings is the belief that human conduct is only partially based on reason. This chapter has explored how Keynes developed his understanding of the role of reason in the context of economic behaviour under uncertainty. It has been argued that the starting point for Keynes's analysis of economic behaviour under uncertainty is *A Treatise on Probability* in which he developed the logical theory of probability as a formal logic of partial belief. Importantly, in the *Treatise*, Keynes recognised the limitations of probability alone as a guide to human conduct and suggested that the weight of argument and the risk of expected loss would also be important in determining actual behaviour. From this perspective, it has been argued that *The General Theory* should be interpreted as, in part, an attempt by Keynes to develop the logical theory of probability into a general theory of economic behaviour under uncertainty that could deal with situations of fundamental uncertainty. Keynes argued that, under conditions of fundamental uncertainty characterised by a limited evidential base, economic behaviour depends on the state of long-term expectations, which consist of the most probable forecast and the state of confidence. The state of long-term expectations should be seen as the practical expression of the concepts of probability, weight and risk that Keynes had developed in *A Treatise on Probability*. It has also been shown that Keynes assigned a key role to the stock market as the source of conventional valuations as a basis for action when fundamental uncertainty prevails.

Although this chapter has been primarily concerned with providing an interpretation of Keynes's writings on probability and uncertainty, the aim has been to develop a constructive interpretation that shows the modern relevance of Keynes's contribution. In particular, it has been argued that Keynes's proposition that economic behaviour under uncertainty depends on probability and weight of argument sets out the basis of a more general theory that can encompass the more restrictive mainstream analyses of risk and ambiguity. Furthermore, Keynes's analysis can provide the starting point for the development of a Keynesian theory of stock-market behaviour under fundamental uncertainty that recognises the importance of the precariousness of conventional market valuations. By moving beyond the characteristic mainstream assumption that share prices reflect fundamental valuations, a Keynesian theory of stock-market behaviour may be more able to give a satisfactory account of stock-market bubbles in terms of the dynamics of conventional valuations under fundamental uncertainty.

Bibliography

Works by Keynes

Unpublished works

Keynes, J. M. (1904) 'Ethics in relation to conduct', unpublished paper, King's College, Cambridge University.
—— (1905) 'Miscellanea ethica', unpublished paper, King's College, Cambridge University.
—— (1907) 'The principles of probability', submitted as a fellowship dissertation to King's College, Cambridge, December 1907. Microfilmed in 1995 by Chadwyck-Healey Ltd, Cambridge: *John Maynard Keynes Papers*, Reel 22, TP/A/1–2.
—— (1908) 'The principles of probability', submitted as a fellowship dissertation to King's College, Cambridge, December 1908. Microfilmed in 1995 by Chadwyck-Healey Ltd, Cambridge: *John Maynard Keynes Papers*, Reel 168, MM/6.

The collected writings of John Maynard Keynes

CWIV (1971) *A Tract on Monetary Reform*, The Collected Writings of John Maynard Keynes, vol. IV, London: Macmillan for the Royal Economic Society (first published 1923).
CWV (1971) *A Treatise on Money: 1 The Pure Theory of Money*, The Collected Writings of John Maynard Keynes, vol. V, London: Macmillan for the Royal Economic Society (first published 1930).
CWVI (1971) *A Treatise on Money: 2 The Applied Theory of Money*, The Collected Writings of John Maynard Keynes, vol. VI, London: Macmillan for the Royal Economic Society (first published 1930).
CWVII (1973) *The General Theory of Employment, Interest and Money*, The Collected Writings of John Maynard Keynes, vol. VII, London: Macmillan for the Royal Economic Society (first published 1936).
CWVIII (1973) *A Treatise on Probability*, The Collected Writings of John Maynard Keynes, vol. VIII, London: Macmillan for the Royal Economic Society (first published 1921).
CWIX (1972) *Essays in Persuasion*, The Collected Writings of John Maynard Keynes, vol. IX, London: Macmillan for the Royal Economic Society.

CWIXa (1972) 'Can Lloyd George do it? – The pledge examined', in *Essays in Persuasion, The Collected Writings of John Maynard Keynes*, vol. IX, London: Macmillan for the Royal Economic Society (first published 1929), pp. 86–125.

CWIXb (1972) 'The end of laissez faire', in *Essays in Persuasion, The Collected Writings of John Maynard Keynes*, vol. IX, London: Macmillan for the Royal Economic Society (first published 1926), pp. 272–94.

CWIXc (1972) 'Review of H. G. Wells's *The World of William Clissold*', in *Essays in Persuasion, The Collected Writings of John Maynard Keynes*, vol. IX, London: Macmillan for the Royal Economic Society (first published 1927), pp. 315–20.

CWIXd (1972) 'The means to prosperity', in *Essays in Persuasion, The Collected Writings of John Maynard Keynes*, vol. IX, London: Macmillan for the Royal Economic Society (first published 1933), pp. 335–66.

CWIXe (1972) 'The economic possibilities for our grandchildren', in *Essays in Persuasion, The Collected Writings of John Maynard Keynes*, vol. IX, London: Macmillan for the Royal Economic Society, pp. 321–32.

CWIXf (1972) 'Am I a liberal?', in *Essays in Persuasion, The Collected Writings of John Maynard Keynes*, vol. IX, London: Macmillan for the Royal Economic Society, pp. 295–306

CWXa (1972) 'F. P. Ramsey', in *Essays in Biography, The Collected Writings of John Maynard Keynes*, vol. X, London: Macmillan for the Royal Economic Society (reprinted from *The New Statesman and Nation*, 3 October 1931), pp. 335–46.

CWXb (1972) 'My early beliefs', in *Essays in Biography, The Collected Writings of John Maynard Keynes*, vol. X, London: Macmillan for the Royal Economic Society (first published 1938), pp. 433–50.

CWXc (1972) 'Alfred Marshall', in *Essays in Biography, The Collected Writings of John Maynard Keynes*, vol. X, London: Macmillan for the Royal Economic Society (reprinted from the *Economic Journal*, September 1924), pp. 161–231.

CWXd (1972) 'Two memoirs', in *Essays in Biography, The Collected Writings of John Maynard Keynes*, vol. X, London: Macmillan for the Royal Economic Society (reprinted from *Two Memoirs*, London: Rupert Hart-Davis, 1949), pp. 389–450.

CWXe (1972) 'Francis Ysidro Edgeworth', in *Essays in Biography, The Collected Writings of John Maynard Keynes*, vol. X, London: Macmillan for the Royal Economic Society (reprinted from the *Economic Journal* 36: 140–53, 1926), pp. 251–66.

CWXf (1972) 'Robert Malthus: centenary allocution', in *Essays in Biography, The Collected Writings of John Maynard Keynes*, vol. X, London: Macmillan for the Royal Economic Society (first published 1933), pp. 104–8.

CWXg (1972) 'Newton, the man', in *Essays in Biography, The Collected Writings of John Maynard Keynes*, vol. X, London: Macmillan for the Royal Economic Society, pp. 363–74.

CWXII (1978) *Activities 1939–45: Internal War Finance, The Collected Writings of John Maynard Keynes*, vol. XII, London: Macmillan for the Royal Economic Society.

CWXIII (1973) *The General Theory and After: Part 1, Preparation, The Collected Writings of John Maynard Keynes*, vol. XIII, London: Macmillan for the Royal Economic Society.

CWXIVa (1973) 'The general theory of employment', in *The General Theory and After: Part II, Defence and Development, The Collected Writings of John Maynard Keynes*, vol. XIV, London: Macmillan for the Royal Economic Society (reprinted from the *Quarterly Journal of Economics* 51: 209–23, 1937), pp. 109–123.

CWXIVb (1973) Letters to Roy Harrod dated 4 and 16 July 1938, in *The General Theory and After: Part II, Defence and Development, The Collected Writings of John Maynard Keynes*, vol. XIV, London: Macmillan for the Royal Economic Society, pp. 295–7 and 299–301.

CWXIVc (1973) Letter to Tinbergen dated 28 September 1938, in *The General Theory and After: Part II, Defence and Development, The Collected Writings of John Maynard Keynes*, vol. XIV, London: Macmillan for the Royal Economic Society, pp. 293–5.

CWXIVd (1973) 'Some economic consequences of a declining population', in '*The General Theory and After: Part II, Defence and Development, The Collected Writings of John Maynard Keynes*, vol. XIV, London: Macmillan for the Royal Economic Society (the Galton Lecture, delivered before the Eugenics Society, 16 February 1937), pp. 124–33.

CWXIVe (1973) 'Professor Tinbergen's method', in *The General Theory and After: Part II, Defence and Development, The Collected Writings of John Maynard Keynes*, vol. XIV, London: Macmillan (reprinted from the *Economic Journal* 47, September 1939), pp. 306–18.

CWXIVf (1973) Letter to R. Tyler dated 23 August 1938, in *The General Theory and After: Part II, Defence and Development, The Collected Writings of John Maynard Keynes*, vol. XIV, London: Macmillan for the Royal Economic Society, pp. 285–9.

CWXV (1971) 'Great Britain's foreign investments', in *Activities 1906–14: India and Cambridge, The Collected Writings of John Maynard Keynes*, vol. XV, London: Macmillan for the Royal Economic Society (reprinted from *New Quarterly* February: 37–53, 1910), pp. 44–59.

CWXXI (1982) *Activities 1931–39: World Crises and Policies in Britain and America, The Collected Writings of John Maynard Keynes*, vol. XXI, London: Macmillan for the Royal Economic Society.

CWXXVII (1980) *Activities 1940–46: Shaping the Post-War World – Employment and Commodities, The Collected Writings of John Maynard Keynes*, vol. XXVII, London: Macmillan for the Royal Economic Society.

CWXXVIII (1982) *Social, Political and Literary Writings, The Collected Writings of John Maynard Keynes*, vol. XXVIII, London: Macmillan for the Royal Economic Society.

CWXXIX (1979) *The General Theory and After: A Supplement to Vols XIII and XIV, The Collected Writings of John Maynard Keynes*, vol. XXIX, London: Macmillan for the Royal Economic Society.

Other published work by J. M. Keynes

Keynes, J. M. (1911) 'The principal averages and the laws of error which lead to them', *Journal of the Royal Statistical Society* 74: 323–36.

Works by other authors

Baccini, A. (forthcoming) 'High pressure and black clouds: Keynes and the frequentist theory of probability', *Cambridge Journal of Economics*.

Barsalou, L.W. (1987) 'The instability of graded structure: implications for the nature of concepts', in U. Neisser (ed.) *Concepts and Conceptual Development: Ecological and Intellectual Factors in Categorization*, Cambridge: Cambridge University Press.

Bateman, B. W. (1987) 'Keynes's changing conception of probability', *Economics and Philosophy* 3: 97–119.

—— (1988) 'G. E. Moore and J. M. Keynes: a missing chapter in the history of the Expected Utility Model', *American Economic Review* 78: 1098–106.

—— (1991) 'Das Maynard Keynes Problem', *Cambridge Journal of Economics* 15: 101–11.

—— (1996) *Keynes's Uncertain Revolution*, Ann Arbor: The University of Michigan Press.

Bateman, B. and Davis, J. B. (eds) (1991) *Keynes and Philosophy: Essays on the Origins of Keynes's Thought*, Aldershot: Edward Elgar.

Blanchard, O. and Fischer, S. (1989) *Lectures in Macroeconomics*, Cambridge, MA: MIT Press.

Braithwaite, R. B. (1973) 'Editorial foreword' in *A Treatise on Probability*, *The Collected Writings of John Maynard Keynes*, vol. VIII, London: Macmillan for the Royal Economic Society.

Broad, C. (1934) 'Is "goodness" a name of a simple non-natural quality?', *Proceedings of the Aristotelian Society* 1934: 249–68.

Brown-Collier, E. K. (1985) 'Keynes's view of an organic universe: the implications', *Review of Social Economy* 43: 14–23.

Carabelli, A. (1988) *On Keynes's Method*, London and New York: Macmillan and St Martin's Press.

—— (1991) 'The methodology of the critique of the classical theory: Keynes on organic interdependence', in B. Bateman and J. B. Davis (eds) (1991), pp. 104–25

—— (1995) 'Uncertainty and measurement in Keynes: probability and organicness', in S. Dow and J. Hillard (eds.) (1995).

—— (1998) 'Keynes on probability, uncertainty and tragic choices', *Cahiers d'Economie Politique* 30–1: 187–226.

Carabelli, A. and De Vecchi, N. (1999a) 'Where to draw the line? Hayek and Keynes on knowledge, ethics and economics', *European Journal of the History of Economic Thought* 6(2): 271–96.

—— (1999b) 'Hayek and Keynes: two travelling companions in the critique of economic method?', paper presented at the European Journal of the History of Economic Thought Conference, Valencia, Spain, February 1999; published (2001) as 'Hayek and Keynes: from a common critique of economic method to different theories of expectations', *Review of Political Economy*, 13: 269–85.

—— (2001) 'Individuals, public institutions and knowledge: Hayek and Keynes', in P. L. Porta, R. Scazzieri and A. Skinner (eds) *Knowledge, Social Institutions and the Division of Labour*, Aldershot: Edward Elgar, pp. 229–48.

Chappell, V. C. (ed.) (1966) *Hume*, London: Macmillan.

Chick, V. (1983) *Macroeconomics after Keynes: A Reconsideration of the General Theory*, Oxford: Philip Allan.

Clarke, P. F. (1988) *The Keynesian Revolution in the Making*, Oxford: Oxford University Press.

Coates, J. M. (1996) *The Claims of Common Sense: Moore, Wittgenstein, Keynes and the Social Sciences*, Cambridge: Cambridge University Press.

Coddington, A. (1976) 'Keynesian economics: the search for first principles', *Journal of Economic Literature* 14: 1258–73.
—— (1982) 'Deficient foresight: a troublesome theme in Keynesian economics', *American Economic Review* 72: 480–7.
—— (1983) *Keynesian Economics: The Search for First Principles*, London: Allen & Unwin.
Committee on Finance and Industry (1931) *Minutes of Evidence*, 2 vols, London: HMSO.
Conniffe, D. (1992) 'Keynes on probability and statistical inference and the links to Fisher', *Cambridge Journal of Economics* 16: 475–89.
Cottrell, A. (1993) 'Keynes's theory of probability and its relevance to his economics: three theses', *Economics and Philosophy* 9: 25–51.
Cottrell, A. F. and Lawlor, M. S. (eds) (1995) 'New perspectives on Keynes', annual supplement to vol. 27 of *History of Political Economy*.
Davidson, P. (1978) *Money and the Real World*, second edition, London: Macmillan.
—— (1982–83) 'Rational expectations: a fallacious foundation for studying crucial decision-making processes', *Journal of Post Keynesian Economics* 10: 146–53.
—— (1988) 'A technical definition of uncertainty and the non-neutrality of money', *Cambridge Journal of Economics* 12: 329–37.
—— (1991) 'Is probability theory relevant for uncertainty? A Post Keynesian perspective', *Journal of Economic Perspectives*, 5: 129–43.
—— (1994) *Post Keynesian Macroeconomic Theory*, Aldershot: Edward Elgar.
——(1996) 'Reality and economic theory', *Journal of Post Keynesian Economics* 18: 479–508.
Davis, J. B. (1994a) 'Keynes's philosophical thinking', in J. B. Davis (ed.) *The State of Interpretation of Keynes*, Boston: Kluwer Academic Publishers, pp. 223–44.
—— (1994b) *Keynes's Philosophical Development*, Cambridge: Cambridge University Press.
—— (1994c) 'The locus of Keynes's philosophical thinking in the *General Theory*: the concept of convention', in Karen I. Vaughn (ed.) *Perspectives on the History of Economic Thought*, vol. X, Aldershot: Edward Elgar, pp. 157–78.
—— (1996) 'Convergences in Keynes and Wittgenstein's later views', *European Journal of the History of Economic Thought* 3: 433–48.
—— (1997) 'J. M. Keynes on history and convention,' in G. C. Harcourt and P. A. Riach (eds) *A 'Second Edition' of The General Theory*, vol. 2, London: Routledge, pp. 203–21.
—— (1998) 'Conventions', in J. B. Davis, D. W. Hands and U. Mäki (eds) *The Handbook of Economic Methodology*, Cheltenham: Edward Elgar, pp. 83–6.
de Finetti, B. (1931) 'Sul significato soggettivo della probabilità', *Fundamenta Mathematicae* 17: 298–329.
Dequech, D. (1999a) 'Expectations and confidence under uncertainty', *Journal of Post Keynesian Economics* 21: 415–30.
—— (1999b) 'On some arguments for the rationality of conventional behaviour under uncertainty – concepts, applicability and criticisms', in C. Sardoni and P. Kriesler (eds) *Keynes, Post-Keynesianism and Political Economy: Essays in Honour of Geoff Harcourt*, vol. 3, London: Routledge, pp. 176–95.
—— (2000) 'Asset choice, liquidity preference, and rationality under uncertainty', *Journal of Economic Issues* 34: 159–76.

Dow, A. and Dow, S. (1985) 'Animal spirits and rationality', in T. Lawson and H. Pesaran (eds) (1985).

Dow, S. C. (1995) 'Uncertainty about uncertainty', in S. C. Dow and J. Hillard (eds) (1995), pp. 117–27.

Dow, S. C. and Hillard, J. V. (eds.) (1995) *Keynes, Knowledge and Uncertainty*, Aldershot: Edward Elgar.

—— (2002) *Keynesian Econometrics, Microeconomics and the Theory of the Firm, Volume 1: Beyond Keynes*, Cheltenham: Edward Elgar.

Drakopoulos, S. (1991) *Values in Economic Theory*, Aldershot: Avebury.

Dunn, S. P. (2001) 'Bounded rationality is not fundamental uncertainty: a Post Keynesian perspective', *Journal of Post Keynesian Economics* 23: 567–87.

Dupuy, J. P. (1989a) 'Common knowledge, common sense', *Theory and Decision* 27: 37–62.

—— (1989b) 'Convention et common knowledge', *Revue Economique* 40: 361–400.

—— (1994) 'The self-deconstruction of convention', *Substance* 74: 86–97.

—— (forthcoming) 'Economics as symptom', in P.A. Lewis (ed.) *Transforming Economics: Perspectives on the Critical Realist Project*, London and New York: Routledge.

ECB (European Central Bank) (2001) 'Monetary policy-making under uncertainty', *ECB Monthly Bulletin* January: 43–55.

Ellsberg, D. (1961) 'Risk, ambiguity, and the Savage axioms', *Quarterly Journal of Economics* 75: 643–69.

Evans, G. W. and Honkapohja, S. (2001) *Learning and Expectations in Macroeconomics*, Princeton: Princeton University Press.

Favereau, O. (1988) 'Probability and uncertainty: after all, Keynes was right', *Economia* 10: 133–67.

Fioretti, G. (1998) 'John Maynard Keynes and Johannes von Kries', *History of Economic Ideas* 6: 51–80.

—— (2001) 'Von Kries and the other "German logicians": non-numerical probabilities before Keynes', *Economics and Philosophy* 17: 245–73.

Fitzgibbons A. (1988) *Keynes's Vision: A New Political Economy*, Oxford: Oxford University Press.

—— (2000) *The Nature of Macroeconomics: Change and Instability in the Capitalist System*, Cheltenham: Edward Elgar.

Franklin, J. (2001) 'Resurrecting logical probability', *Erkenntnis* 55: 277–305.

Galavotti, M. C. (1991) 'The notion of subjective probability in the work of Ramsey and de Finetti', *Theoria* 62(3): 239–59.

Gerrard, B. (1992) 'From *A Treatise on Probability* to the *General Theory*: continuity or change in Keynes's thought?', in W. J. Gerrard and J. V. Hillard (eds) (1993).

—— (1994) 'Beyond rational expectations: a constructive interpretation of Keynes's analysis of behaviour under uncertainty', *Economic Journal* 104: 327–37.

—— (1995) 'Probability, uncertainty and behaviour: a Keynesian perspective', in S. C. Dow and J. V. Hillard (eds) (1995).

—— (1997) 'Method and methodology in Keynes's *General Theory*', in G. C. Harcourt and P. A. Riach (eds), pp. 166–202.

Gerrard, W. J. and Hillard, J. V. (eds) (1993) *The Philosophy and Economics of J. M. Keynes*, Cheltenham: Edward Elgar.

Gillies, D. A. (2000) *Philosophical Theories of Probability*, London: Routledge.

Gillies, D. and Ietto-Gillies, G. (1991) 'Intersubjective probability and economics', *Review of Political Economy* 3(4): 393–417.

Goodman, N. (1954) *Fact, Fiction and Forecast*, Indianapolis and New York: Bobbs-Merrill Company.

Hahn, F. and Hollis, M. (eds) (1979) *Philosophy and Economic Theory*, Oxford: Oxford University Press.

Hall, P.A. (ed.) (1989) *The Political Power of Economic Ideas: Keynesianism across Nations*, Princeton: Princeton University Press.

Hampton, J. (1993) 'Prototype models of concept representation', in I. Van Mechelen, J. Hampton, R. Michalski and P. Thenus (eds) *Categories and Concepts: Theoretical Views and Inductive Data Analysis*, New York: Academic Press.

Harcourt, G. C. and Riach, P. A. (eds) (1997) *A 'Second Edition' of The General Theory*, London: Routledge.

Harrod, R. F (1951) *The Life of John Maynard Keynes*, London: Macmillan.

Hayek, F. A. (1975) 'Full employment at any price', *Hobart Paper* 45, London: IEA.

Heiner, R. A. (1983) 'The origin of predictable behaviour', *American Economic Review* 73: 560–95.

Hicks, J. R. (1936) 'Mr Keynes' theory of employment', *Economic Journal* 46: 238–53.

—— (1977) *Economic Perspectives*, Oxford: Oxford University Press.

—— (1979) *Causality in Economics*, Oxford: Basil Blackwell.

Hodgson, G. M. (2001) *How Economics Forgot History: The Problem of Historical Specificity in Social Science*, London: Routledge.

Hollis, M. (1977) 'Rational man and social science', unpublished paper, University of East Anglia.

Hoogduin, L. (1987) 'On the difference between the Keynesian, Knightian and the "classical" analysis of uncertainty and the development of a more general monetary theory', *De Economist* 135: 54–65.

Hume, D. (1938) *An Abstract of a Treatise of Human Nature*, (ed.) J. M. Keynes and P. Sraffa, Cambridge: Cambridge University Press.

—— (1948) *Dialogues concerning Natural Religion*, New York: Hafner.

—— (1975) *Enquiries concerning the Human Understanding and concerning the Principles of Morals*, (ed.) L. A. Selby-Bigge, third edition, Oxford: Oxford University Press (first published 1748).

—— (1978) *A Treatise of Human Nature*, (ed.) L. A. Selby-Bigge and P. H. Nedditch, second edition, Oxford: Clarendon Press (first published 1739–40).

Jeffreys, H. (1931) *Scientific Inference*, Cambridge: Cambridge University Press.

—— (1948) *Theory of Probability*, second edition, Oxford: Oxford University Press.

Kahn, R. F. (1984) *The Making of Keynes's General Theory*, Cambridge: Cambridge University Press.

Knight, F. H. (1921) *Risk, Uncertainty and Profit*, Chicago: Chicago University Press.

Koopman, B. O. (1940) 'The axioms and algebra of intuitive probability', *Annals of Mathematics* 41: 269–92.

Kuhn, T. S. (1962) *The Structure of Scientific Revolutions*, Chicago: University of Chicago Press.

Lakoff, G. (1987) *Women, Fire, and Dangerous Things*, Chicago: University of Chicago Press.

Lavington, F. (1922) *The Trade Cycle: An Account of the Causes Producing Rhythmical Changes in the Activity of Business*, London: P. S. King and Staples.

Lawson, T. (1985) 'Uncertainty and economic analysis', *Economic Journal* 95: 909–27.

—— (1989) 'Realism and instrumentalism in the development of econometrics', *Oxford Economic Papers* 41: 236–58, reprinted in N. De Marchi and C. Gilbert (eds) (1990) *The History and Methodology of Econometrics*, Oxford: Oxford University Press; also reprinted in O. F. Hamouda and J. C. R. Rowley (eds) (1996) *Foundations of Probability, Econometrics and Economic Games*, Cheltenham: Edward Elgar.

—— (1993) 'Keynes and conventions', *Review of Social Economy* 51: 174–200.

—— (1996) 'Hayek and Keynes: a commonality', *History of Economics Review* 25: 96–114.

—— (1997a) *Economics and Reality*, London: Routledge.

—— (1997b) 'Horses for courses', in P. Arestis, G. Palma and M. Sawyer (eds) *Markets, Unemployment and Economic Policy: Festschrift for Geoff Harcourt*, London: Routledge, pp. 1–15.

—— (forthcoming) *Reorientating Economics*, London: Routledge.

Lawson, T. and Pesaran, H. (eds) (1985) *Keynes' Economics: Methodological Issues*, Beckenham: Croom Helm.

Lenz, J. W. (1958) 'Hume's defense of casual inference', in Chappell (ed.) (1966), reprinted from the *Journal of the History of Ideas* 19: 559–67.

Levine, D. (1984) 'Long period expectations and investment', *Social Concept* 1: 42–51.

Lewis, D. (1969) *Convention: A Philosophical Study*, Cambridge, MA: Harvard University Press.

Littleboy, B. (1990) *On Interpreting Keynes: A Study in Reconciliation*, London: Routledge.

Loasby, B. J. (1976) *Choice, Complexity and Ignorance*, Cambridge: Cambridge University Press.

Lucas, R. E. (1972) 'Expectations and the neutrality of money', *Journal of Economic Theory* 4: 103–24.

Lucas, R. E. and Sargent, T. J. (1981) *Rational Expectations and Econometric Practices*, Minneapolis: University of Minnesota Press.

Luce, R. D. and Raiffa, H. (1957) *Games and Decisions*, New York: Wiley.

McCann, C. R., Jr (1994) *Probability Foundations of Economic Theory*, London: Routledge.

Machina, M. J. (1987) 'Choice under uncertainty: problems solved and unsolved', *Journal of Economic Perspectives* 1: 121–54.

Mäki, U. (ed.) (2001) *The Economic Worldview*, Cambridge: Cambridge University Press.

Malthus, T. R. (1800) *An Investigation of the Cause of the Present High Price of Provisions*, London: J. Johnson.

Marchionatti, R. (1999) 'On Keynes's animal spirits', *Kyklos* 52: 415–39.

Marshak, J. (1941) 'Lack of confidence', *Social Research* 8: 41–62.

Marshall, A. (1961) *Principles of Economics*, 2 vols, ninth (variorum) edition, ed. and annotated C.W. Guillebaud, London: Macmillan.

Matthews, R. (1991) 'Animal spirits', in J. G. T. Meeks (ed.) (1991), reprinted from the *Proceedings of the British Academy* (1984) 70: 209–29.

Meeks, J. G. T. (1991) 'Keynes on the rationality of decision procedures under uncertainty: the investment decision', in J. G. T. Meeks (ed.) (1991).

Meeks, J. G. T. (ed.) (1991) *Thoughtful Economic Man: Essays on Rationality, Moral Rules and Benevolence*, Cambridge: Cambridge University Press.

Meinong, A. (1890) 'Kries, Johannes v., Die Principien der Wahrscheinlichkeitsrechnung', *Göttingische gelehrte Anzeigen* 1: 56–75.

Meltzer, A. H. (1988) *Keynes's Monetary Theory: A Different Interpretation*, Cambridge: Cambridge University Press.

Miller, E. M. (1977) 'Risk, uncertainty and divergence of opinion', *The Journal of Finance* 32: 1151–68.

Minsky, H. P. (1975) *John Maynard Keynes*, New York: Macmillan.

Mizuhara, S. (2002) 'Keynes's views on information', in S. C. Dow and J. Hillard (eds) pp. 97–109.

Moggridge, D. E. (1986) 'Keynes in historical perspective', *Eastern Economic Journal* 12: 357–69.

Moore, G. E. (1903a) *Principia Ethica*, Cambridge: Cambridge University Press.

—— (1903b) 'Refutation of idealism', in (1922) *Philosophical Studies*, London: Routledge and Kegan Paul.

Nitsche, A. (1892) 'Die Dimensionen der Wahrscheinlichkeit und die Evidenz der Ungewissheit', *Vierteljahrschrift für wissenschaftliche Philosophie* 16: 20–35.

O'Donnell, R. M. (1989) *Keynes: Philosophy, Economics and Politics*, London: Macmillan.

—— (1991a) 'Keynes on probability, expectations and uncertainty', in R. M. O'Donnell (ed.) (1991b), pp. 3–60.

—— (1992) 'The unwritten books and papers of J. M. Keynes', *History of Political Economy*, 24: 767–817.

O'Donnell, R. M. (ed.) (1991b) *Keynes as Philosopher-Economist*, London: Macmillan.

O'Driscoll, G. P. and Rizzo, M. J. (1985) *The Economics of Time and Ignorance*, London: Basil Blackwell.

Orléan, A. (1989) 'Mimetic contagion and speculative bubbles', *Theory and Decision*, 27: 63–92.

Patinkin, D. (1976) *Keynes's Monetary Thought*, Durham: Duke University Press.

—— (1990) 'On different interpretations of the *General Theory*', *Journal of Monetary Economics* 26: 205–43.

Peden, G. C. (1988) *Keynes, the Treasury, and British Economic Policy*, London: Macmillan.

Plato (1892) 'The Republic' in *The Dialogues of Plato*, trans. B. Jowett, Oxford: Oxford University Press.

Plumptre, A. F. W. (1983) 'Keynes in Cambridge', in J. C. Wood (ed.) *John Maynard Keynes: Critical Assessments*, vol. I, London: Croom Helm, reprinted from *Canadian Journal of Economics* August 1947: 366–71.

Popkin, R. H. (1951) 'David Hume: his Pyrrhonism and his critique of Pyrrhonism', *The Philosophical Quarterly* 1: 385–407, reprinted in Chappell (ed.) (1966).

Pratten, C. (1993) *The Stock Market*, Cambridge: Cambridge University Press.

Ramsey, F. P. (1978) 'Truth and probability', in D. H. Mellor (ed.) *Foundations: Essays in Philosophy, Logic, Mathematics and Economics*, London: Routledge and Kegan Paul (first published posthumously in R. B. Braithwaite (ed.) (1931) *The Foundations of Mathematics and Other Logical Essays*, London: Routledge and Kegan Paul).

Raz, J. (1975) *Practical Reason and Norms*, London: Hutchinson.

Ricardo, D. (1817) *On the Principles of Political Economy and Taxation*, third edition, in P. Sraffa (ed.) with M. H. Dobb (1951) *The Works and Correspondence of David Ricardo*, vol. I, Cambridge: Cambridge University Press

Robinson, J. (1964) *Economic Philosophy*, Harmondsworth: Penguin.

Rotheim, R. (1998) *New Keynesian Economics/Post Keynesian Alternatives*, London: Routledge.

Runde, J. H. (1990) 'Keynesian uncertainty and the weight of arguments', *Economics and Philosophy* 6: 275–92.

—— (1991) 'Keynesian uncertainty and the instability of beliefs', *Review of Political Economy* 3: 125–45.

—— (1994a) 'Keynesian uncertainty and liquidity preference', *Cambridge Journal of Economics* 18: 129–44.

—— (1994b) 'Keynes after Ramsey: in defence of *A Treatise on Probability*', *Studies in History and Philosophy of Science* 25: 97–121.

—— (1994c) 'The Keynesian probability-relation: in search of a substitute', in J. B. Davis (ed.) *The State of Interpretation of Keynes*, Boston: Kluwer Academic Publishers, pp. 245–51.

—— (1995) 'Risk, uncertainty and Bayesian decision theory: a Keynesian view', in S. C. Dow and J. V. Hillard (eds) (1995).

—— (1996) 'On Popper, probabilities and propensities', *Review of Social Economy* LIV: 465–85.

—— (1997) 'Keynesian methodology', in G. C. Harcourt and P. A. Riach (eds.) (1997), pp. 222–43.

Runde, J. and Bibow, J. (1998) 'Expectations and stock market prices', in R. Koppl and G. Mongiovi (eds) *Subjectivism and Economic Analysis: Essays in Memory of Ludwig M. Lachmann*, London: Routledge, pp. 183–200.

Russell, B. (1912) *The Problems of Philosophy*, Oxford: Oxford University Press (references are to the OPUS edition).

—— (1948) *Human Knowledge: Its Scopes and Limits*, New York: Simon & Schuster.

Rymes, T. K. (ed.) (1989) *Keynes's Lectures, 1932–35*, Ann Arbor: University of Michigan Press.

Samuelson, P. A. (1947) *Foundations of Economic Analysis*, Cambridge, MA.: Harvard University Press.

—— (1969) 'Classical and neoclassical monetary theory', in R. W. Clower (ed.) *Monetary Theory*, Harmondsworth: Penguin.

Sargent, T. J. (1993) *Bounded Rationality in Macroeconomics*, Oxford: Clarendon Press.

Savage, L. (1954) *The Foundations of Statistics*, New York: Wiley.

Schelling, T. C. (1960) *The Strategy of Conflict*, Cambridge, MA: Harvard University Press.

Schumpeter, J. A. (1936) 'Review of *The General Theory of Employment, Interest and Money* by John Maynard Keynes', *Journal of the American Statistical Association* 31: 791–6.

—— (1942) *Capitalism, Socialism and Democracy*, London: Allen & Unwin.

—— (1954) *A History of Economic Analysis*, London: Routledge.

Schwartz, S. (ed.) (1977) *Naming, Necessity, and Natural Kinds*, Ithaca: Cornell University Press.

Sen, A. K. (1987) 'Rational behaviour', in J. Eatwell, M. Milgate and P. Newman (eds) *New Palgrave Dictionary of Economics*, vol. IV, London: Macmillan, pp. 68–76.

Sent, E.-M. (1998) *The Evolving Rationality of Rational Expectations*, Cambridge: Cambridge University Press.

Shackle, G. L. S. (1955) *Uncertainty in Economics*, Cambridge: Cambridge University Press.

—— (1961a) *Decision, Order and Time*, Cambridge: Cambridge University Press.

—— (1961b) 'Recent theories concerning the nature and role of interest', *Economic Journal* 71: 421–36.

—— (1967) *The Years of High Theory: Invention and Tradition in Economic Thought 1926–1939*, Cambridge: Cambridge University Press.

—— (1972) *Epistemics and Economics*, Cambridge: Cambridge University Press.

—— (1979) *Imagination and the Nature of Choice*, Edinburgh: Edinburgh University Press.

Shiller, R. J. (2000) *Irrational Exuberance*, Princeton: Princeton University Press.

Simon, H. A. (1976), 'From substantive to procedural rationality', reprinted in F. Hahn and M. Hollis (eds) (1979).

Skidelsky, R. (1983) *John Maynard Keynes, Volume I: Hopes Betrayed 1883–1920*, London: Macmillan.

—— (1992) *John Maynard Keynes, Volume II: The Economist as Saviour 1920–1937*, London: Macmillan.

—— (2000) *John Maynard Keynes, Volume III: Fighting for Britain 1937–1946*, London: Macmillan.

Solow, R. M. (1985) 'Economic history and economics', *American Economic Review Papers and Proceedings* 75: 328–31.

Stove, D. C. (1965) 'Hume, probability, and induction', in Chappell (ed.) (1966), reprinted from the *Philosophical Review* LXXIV: 160–77.

—— (1973) *Probability and Hume's Inductive Scepticism*, Oxford: Oxford University Press.

Strawson, P. F. (1952) *Introduction to Logical Theory*, London: Methuen.

Sugden, R. (1991) 'Rational choice: a survey of contributions from economics and philosophy', *Economic Journal* 101: 751–85.

Urmson, J. (1956) *Philosophical Analysis*, Oxford: Clarendon Press.

von Kries, J. (1886) *Die Principien der Wahrscheinlichkeitsrechnung*, Tübingen: Verlag von J. C. B. Mohr (Paul Siebeck) (reprinted in 1927 by the same publisher).

—— (1888) 'Ueber den Begriff der objectiven Möglichkeit und einige Anwendungen desselben', *Vierteljahrschrift für wissenschaftliche Philosophie* 12: 179–240, 287–323, 393–428.

—— (1892) 'Ueber Real- und Beziehungs-Urtheile', *Vierteljahrschrift für wissenschaftliche Philosophie* 16: 253–88.

—— (1899) 'Zur Psychologie der Urteile', *Vierteljahrschrift für wissenschaftliche Philosophie* 23: 1–48.

—— (1901) *Über die materiellen Grundlagen der Bewusstseins-Erscheinungen*, Tübingen: Verlag von J. C. B. Mohr (Paul Siebeck).

—— (1916) *Logik*, Tübingen: Verlag von J. C. B. Mohr (Paul Siebeck).

—— (1923) *Allgemeine Sinnesphysiologie*, Leipzig: Verlag von F. C. W. Vogel.

—— (1924a) 'Goethe als Psycholog', in *Philosophie und Geschichte*, Tübingen: Verlag von J. C. B. Mohr (Paul Siebeck).

—— (1924b) *Immanuel Kant und seine Bedeutung für die Naturforschung der Gegenwart*, Berlin: Verlag von Julius Springer.

—— (1925) 'Johannes von Kries', in L. R. Grote (ed.) *Die Medizin der Gegenwart*, Leipzig: Verlag von Felix Meiner.

von Mises, L. (1981) *Epistemological Problems of Economics*, trans. G. Reisman, New York and London: New York University Press.

Weatherford, R. (1982) *Philosophical Foundations of Probability Theory*, London: Routledge and Kegan Paul.

Weatherson, B. (2002) 'Keynes, uncertainty and interest rates', *Cambridge Journal of Economics* 26: 47–62.

Westall, O. M. (1992) *The Provincial Insurance Company, 1903–38: Family, Markets, and Competitive Growth*, Manchester: Manchester University Press.

Whitehead, A. N. (1929) *Process and Reality*, corrected edition, (ed.) D. R. Griffin and D. W. Sherburne, New York: The Free Press, Macmillan.

—— (1948) 'Uniformity and contingency', in *Essays in Science and Philosophy*, New York: Philosophical Library, pp. 100–11.

—— (1958) *The Function of Reason*, Boston: Beacon Press.

—— (1967a) *The Aims of Education*, New York: The Free Press, Macmillan.

—— (1967b) *Adventures of Ideas*, New York: The Free Press, Macmillan

—— (1968) *Modes of Thought*, New York: The Free Press, Macmillan.

Winslow, E. G. (1986a) ' "Human logic" and Keynes's economics', *Eastern Economic Journal* 12: 413–30.

—— (1986b) 'Keynes and Freud: psychoanalysis and Keynes's account of the "animal spirits" of capitalism', *Social Research* 53: 549–78.

—— (1989) 'Organic interdependence, uncertainty and economic analysis', *Economic Journal* 99: 1173–82.

—— (1990) 'Bloomsbury, Freud, and the vulgar passions', *Social Research* 57: 785–819.

—— (1993a) 'Keynes on rationality', in W. J. Gerrard (ed.) *The Economics of Rationality*, London: Routledge.

—— (1993b) 'Atomism and organicism', in G. Hodgson, W. Samuels and M. Tool (eds) *Handbook of Institutional and Evolutionary Economics*, Cheltenham: Edward Elgar.

—— (1993c) 'Psychoanalysis and Keynes's account of the psychology of the trade cycle', in W. J. Gerrard and J. V. Hillard (eds) (1993).

—— (1995) 'Uncertainty and liquidity-preference', in S. C. Dow and J. V. Hillard (eds) (1995).

Wittgenstein, L. (1953) *Philosophical Investigations*, second edition, Oxford: Blackwell (revised in 1958).

Index

abstract rules of conduct 224–5
accumulation of wealth 22, 197
actions have consequences in the future 20, 30
aleatory approach, decision-making and 246
amount of investment, key in determining
  performance of economy 113
animal spirits, description of 124; Keynesian
  scholars and 139; plunge into abyss of the
  unknown 176; role of 4, 14, 23–5, 32, 59,
  81, 108, 248, 250; *Treatise on Probability, A*
  and 137
Apostles, Moore's neo-Platonism 135; papers
  100; 'Ethics in relation to conduct' 104,
  106
Appendix: Keynes–Plato dialogues 65;
  democracy and individualism 65–6; money
  and power 66–7; money and virtue 67
'approximate uniformity of human organs'
  222–3
asset choice 51–2
atomic character, natural law and 9–10, 162
atomic hypothesis, abandoned by Keynes 145,
  154, 242; Keynes's discussions on limits of
  application 218; relations as 'external' 146
atomism, theory of induction and 133, 135–6,
  144, 163
Austrian theory 213
average expectation, financial markets and 200

Barsalou, L.W. 138
Bateman, Brad 1, 5, 7, 53, 85, 102; arguments
  against continuity view 6, 121; concept of
  confidence and 95, 98–9; differences
  between young and mature Keynes 135;
  Hacking's bipartite (aleatory/epistemic)
  classification 93–4; history of economic
  thought and 85–7; Keynes's actual beliefs
  and imperfect expression 87; Keynes and
  intersubjective probabilities 94–5, 97;
  'Keynes's changing conception of

probability' 121; Keynes's ideas on
  liquidity preference 96; on Keynes's
  philosophy 88–9; 'new' Keynesian
  fundamentalist research 243; on
  O'Donnell's interpretation of Keynes
  89–90; promise to show history necessary
  to understanding 88; on Ramsey's critique
  of *Treatise* 90; Ramsey's theory of
  subjective probabilities 89; treatment of
  conventions 97–8; tripartite division of
  probability 94
behaviour under uncertainty, four
  determinants 242
belief, degrees part of our human outfit 53;
  rational belief 38
Benthamite tradition 123, 137, 170, 202, 222
betting quotients, axioms of probability 118,
  126
Bibow, Jörg 11, 194
Bosanquet, Bernard 102
Bradley, F.H. 102
Braithwaite, R.B. 42, 63
Broad, C.D. 105
Brown-Collier, E.K. 242
budget deficits, Great Depression and 71
business cycles, changes in aggregate demand
  and 64; Keynes and 10; Tinbergen's
  econometric work on 167
business entrepreneurs, stock-market
  behaviour and 249

calculus of probability 59–60, 121, 144, 224,
  239
Cambridge theory of trade cycle, expectations
  and uncertainty 73–4, 76
Cambridge trade cycle theorists 76, 79
capital markets, chaos or irrational behaviour
  60; entrepreneur and mass valuation of
  market 26; Keynesian Synthesis and 64
capitalism, explosive energy to long-run